FANTASY FOOTBALL 2024

Jalen Hurts
Philadelphia Eagles
No. 2 Quarterback

CONTENTS

FEATURES

POSITIONAL PREVIEWS & RANKINGS

TEAM PREVIEWS

This ESPN special edition has four regional covers.

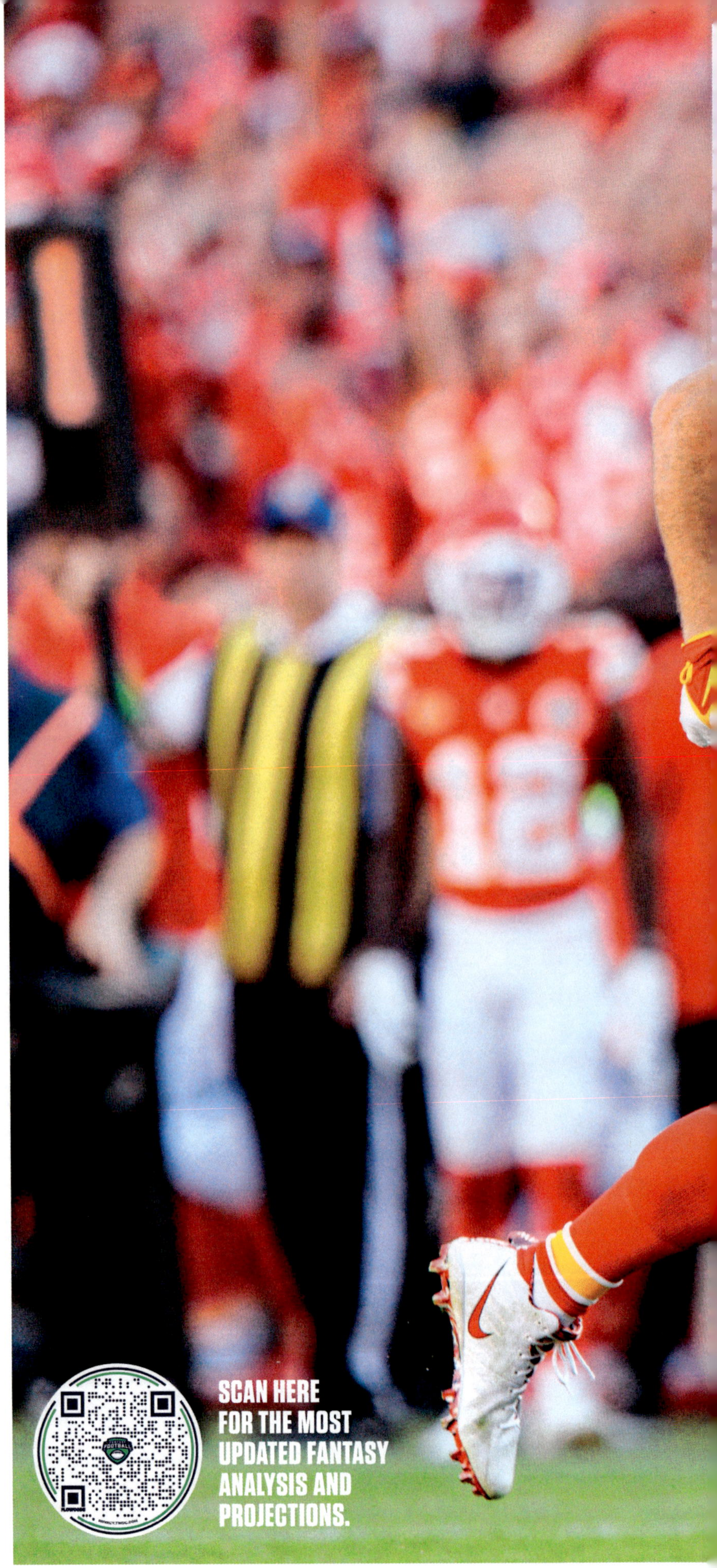

SCAN HERE FOR THE MOST UPDATED FANTASY ANALYSIS AND PROJECTIONS.

He turns 35 this fall, but the Chiefs' Travis Kelce remains one of the top tight ends in fantasy football.

TRUST YOUR GUT

Analytics are critical when building your roster, but you shouldn't ignore your feelings about a long shot

BY MIKE CLAY

If you've watched television during the past couple decades, you are at least somewhat familiar with The Confessional. In a nutshell, it's a concept often used in reality shows and mockumentaries in which cast members are pulled aside to narrate their true thoughts about a person or subject.

It's a device we don't get to use much in the fantasy football industry, but I'm going to attempt it right now.

Why? Because this is something I can't say publicly without ridicule, smirks and eyerolls from my *Fantasy Focus Football* podcast mates, Field Yates, Daniel Dopp and Stephania Bell, who have had to deal with my analytics and stats for nearly a decade. (They won't read this, right?)

So grab your popcorn, settle in, and—if you can stomach it—imagine I'm staring right at you down the barrel of the camera.

Ready? Good. Here we go.

Fantasy football is supposed to be fun, and it's OK to go with your gut.

I know, I know, I know.

"Trust the process!"

"Regression to the mean!"

"Fade the outliers!"

"Boneless wings are a fraud and should be banned!"

These are things I say, and I stand by them. At the end of the day, the goal is to score the most points, and the best way to get there is with a good process. However, we're playing a high-variance and unpredictable game with loads of talented players—literally the best football players in the world—and you should never feel bad or wrong about reaching a bit for a player you have a good feeling about or you just plain like. (Field will never not draft a former lacrosse player, for example.)

The 2023 season gave us several examples of these outliers who proved to be league winners—and I'm not even talking about Taylor Swift, who took the NFL by storm and rallied the Chiefs to yet another Lombardi Trophy.

No one saw that coming, but I bet a few of you were intrigued by these emerging stars:

• The rule is that rookie quarterbacks make for poor fantasy options unless they add substantial value with their legs. And yet C.J. Stroud, last year's No. 2 overall pick, defied the odds and finished eighth in fantasy PPG despite rushing for only 167 yards.

• Over the past decade, only one rookie wide receiver selected on Day 3 of the draft has averaged at least 14.0 fantasy PPG. That player is, of course, Puka Nacua. The 2023 fifth-round pick's 17.6 fantasy PPG ranked fifth among all WRs last season.

• And of course, the biggest outlier of all: Sam LaPorta. The Iowa product

ILLUSTRATION BY RAFA ALVAREZ

led all fantasy tight ends with 239.3 points, which also happens to be the most points *ever* scored by a rookie at the position.

If you felt good about these players but passed on them on draft day because they were long shots, you surely were kicking yourself all season long. Yes, it's important not to lose your league early on by making ridiculous dart throws, but there's no harm in planting a flag on an early-rounder you expect to make a leap to the elite and using your gut for some late-round sleeper hunting. Hitting on those players is how leagues are won.

The funny thing about using your gut is that it's generally leading you in a certain direction for a good reason. Some of my favorite "hits" of all time were driven by things I witnessed on film or stats that jumped off the page. RBs like Chris Carson and Jordan Howard (both Day 3 draft picks) weren't "supposed" to be good, but I had a man crush and couldn't leave a draft without taking a late flier. Last season, Jakobi Meyers was an example of a boring draft-day target, but if you agreed he was an underrated player and could soak up a ton of targets opposite Davante Adams in Las Vegas, you stumbled upon fantasy's No. 24–scoring WR with a late pick. It doesn't always work out (let's not talk about the repercussions of Aaron Rodgers' Week 1 torn Achilles), but it's low risk, and when it does work, it can win you your league.

So, what is your gut telling you will happen in 2024?

Perhaps J.J. McCarthy will prove a perfect fit for Kevin O'Connell's offense and deliver QB1 numbers.

Maybe a fresh start in Cleveland is what Jerry Jeudy needs to finally live up to his lofty ADP.

Will Jonathon Brooks follow in Breece Hall's footsteps and put up RB1 production in his first season off a torn ACL?

Dare I suggest that another celebrity (Jennifer Coolidge?) will create headlines by dating someone from the NFL world (Zach Wilson?).

Who's to say?

But the fun of it is that you can circle the players you have a good feeling about on your cheat sheet and make sure you get them on your team, even if you have to reach a bit. And if your league mates laugh at you for reaching, be sure to keep the receipt. There's not much better than some post-championship smack talk, especially when you're led to the title by a player you just had to have.

OK, so that's that. Thanks for bearing with me. I hope it helps. I need to head back to the set now before Daniel realizes I'm gone and starts spreading rumors that I'm a traitor. Thanks for listening, enjoy the rest of our guide to fantasy football in 2024...and have a great season! ■

New Chargers head coach Jim Harbaugh has been making big changes to the roster.

56
85
McDONALD IV
99

Marvin Harrison Jr.

ARIZONA CARDINALS

THE SKINNY

The arrival of Marvin Harrison Jr. turns this offense into a playoff-caliber outfit. Between his addition and QB Kyler Murray getting an entire offseason in the scheme, Arizona will be able to not only hit the ground running, but Murray will have the best offensive weapon in this year's draft to throw to.

Over/Under: 82 receptions for Harrison. **Prediction:** **Over.** Harrison will come in as WR1 and instantly become Murray's favorite target. Even with defenses scheming against Harrison, Murray will look to him enough for Harrison to get his share of targets and catches. *–Josh Weinfuss*

SCORE PROJECTIONS

WK	OPP	LOC	TM	OPP	WIN PROB
1	BUF	A	19.9	28.1	22%
2	LAR	H	23.8	26.5	40%
3	DET	H	21.0	28.1	25%
4	WAS	H	23.5	21.7	56%
5	SF	A	17.4	30.1	11%
6	GB	A	20.6	27.2	27%
7	LAC	H	23.1	25.1	43%
8	MIA	A	18.5	27.2	21%
9	CHI	H	20.6	24.6	36%
10	NYJ	H	19.2	27.9	21%
11					
12	SEA	A	20.2	25.4	32%
13	MIN	A	21.3	24.4	39%
14	SEA	H	21.3	24.3	39%
15	NE	H	21.3	21.3	50%
16	CAR	A	21.3	24.3	39%
17	LAR	A	22.7	27.6	33%
18	SF	H	18.5	29.0	16%
			354	443	32%

Projected Wins: 5.5 (NFL Rank: 29)
Strength of Schedule Ranking: 28

FANTASY DEPTH CHART

QB
Kyler Murray
Desmond Ridder

RB
James Conner
Trey Benson
Michael Carter

WR
Marvin Harrison Jr.
Zay Jones
Michael Wilson
Greg Dortch
Zach Pascal
Chris Moore

TE
Trey McBride
Elijah Higgins
Tip Reiman

K
Matt Prater

USAGE PROJECTIONS

TARGET SHARES

Marvin Harrison Jr.	23%
Trey McBride	20%
Zay Jones	14%
Michael Wilson	13%
James Conner	7%

CARRY SHARES

James Conner	43%
Trey Benson	28%
Kyler Murray	12%

TEAM SCORING FORECAST

Passing TD	Rushing TD	FG
20	16	29

ATLANTA FALCONS

THE SKINNY

The Falcons already had exciting, young skill-position players like RB Bijan Robinson, WR Drake London and TE Kyle Pitts. The question was who would throw to them, and the front office answered that question by signing Kirk Cousins to a hefty $180 million contract in March.

Over/Under: 60 receptions for Pitts. **Prediction:** **Over.** More than 26% of Cousins' passes went to tight ends in 2023, the fifth-highest rate in the NFL. Coach Raheem Morris will bring in a Sean McVay-influenced scheme that will get Pitts the targets he needs to break out. *–Marc Raimondi*

SCORE PROJECTIONS

WK	OPP	LOC	TM	OPP	WIN PROB
1	PIT	H	22.0	21.0	54%
2	PHI	A	24.5	27.0	41%
3	KC	H	23.8	28.0	35%
4	NO	H	23.1	21.4	56%
5	TB	H	25.2	22.3	60%
6	CAR	A	24.1	22.5	56%
7	SEA	H	24.2	22.5	56%
8	TB	A	24.1	23.4	53%
9	DAL	H	22.0	25.4	38%
10	NO	A	22.0	22.5	48%
11	DEN	A	25.2	20.9	65%
12					
13	LAC	H	25.9	23.3	59%
14	MIN	A	24.1	22.7	55%
15	LV	A	23.8	20.6	61%
16	NYG	H	26.6	18.9	76%
17	WAS	A	25.2	21.0	65%
18	CAR	H	25.2	21.4	64%
			411	385	55%

Projected Wins: 9.4 (NFL Rank: 11)
Strength of Schedule Ranking: 1

FANTASY DEPTH CHART

QB
Kirk Cousins
Michael Penix Jr.

RB
Bijan Robinson
Tyler Allgeier
Jase McClellan

WR
Drake London
Darnell Mooney
Rondale Moore
KhaDarel Hodge
Ray-Ray McCloud
Casey Washington

TE
Kyle Pitts
Ross Dwelley
Charlie Woerner

K
Younghoe Koo

USAGE PROJECTIONS

TARGET SHARES

Drake London	22%
Kyle Pitts	17%
Darnell Mooney	16%
Bijan Robinson	15%
Rondale Moore	10%

CARRY SHARES

Bijan Robinson	50%
Tyler Allgeier	33%
Jase McClellan	8%

TEAM SCORING FORECAST

Passing TD	Rushing TD	FG
28	16	28

Kyle Pitts

BALTIMORE RAVENS

THE SKINNY

The Ravens are going to rely more on the arm of Lamar Jackson and less on the reigning NFL MVP's legs. Last season, he threw a career-high 457 passes and averaged a career-low 9.3 rushing attempts per game. Baltimore helped Jackson even more by adding Derrick Henry, who has totaled a league-best 8,295 yards from scrimmage over the past five years.

Over/Under: 252 carries for Henry. **Prediction:** Over. The Ravens love rotating their backs, which is why no one has exceeded 235 carries since 2012. But Henry averaged 327 carries over his past four full seasons. *–Jamison Hensley*

SCORE PROJECTIONS

WK	OPP	LOC	TM	OPP	WIN PROB
1	KC	A	24.7	25.8	46%
2	LV	H	26.9	16.3	84%
3	DAL	A	23.0	23.3	49%
4	BUF	H	25.8	22.1	63%
5	CIN	A	24.7	23.6	54%
6	WAS	H	28.3	16.7	87%
7	TB	A	26.2	20.2	71%
8	CLE	A	21.9	20.9	53%
9	DEN	H	28.3	16.6	87%
10	CIN	H	25.8	22.5	62%
11	PIT	A	23.0	18.9	64%
12	LAC	A	26.9	21.2	70%
13	PHI	H	27.6	22.7	67%
14					
15	NYG	A	27.6	16.8	85%
16	PIT	H	24.1	17.8	72%
17	HOU	A	25.5	23.3	58%
18	CLE	H	23.0	19.8	61%
			433	349	67%

Projected Wins: 11.3 (NFL Rank: 4)
Strength of Schedule Ranking: 15

FANTASY DEPTH CHART

QB
Lamar Jackson
Josh Johnson

RB
Derrick Henry
Keaton Mitchell
Justice Hill

WR
Zay Flowers
Rashod Bateman
Nelson Agholor
Devontez Walker
Deonte Harty
Tylan Wallace

TE
Mark Andrews
Isaiah Likely
Charlie Kolar

K
Justin Tucker

USAGE PROJECTIONS

TARGET SHARES

Zay Flowers	23%
Mark Andrews	21%
Rashod Bateman	15%
Nelson Agholor	9%
Derrick Henry	7%

CARRY SHARES

Derrick Henry	56%
Lamar Jackson	16%
Justice Hill	12%

TEAM SCORING FORECAST

Passing TD	Rushing TD	FG
25	22	29

BUFFALO BILLS

THE SKINNY

The Bills are undergoing a shake-up, with Stefon Diggs no longer the focal point for Josh Allen. Rookie receiver Keon Coleman is expected to start at X while tight end Dalton Kincaid's role should only get bigger. Running the ball will be an integral part of the offensive attack.

Over/Under: 258 touches for James Cook. **Prediction:** Over. Cook's involvement in the offense should only continue to increase in his third season. His touches in 2023 increased from 14.4 per game with Ken Dorsey calling the plays to 20.1 after Joe Brady took over. *–Alaina Getzenberg*

SCORE PROJECTIONS

WK	OPP	LOC	TM	OPP	WIN PROB
1	ARI	H	28.1	19.9	78%
2	MIA	A	22.1	23.7	44%
3	JAX	H	23.9	20.5	62%
4	BAL	A	22.1	25.8	37%
5	HOU	A	24.2	24.8	48%
6	NYJ	A	21.8	25.4	37%
7	TEN	H	27.1	18.6	79%
8	SEA	A	23.9	21.8	57%
9	MIA	H	23.2	22.6	52%
10	IND	A	24.6	22.4	58%
11	KC	H	24.6	26.2	44%
12					
13	SF	H	22.1	25.5	38%
14	LAR	A	26.3	24.1	58%
15	DET	A	23.5	25.7	42%
16	NE	H	25.0	17.8	75%
17	NYJ	H	22.8	24.4	45%
18	NE	A	23.9	18.9	68%
			409	388	54%

Projected Wins: 9.2 (NFL Rank: 12)
Strength of Schedule Ranking: 31

FANTASY DEPTH CHART

QB
Josh Allen
Mitchell Trubisky

RB
James Cook
Ray Davis
Ty Johnson

WR
Keon Coleman
Curtis Samuel
Khalil Shakir
Marquez Valdes-Scantling
Mack Hollins
Chase Claypool

TE
Dalton Kincaid
Dawson Knox
Quintin Morris

K
Tyler Bass

USAGE PROJECTIONS

TARGET SHARES

Dalton Kincaid	18%
Keon Coleman	17%
Curtis Samuel	16%
Khalil Shakir	13%
James Cook	11%

CARRY SHARES

James Cook	50%
Ray Davis	20%
Josh Allen	13%

TEAM SCORING FORECAST

Passing TD	Rushing TD	FG
26	19	27

James Cook

Jonathon Brooks

CAROLINA PANTHERS

THE SKINNY

New coach Dave Canales has already gotten the best out of quarterbacks Baker Mayfield and Geno Smith in previous stops. Now he's surrounded Bryce Young with a much-improved offensive line and a supporting cast that is far more dynamic than it was a year ago.

Over/Under: 230 touches for Jonathon Brooks. **Prediction:** **Under.** The Panthers didn't take Brooks in the second round not to use him heavily, and Canales is committed to the run game. Ideally, though, the load will be split between Brooks, Chuba Hubbard and Miles Sanders. *–David Newton*

SCORE PROJECTIONS

WK	OPP	LOC	TM	OPP	WIN PROB
1	NO	A	18.9	22.1	39%
2	LAC	H	22.8	23.0	50%
3	LV	A	20.7	20.2	52%
4	CIN	H	20.7	25.4	34%
5	CHI	A	19.3	23.6	35%
6	ATL	H	22.5	24.1	44%
7	WAS	A	22.1	20.7	55%
8	DEN	A	22.1	20.5	56%
9	NO	H	20.0	21.0	46%
10	NYG	H	23.0	19.1	64%
11					
12	KC	H	20.7	27.6	26%
13	TB	H	22.1	22.0	51%
14	PHI	A	21.4	26.6	32%
15	DAL	H	18.9	25.1	29%
16	ARI	H	24.3	21.3	61%
17	TB	A	21.0	23.1	43%
18	ATL	A	21.4	25.2	36%
			362	391	44%

Projected Wins: 7.5 (NFL Rank: 24)
Strength of Schedule Ranking: 3

FANTASY DEPTH CHART

QB
Bryce Young
Andy Dalton

RB
Jonathon Brooks
Chuba Hubbard
Miles Sanders

WR
Diontae Johnson
Adam Thielen
Xavier Legette
Jonathan Mingo
David Moore
Ihmir Smith-Marsette

TE
Tommy Tremble
Ja'Tavion Sanders
Stephen Sullivan

K
Eddy Pineiro

USAGE PROJECTIONS

TARGET SHARES

Diontae Johnson	20%
Adam Thielen	18%
Xavier Legette	16%
Jonathon Brooks	8%
Jonathan Mingo	8%

CARRY SHARES

Jonathon Brooks	46%
Chuba Hubbard	24%
Miles Sanders	20%

TEAM SCORING FORECAST

Passing TD	Rushing TD	FG
23	14	29

CHICAGO BEARS

THE SKINNY

With a receiving corps that includes DJ Moore, Keenan Allen and Rome Odunze, plus a rookie QB (Caleb Williams) who provides the Bears with a major passing upgrade, Chicago's offense could very well become a top-10 unit. That's a far cry from the imbalanced attack the Bears fielded last season.

Over/Under: 56 receptions for Rome Odunze. **Prediction:** **Over.** It's easy to envision Odunze becoming one of Williams' favorite targets as the Bears' passing offense increases its sheer volume of opportunities for all of the team's top weapons. *–Courtney Cronin*

SCORE PROJECTIONS

WK	OPP	LOC	TM	OPP	WIN PROB
1	TEN	H	24.6	18.2	72%
2	HOU	A	21.8	24.4	41%
3	IND	A	22.1	22.1	50%
4	LAR	H	25.0	22.6	58%
5	CAR	H	23.6	19.3	65%
6	JAX	H	20.9	20.7	51%
7					
8	WAS	A	23.5	18.9	66%
9	ARI	A	24.6	20.6	64%
10	NE	H	22.5	17.4	68%
11	GB	H	22.9	22.2	52%
12	MIN	H	23.6	19.5	65%
13	DET	A	21.1	25.3	35%
14	SF	A	18.6	26.2	24%
15	MIN	A	22.5	20.6	57%
16	DET	H	22.1	24.2	43%
17	SEA	H	22.5	20.4	58%
18	GB	A	21.8	23.3	45%
			384	366	54%

Projected Wins: 9.1 (NFL Rank: 14)
Strength of Schedule Ranking: 8

FANTASY DEPTH CHART

QB
Caleb Williams
Tyson Bagent

RB
D'Andre Swift
Roschon Johnson
Khalil Herbert

WR
DJ Moore
Keenan Allen
Rome Odunze
Tyler Scott
Velus Jones Jr.
Collin Johnson

TE
Cole Kmet
Gerald Everett
Stephen Carlson

K
Cairo Santos

USAGE PROJECTIONS

TARGET SHARES

Keenan Allen	22%
DJ Moore	22%
Rome Odunze	18%
Cole Kmet	14%
D'Andre Swift	8%

CARRY SHARES

D'Andre Swift	44%
Khalil Herbert	25%
Roschon Johnson	18%

TEAM SCORING FORECAST

Passing TD	Rushing TD	FG
26	14	29

Rome Odunze

Tee Higgins

CINCINNATI BENGALS

THE SKINNY

Expect a more dynamic offense this season. New RB Zack Moss is a better fit for Cincinnati's scheme than Joe Mixon was. Ja'Marr Chase could see more reps at slot receiver, and TE Mike Gesicki is a viable downfield threat. All that should lead to a more-explosive unit in Cincinnati.

Over/Under: 1,029 receiving yards for Tee Higgins. **Prediction: Over.** Higgins should see a return to form after injuries and the lack of a long-term deal loomed over him last season. He'll be playing for a big contract in the next round of free agency. *–Ben Baby*

SCORE PROJECTIONS

WK	OPP	LOC	TM	OPP	WIN PROB
1	NE	H	25.4	17.8	76%
2	KC	A	24.0	27.3	38%
3	WAS	H	27.5	18.2	81%
4	CAR	A	25.4	20.7	66%
5	BAL	H	23.6	24.7	46%
6	NYG	A	26.8	18.2	79%
7	CLE	A	21.1	22.4	46%
8	PHI	H	26.8	24.1	60%
9	LV	H	26.1	17.7	78%
10	BAL	A	22.5	25.8	38%
11	LAC	A	26.1	22.6	62%
12					
13	PIT	H	23.3	19.2	64%
14	DAL	A	22.2	24.7	41%
15	TEN	A	26.4	19.7	73%
16	CLE	H	22.2	21.3	53%
17	DEN	H	27.5	18.0	82%
18	PIT	A	22.2	20.3	57%
			419	363	61%

Projected Wins: 10.4 (NFL Rank: 7)
Strength of Schedule Ranking: 6

FANTASY DEPTH CHART

QB
Joe Burrow
Jake Browning

RB
Zack Moss
Chase Brown
Trayveon Williams

WR
Ja'Marr Chase
Tee Higgins
Jermaine Burton
Andrei Iosivas
Trenton Irwin
Charlie Jones

TE
Mike Gesicki
Drew Sample
Tanner Hudson

K
Evan McPherson

USAGE PROJECTIONS

TARGET SHARES

Ja'Marr Chase	25%
Tee Higgins	19%
Jermaine Burton	12%
Chase Brown	8%
Zack Moss	6%

CARRY SHARES

Zack Moss	51%
Chase Brown	25%
Trayveon Williams	11%

TEAM SCORING FORECAST

Passing TD	Rushing TD	FG
30	15	28

CLEVELAND BROWNS

THE SKINNY

Even if Nick Chubb, who is returning to the field after a pair of knee surgeries, is back for Week 1, he might not be ready for a full workload. And the Browns' offseason trade for WR Jerry Jeudy signals a team seeking to unlock its passing game with quarterback Deshaun Watson in 2024.

Over/Under: 23 total TDs for Watson. **Prediction: Over.** If Watson stays healthy, he has his best group of pass-catchers since joining Cleveland and a new offensive coordinator in Ken Dorsey, who has a history of working with mobile quarterbacks. *–Daniel Oyefusi*

SCORE PROJECTIONS

WK	OPP	LOC	TM	OPP	WIN PROB
1	DAL	H	20.6	20.8	49%
2	JAX	A	20.5	18.7	56%
3	NYG	H	25.2	14.3	85%
4	LV	A	22.3	16.0	72%
5	WAS	A	23.8	16.4	75%
6	PHI	A	23.0	22.3	53%
7	CIN	H	22.4	21.1	54%
8	BAL	H	20.9	21.9	47%
9	LAC	H	24.5	18.7	70%
10					
11	NO	A	20.5	17.9	60%
12	PIT	H	20.6	16.4	65%
13	DEN	A	23.8	16.3	76%
14	PIT	A	19.5	17.5	57%
15	KC	H	22.4	23.3	46%
16	CIN	A	21.3	22.2	47%
17	MIA	H	20.9	19.7	54%
18	BAL	A	19.8	23.0	39%
			372	326	59%

Projected Wins: 10 (NFL Rank: 8)
Strength of Schedule Ranking: 22

FANTASY DEPTH CHART

QB
Deshaun Watson
Jameis Winston

RB
Nick Chubb
Jerome Ford
Nyheim Hines

WR
Amari Cooper
Jerry Jeudy
Elijah Moore
Cedric Tillman
David Bell
Jamari Thrash

TE
David Njoku
Jordan Akins
Giovanni Ricci

K
Dustin Hopkins

USAGE PROJECTIONS

TARGET SHARES

Amari Cooper	22%
Jerry Jeudy	18%
David Njoku	18%
Elijah Moore	12%
Jerome Ford	6%

CARRY SHARES

Nick Chubb	43%
Jerome Ford	28%
D'Onta Foreman	15%

TEAM SCORING FORECAST

Passing TD	Rushing TD	FG
23	15	29

Deshaun Watson

Brandin Cooks

DALLAS COWBOYS

THE SKINNY

The offense will look different than it has in recent years, especially in the running game, where a committee approach is expected. Along with better pass protection—despite two losses on the offensive line—the Cowboys will go as far as the passing game can take them.

Over/Under: 716 receiving yards for Brandin Cooks. **Prediction:** **Over.** Cooks had a slow start last season, but in the final nine games he had 37 catches and six TDs. Cooks should clear this number and potentially rack up a 1,000-yard season with his fifth franchise. *–Todd Archer*

SCORE PROJECTIONS

WK	OPP	LOC	TM	OPP	WIN PROB
1	CLE	A	20.8	20.6	51%
2	NO	H	24.0	17.9	71%
3	BAL	H	23.3	23.0	51%
4	NYG	A	26.5	16.5	83%
5	PIT	A	21.9	18.5	62%
6	DET	H	24.7	22.8	57%
7					
8	SF	A	21.1	24.8	37%
9	ATL	A	25.4	22.0	62%
10	PHI	H	26.5	22.3	65%
11	HOU	H	25.4	21.9	63%
12	WAS	A	26.1	17.5	79%
13	NYG	H	27.6	15.4	88%
14	CIN	H	24.7	22.2	59%
15	CAR	A	25.1	18.9	71%
16	TB	H	26.2	18.8	75%
17	PHI	A	25.4	23.4	57%
18	WAS	H	27.2	16.4	85%
			422	343	66%

Projected Wins: 11.2 (NFL Rank: 5)
Strength of Schedule Ranking: 13

FANTASY DEPTH CHART

QB
Dak Prescott
Cooper Rush

RB
Ezekiel Elliott
Rico Dowdle
Deuce Vaughn

WR
CeeDee Lamb
Brandin Cooks
Jalen Tolbert
KaVontae Turpin
Ryan Flournoy
Jalen Brooks

TE
Jake Ferguson
Peyton Hendershot
Luke Schoonmaker

K
Brandon Aubrey

USAGE PROJECTIONS

TARGET SHARES

CeeDee Lamb	27%
Jake Ferguson	15%
Brandin Cooks	14%
Jalen Tolbert	12%
Ezekiel Elliott	7%

CARRY SHARES

Ezekiel Elliott	46%
Rico Dowdle	27%
Deuce Vaughn	7%

TEAM SCORING FORECAST

Passing TD	Rushing TD	FG
30	15	29

DENVER BRONCOS

THE SKINNY

There are plenty of unknowns within the Broncos' offense, including who the starting QB will be after the first-round selection of Bo Nix. Head coach Sean Payton will be on the hunt for solutions in the red zone—the Broncos were one of the league's worst offenses in goal-to-go situations, had just eight rushing touchdowns overall and got little production from the tight end spot.

Over/Under: 48 receptions for Marvin Mims Jr. **Prediction:** **Over.** Even with his limited snap count last season, Mims finished with 22 receptions and a team-leading 17.1 yards per catch. *–Jeff Legwold*

SCORE PROJECTIONS

WK	OPP	LOC	TM	OPP	WIN PROB
1	SEA	A	18.4	24.3	29%
2	PIT	H	17.3	21.7	35%
3	TB	A	19.4	24.1	33%
4	NYJ	A	16.2	27.9	13%
5	LV	H	20.1	20.2	50%
6	LAC	H	21.2	24.0	40%
7	NO	A	17.3	23.2	30%
8	CAR	H	20.5	22.1	44%
9	BAL	A	16.6	28.3	13%
10	KC	A	18.0	29.8	13%
11	ATL	H	20.9	25.2	35%
12	LV	A	19.0	21.3	42%
13	CLE	H	16.3	23.8	24%
14					
15	IND	H	20.2	23.8	37%
16	LAC	A	20.1	25.1	33%
17	CIN	A	18.0	27.5	18%
18	KC	H	19.1	28.7	18%
			319	421	30%

Projected Wins: 5.1 (NFL Rank: 31)
Strength of Schedule Ranking: 25

FANTASY DEPTH CHART

QB
Bo Nix
Jarrett Stidham

RB
Javonte Williams
Samaje Perine
Jaleel McLaughlin

WR
Courtland Sutton
Marvin Mims Jr.
Tim Patrick
Josh Reynolds
Troy Franklin
Brandon Johnson

TE
Adam Trautman
Greg Dulcich
Lucas Krull

K
Wil Lutz

USAGE PROJECTIONS

TARGET SHARES

Courtland Sutton	21%
Marvin Mims Jr.	14%
Javonte Williams	10%
Greg Dulcich	8%
Samaje Perine	8%

CARRY SHARES

Javonte Williams	46%
Jaleel McLaughlin	25%
Samaje Perine	15%

TEAM SCORING FORECAST

Passing TD	Rushing TD	FG
20	11	27

Marvin Mims Jr.

Jameson Williams

DETROIT LIONS

THE SKINNY

After reaching multiyear extensions for WR Amon-Ra St. Brown and OT Penei Sewell, the Lions will look to pick up where they left off last season as one of the league's most explosive offenses. An underrated win for them was also keeping offensive coordinator Ben Johnson, who is well respected among players and members of the staff for his creative approach to playcalling.

Over/Under: 677 receiving yards for Jameson Williams. **Prediction:** **Over.** This year, he will have his first full training camp and has built trust with the coaching staff and QB Jared Goff to earn more opportunities. *–Eric Woodyard*

SCORE PROJECTIONS

WK	OPP	LOC	TM	OPP	WIN PROB
1	LAR	H	28.5	23.0	69%
2	TB	H	27.1	20.6	73%
3	ARI	A	28.1	21.0	75%
4	SEA	H	26.0	20.7	68%
5					
6	DAL	A	22.8	24.7	43%
7	MIN	A	26.0	20.9	68%
8	TEN	H	28.1	18.6	82%
9	GB	A	25.3	23.6	56%
10	HOU	A	25.3	24.8	52%
11	JAX	H	24.9	20.5	66%
12	IND	A	25.6	22.4	61%
13	CHI	H	25.3	21.1	65%
14	GB	H	26.4	22.5	64%
15	BUF	H	25.7	23.5	58%
16	CHI	A	24.2	22.1	57%
17	SF	A	22.1	26.6	34%
18	MIN	H	27.1	19.8	75%
			438	376	63%

Projected Wins: 10.6 (NFL Rank: 6)
Strength of Schedule Ranking: 14

FANTASY DEPTH CHART

QB
Jared Goff
Hendon Hooker

RB
Jahmyr Gibbs
David Montgomery
Craig Reynolds

WR
Amon-Ra St. Brown
Jameson Williams
Kalif Raymond
Donovan Peoples-Jones
Antoine Green
Maurice Alexander

TE
Sam LaPorta
Brock Wright
James Mitchell

K
Michael Badgley

USAGE PROJECTIONS

TARGET SHARES

Amon-Ra St. Brown	27%
Sam LaPorta	21%
Jameson Williams	16%
Jahmyr Gibbs	12%
Kalif Raymond	8%

CARRY SHARES

David Montgomery	41%
Jahmyr Gibbs	41%
Craig Reynolds	8%

TEAM SCORING FORECAST

Passing TD	Rushing TD	FG
26	22	28

GREEN BAY PACKERS

THE SKINNY

It took Matt LaFleur half the season to find a rhythm with Jordan Love last year, but once he found it, it sure worked, as Love threw 18 TDs and just one interception over the final eight games. Love should be able to do even more considering he returns all of his top receivers and tight ends.

Over/Under: 75 touches for Jayden Reed. **Prediction:** **Over.** It's not often a slot receiver is a team's No. 1 target, but Reed is so dynamic. He was also so effective as a rusher (119 yards on just 11 attempts) that the Packers will likely design more plays to take advantage of that. *–Rob Demovsky*

SCORE PROJECTIONS

WK	OPP	LOC	TM	OPP	WIN PROB
1	PHI	A	24.9	25.3	48%
2	IND	H	24.7	22.0	59%
3	TEN	A	25.0	20.4	66%
4	MIN	H	25.0	20.5	66%
5	LAR	A	25.4	24.8	52%
6	ARI	H	27.2	20.6	73%
7	HOU	H	24.3	24.4	50%
8	JAX	A	21.8	22.3	48%
9	DET	H	23.6	25.3	44%
10					
11	CHI	A	22.2	22.9	48%
12	SF	H	21.2	26.2	32%
13	MIA	H	22.2	23.3	46%
14	DET	A	22.5	26.4	36%
15	SEA	A	22.9	22.5	51%
16	NO	H	22.9	20.3	59%
17	MIN	A	24.0	21.6	58%
18	CHI	H	23.3	21.8	55%
			403	391	53%

Projected Wins: 8.9 (NFL Rank: 15)
Strength of Schedule Ranking: 21

FANTASY DEPTH CHART

QB
Jordan Love
Sean Clifford

RB
Josh Jacobs
MarShawn Lloyd
AJ Dillon

WR
Christian Watson
Romeo Doubs
Jayden Reed
Dontayvion Wicks
Bo Melton
Malik Heath

TE
Tucker Kraft
Luke Musgrave
Ben Sims

K
Anders Carlson

USAGE PROJECTIONS

TARGET SHARES

Christian Watson	17%
Jayden Reed	17%
Romeo Doubs	16%
Dontayvion Wicks	10%
Tucker Kraft	10%

CARRY SHARES

Josh Jacobs	59%
MarShawn Lloyd	18%
AJ Dillon	12%

TEAM SCORING FORECAST

Passing TD	Rushing TD	FG
30	14	27

Jayden Reed

Stefon Diggs

HOUSTON TEXANS

THE SKINNY

Texans offensive coordinator Bobby Slowik wants to be balanced. So while C.J. Stroud has weapons to throw to, Slowik still wants to run the ball effectively to keep defenses guessing. Before acquiring wideout Stefon Diggs, the Texans added RB Joe Mixon, so it's clear they want to run the ball, too.

Over/Under: 86 receptions for Diggs. **Prediction: Under.** Diggs will have to share touches with receivers Tank Dell and Nico Collins, so it's hard to envision him being force-fed. Even if he goes under this total, his opportunities should lead to explosive results. *–DJ Bien-Aime*

SCORE PROJECTIONS

WK	OPP	LOC	TM	OPP	WIN PROB
1	IND	A	24.7	23.1	56%
2	CHI	H	24.4	21.8	59%
3	MIN	A	25.1	21.6	62%
4	JAX	H	24.1	21.2	60%
5	BUF	H	24.8	24.2	52%
6	NE	A	24.0	19.6	66%
7	GB	A	24.4	24.3	50%
8	IND	H	25.8	22.0	63%
9	NYJ	A	21.9	26.2	35%
10	DET	H	24.8	25.3	48%
11	DAL	A	21.9	25.4	37%
12	TEN	H	27.3	19.3	77%
13	JAX	A	23.0	22.3	52%
14					
15	MIA	H	23.3	23.3	50%
16	KC	A	23.7	28.0	35%
17	BAL	H	23.3	25.5	42%
18	TEN	A	26.2	20.4	70%
			413	393	54%

Projected Wins: 9.2 (NFL Rank: 13)
Strength of Schedule Ranking: 29

FANTASY DEPTH CHART

QB
C.J. Stroud
Case Keenum

RB
Joe Mixon
Dare Ogunbowale
Dameon Pierce

WR
Stefon Diggs
Nico Collins
Tank Dell
Noah Brown
John Metchie III
Xavier Hutchinson

TE
Dalton Schultz
Brevin Jordan
Cade Stover

K
Ka'imi Fairbairn

USAGE PROJECTIONS

TARGET SHARES

Stefon Diggs	22%
Nico Collins	20%
Tank Dell	19%
Dalton Schultz	13%
Joe Mixon	9%

CARRY SHARES

Joe Mixon	58%
Dameon Pierce	20%
Dare Ogunbowale	10%

TEAM SCORING FORECAST

Passing TD	Rushing TD	FG
30	14	29

INDIANAPOLIS COLTS

THE SKINNY

If QB Anthony Richardson and RB Jonathan Taylor stay healthy, the Colts could have one of the NFL's more explosive and unpredictable offenses. Coach Shane Steichen is known for designing creative schemes, and he has the players to enable limitless RPO production in 2024.

Over/Under: 24 total TDs for Richardson. **Prediction: Over.** That's a high bar for a player who isn't yet a polished passer, but Richardson generated seven total touchdowns in just 12 quarters of play spread over four games as a rookie last season. His availability is the biggest variable *–Stephen Holder*

SCORE PROJECTIONS

WK	OPP	LOC	TM	OPP	WIN PROB
1	HOU	H	23.1	24.7	44%
2	GB	A	22.0	24.7	41%
3	CHI	H	22.1	22.1	50%
4	PIT	H	20.6	20.3	51%
5	JAX	A	20.6	22.6	43%
6	TEN	A	23.8	20.7	61%
7	MIA	H	21.0	23.6	41%
8	HOU	A	22.0	25.8	37%
9	MIN	A	22.7	22.0	53%
10	BUF	H	22.4	24.6	42%
11	NYJ	A	19.5	26.5	26%
12	DET	H	22.4	25.6	39%
13	NE	A	21.7	19.9	56%
14					
15	DEN	A	23.8	20.2	63%
16	TEN	H	24.9	19.6	68%
17	NYG	A	24.2	19.3	67%
18	JAX	H	21.7	21.5	51%
			379	384	49%

Projected Wins: 8.3 (NFL Rank: 18)
Strength of Schedule Ranking: 7

FANTASY DEPTH CHART

QB
Anthony Richardson
Joe Flacco

RB
Jonathan Taylor
Trey Sermon
Evan Hull

WR
Michael Pittman Jr.
Adonai Mitchell
Josh Downs
Alec Pierce
Anthony Gould
Ashton Dulin

TE
Jelani Woods
Kylen Granson
Andrew Ogletree

K
Matt Gay

USAGE PROJECTIONS

TARGET SHARES

Michael Pittman Jr.	27%
Josh Downs	15%
Adonai Mitchell	15%
Jonathan Taylor	10%
Jelani Woods	9%

CARRY SHARES

Jonathan Taylor	56%
Anthony Richardson	19%
Trey Sermon	16%

TEAM SCORING FORECAST

Passing TD	Rushing TD	FG
18	22	28

Anthony Richardson

JACKSONVILLE JAGUARS

THE SKINNY

The addition of 6-foot-3 WR Brian Thomas Jr. gives Trevor Lawrence a tall and speedy downfield threat. The biggest reasons for optimism: Everybody is healthy, and the team made a significant upgrade at center with Mitch Morse. The Jaguars should have a top-10 offense again if everyone remains healthy.

Over/Under: 49 receptions for Gabe Davis. **Prediction: Under.** Had the Jaguars not drafted Thomas with the 23rd pick, the over would be the prediction here, because Davis would be the No. 2 behind slot receiver Christian Kirk. *–Michael DiRocco*

SCORE PROJECTIONS

WK	OPP	LOC	TM	OPP	WIN PROB
1	MIA	A	19.1	23.0	36%
2	CLE	H	18.7	20.5	44%
3	BUF	A	20.5	23.9	38%
4	HOU	A	21.2	24.1	40%
5	IND	H	22.6	20.6	57%
6	CHI	A	20.7	20.9	49%
7	NE	H	21.4	17.6	63%
8	GB	H	22.3	21.8	52%
9	PHI	A	22.3	24.5	42%
10	MIN	H	23.0	19.1	64%
11	DET	A	20.5	24.9	34%
12					
13	HOU	H	22.3	23.0	48%
14	TEN	A	23.0	18.9	64%
15	NYJ	H	19.8	23.6	36%
16	LV	A	21.5	18.1	62%
17	TEN	H	24.0	17.8	72%
18	IND	A	21.5	21.7	49%
			364	364	50%

Projected Wins: 8.5 (NFL Rank: 17)
Strength of Schedule Ranking: 17

FANTASY DEPTH CHART

QB
Trevor Lawrence
Mac Jones

RB
Travis Etienne Jr.
Tank Bigsby
D'Ernest Johnson

WR
Christian Kirk
Brian Thomas Jr.
Gabe Davis
Devin Duvernay
Parker Washington
Tim Jones

TE
Evan Engram
Luke Farrell
Brenton Strange

K
Cam Little

USAGE PROJECTIONS

TARGET SHARES

Evan Engram	20%
Christian Kirk	20%
Brian Thomas Jr.	17%
Gabe Davis	16%
Travis Etienne Jr.	10%

CARRY SHARES

Travis Etienne Jr.	57%
Tank Bigsby	21%
D'Ernest Johnson	14%

TEAM SCORING FORECAST

Passing TD	Rushing TD	FG
23	14	28

KANSAS CITY CHIEFS

THE SKINNY

The Chiefs brought in some serious speed in WRs Marquise Brown and Xavier Worthy, which could open up the downfield passing game that has produced few big plays since Tyreek Hill was traded two years ago. They need big seasons from both players, given the uncertainty over Rashee Rice's availability and Travis Kelce's advancing age.

Over/Under: 50 touches for Worthy. **Prediction: Under.** It's difficult to predict a busy season for any Chiefs rookie wide receiver, even a first-round pick like Worthy. Patrick Mahomes has many other targets. *–Adam Teicher*

SCORE PROJECTIONS

WK	OPP	LOC	TM	OPP	WIN PROB
1	BAL	H	25.8	24.7	54%
2	CIN	H	27.3	24.0	62%
3	ATL	A	28.0	23.8	65%
4	LAC	A	28.3	22.6	70%
5	NO	H	26.6	19.6	74%
6					
7	SF	A	23.7	26.6	40%
8	LV	A	27.2	18.8	78%
9	TB	H	28.7	20.6	78%
10	DEN	H	29.8	18.0	87%
11	BUF	A	26.2	24.6	56%
12	CAR	A	27.6	20.7	74%
13	LV	H	28.3	17.7	84%
14	LAC	H	29.4	21.5	77%
15	CLE	A	23.3	22.4	54%
16	HOU	H	28.0	23.7	65%
17	PIT	A	24.4	20.3	64%
18	DEN	A	28.7	19.1	82%
			461	369	68%

Projected Wins: 11.6 (NFL Rank: 3)
Strength of Schedule Ranking: 10

FANTASY DEPTH CHART

QB
Patrick Mahomes
Carson Wentz

RB
Isiah Pacheco
Clyde Edwards-Helaire
Keaontay Ingram

WR
Rashee Rice
Marquise Brown
Xavier Worthy
Justin Watson
Skyy Moore
Kadarius Toney

TE
Travis Kelce
Noah Gray
Irv Smith Jr.

K
Harrison Butker

USAGE PROJECTIONS

TARGET SHARES

Travis Kelce	18%
Marquise Brown	16%
Rashee Rice	16%
Xavier Worthy	15%
Isiah Pacheco	9%

CARRY SHARES

Isiah Pacheco	58%
Clyde Edwards-Helaire	23%
Keaontay Ingram	6%

TEAM SCORING FORECAST

Passing TD	Rushing TD	FG
37	14	28

Brock Bowers

LAS VEGAS RAIDERS

THE SKINNY

The Raiders enter camp with Aidan O'Connell and vet pickup Gardner Minshew at QB. Welp. As such, the offense will be a work in progress under new playcaller Luke Getsy, who has authored top-tier NFL running attacks.

Over/Under: 652 receiving yards for Brock Bowers. **Prediction: Under.** Bowers may be the preeminent tight end of his era, and he is versatile, but with Davante Adams the clear first option, Jakobi Meyers taking another step and either QB throwing the ball in Getsy's run-heavy scheme, there just do not seem to be enough balls to go around. *–Paul Gutierrez*

SCORE PROJECTIONS

WK	OPP	LOC	TM	OPP	WIN PROB
1	LAC	A	19.8	23.7	36%
2	BAL	A	16.3	26.9	16%
3	CAR	H	20.2	20.7	48%
4	CLE	H	16.0	22.3	28%
5	DEN	A	20.2	20.1	50%
6	PIT	H	17.0	20.3	38%
7	LAR	A	20.6	25.1	34%
8	KC	H	18.8	27.2	22%
9	CIN	A	17.7	26.1	22%
10					
11	MIA	A	16.3	24.7	22%
12	DEN	H	21.3	19.0	58%
13	KC	A	17.7	28.3	16%
14	TB	A	19.1	22.7	37%
15	ATL	H	20.6	23.8	39%
16	JAX	H	18.1	21.5	38%
17	NO	A	17.0	21.8	33%
18	LAC	H	20.9	22.6	44%
			318	397	34%

Projected Wins: 5.8 (NFL Rank: 26)
Strength of Schedule Ranking: 20

FANTASY DEPTH CHART

QB
Gardner Minshew
Aidan O'Connell

RB
Zamir White
Ameer Abdullah
Alexander Mattison

WR
Davante Adams
Jakobi Meyers
Michael Gallup
Tre Tucker
Jalen Guyton
DJ Turner

TE
Brock Bowers
Michael Mayer
Harrison Bryant

K
Daniel Carlson

USAGE PROJECTIONS

TARGET SHARES

Davante Adams	27%
Jakobi Meyers	19%
Brock Bowers	15%
Zamir White	8%
Michael Gallup	8%

CARRY SHARES

Zamir White	50%
Alexander Mattison	30%
Ameer Abdullah	6%

TEAM SCORING FORECAST

Passing TD	Rushing TD	FG
18	12	29

LOS ANGELES CHARGERS

THE SKINNY

After hiring coach Jim Harbaugh, the Chargers revamped the offense. Receivers Keenan Allen and Mike Williams, tight end Gerald Everett and running back Austin Ekeler—who accounted for 57% of Herbert's career completions, touchdowns and passing yards—will play elsewhere in 2024.

Over/Under: 66 receptions for Ladd McConkey. **Prediction: Under.** Allen has the team record for receptions by a rookie at 71; no one else has had more than 59, and with the Chargers focused on rushing, 66 seems like somewhat of a long shot for McConkey. *–Kris Rhim*

SCORE PROJECTIONS

WK	OPP	LOC	TM	OPP	WIN PROB
1	LV	H	23.7	19.8	64%
2	CAR	A	23.0	22.8	50%
3	PIT	A	19.7	22.4	40%
4	KC	H	22.6	28.3	30%
5					
6	DEN	A	24.0	21.2	60%
7	ARI	A	25.1	23.1	57%
8	NO	H	21.9	21.8	51%
9	CLE	A	18.7	24.5	30%
10	TEN	H	25.1	20.7	66%
11	CIN	H	22.6	26.1	38%
12	BAL	H	21.2	26.9	30%
13	ATL	A	23.3	25.9	41%
14	KC	A	21.5	29.4	23%
15	TB	H	24.0	22.7	55%
16	DEN	H	25.1	20.1	67%
17	NE	A	21.9	21.0	53%
18	LV	A	22.6	20.9	56%
			386	398	48%

Projected Wins: 8.1 (NFL Rank: 20)
Strength of Schedule Ranking: 2

FANTASY DEPTH CHART

QB
Justin Herbert
Easton Stick

RB
Gus Edwards
J.K. Dobbins
Isaiah Spiller

WR
Ladd McConkey
Josh Palmer
Quentin Johnston
DJ Chark Jr.
Derius Davis
Brenden Rice

TE
Hayden Hurst
Will Dissly
Stone Smartt

K
Cameron Dicker

USAGE PROJECTIONS

TARGET SHARES

Ladd McConkey	18%
Josh Palmer	15%
Quentin Johnston	14%
DJ Chark Jr.	13%
Hayden Hurst	11%

CARRY SHARES

Gus Edwards	40%
J.K. Dobbins	34%
Isaiah Spiller	9%

TEAM SCORING FORECAST

Passing TD	Rushing TD	FG
26	14	29

Ladd McConkey

Cooper Kupp

LOS ANGELES RAMS

THE SKINNY

The Rams return their core of offensive playmakers, including QB Matthew Stafford, RB Kyren Williams and WRs Cooper Kupp and Puka Nacua, and they improved the offensive line in free agency. The health of Stafford and Kupp will be a big determining factor for the team's success in 2024.

Over/Under: 78 receptions for Kupp. **Prediction: Over.** Kupp averaged 4.9 catches per game last season alongside Nacua, catching just 61% of targets, below his 72% career rate. If he remains in good health, Kupp should hit this over. *–Sarah Barshop*

SCORE PROJECTIONS

WK	OPP	LOC	TM	OPP	WIN PROB
1	DET	A	23.0	28.5	31%
2	ARI	A	26.5	23.8	60%
3	SF	H	21.6	28.3	27%
4	CHI	A	22.6	25.0	42%
5	GB	H	24.8	25.4	48%
6					
7	LV	H	25.1	20.6	66%
8	MIN	H	25.5	22.7	60%
9	SEA	A	23.4	24.7	45%
10	MIA	H	22.7	25.4	40%
11	NE	A	23.4	21.7	56%
12	PHI	H	25.9	26.9	46%
13	NO	A	22.3	23.5	46%
14	BUF	H	24.1	26.3	42%
15	SF	A	20.5	29.4	20%
16	NYJ	A	21.2	28.3	26%
17	ARI	H	27.6	22.7	67%
18	SEA	H	24.4	23.6	53%
			405	427	46%

Projected Wins: 7.7 (NFL Rank: 22)
Strength of Schedule Ranking: 27

FANTASY DEPTH CHART

QB
Matthew Stafford
Jimmy Garoppolo

RB
Kyren Williams
Blake Corum
Ronnie Rivers

WR
Puka Nacua
Cooper Kupp
Demarcus Robinson
Tutu Atwell
Jordan Whittington
Tyler Johnson

TE
Tyler Higbee
Colby Parkinson
Hunter Long

K
Joshua Karty

USAGE PROJECTIONS

TARGET SHARES

Puka Nacua	23%
Cooper Kupp	20%
Demarcus Robinson	15%
Tyler Higbee	8%
Kyren Williams	8%

CARRY SHARES

Kyren Williams	59%
Blake Corum	27%
Ronnie Rivers	6%

TEAM SCORING FORECAST

Passing TD	Rushing TD	FG
27	17	27

MIAMI DOLPHINS

THE SKINNY

The NFL's No. 1 offense from a season ago kept its core together with four players who can score from anywhere on the field, as well as quarterback Tua Tagovailoa. Miami also added WR Odell Beckham Jr., TE Jonnu Smith and rookie RB Jaylen Wright to the mix.

Over/Under: 208 touches for De'Von Achane. **Prediction: Under.** Achane was on pace for 201 touches over 17 games last season, but there's only one ball and an offense full of playmakers. Achane's touches should increase from the 130 he saw last season, but not quite to this level. *–Marcel Louis-Jacques*

SCORE PROJECTIONS

WK	OPP	LOC	TM	OPP	WIN PROB
1	JAX	H	23.0	19.1	64%
2	BUF	H	23.7	22.1	56%
3	SEA	A	22.9	20.4	59%
4	TEN	H	26.1	17.1	80%
5	NE	A	22.9	17.4	69%
6					
7	IND	A	23.6	21.0	59%
8	ARI	H	27.2	18.5	79%
9	BUF	A	22.6	23.2	48%
10	LAR	A	25.4	22.7	60%
11	LV	H	24.7	16.3	78%
12	NE	H	24.0	16.4	76%
13	GB	A	23.3	22.2	54%
14	NYJ	H	21.9	22.9	46%
15	HOU	A	23.3	23.3	50%
16	SF	H	21.2	24.1	40%
17	CLE	A	19.7	20.9	46%
18	NYJ	A	20.8	24.0	39%
			396	352	59%

Projected Wins: 10 (NFL Rank: 9)
Strength of Schedule Ranking: 19

FANTASY DEPTH CHART

QB
Tua Tagovailoa
Mike White

RB
Raheem Mostert
De'Von Achane
Jaylen Wright

WR
Tyreek Hill
Jaylen Waddle
Odell Beckham Jr.
Malik Washington
Braxton Berrios
River Cracraft

TE
Jonnu Smith
Durham Smythe
Jody Fortson

K
Jason Sanders

USAGE PROJECTIONS

TARGET SHARES

Tyreek Hill	27%
Jaylen Waddle	21%
De'Von Achane	11%
Odell Beckham Jr.	10%
Jonnu Smith	8%

CARRY SHARES

De'Von Achane	39%
Raheem Mostert	37%
Jaylen Wright	12%

TEAM SCORING FORECAST

Passing TD	Rushing TD	FG
25	17	27

De'Von Achane

Aaron Jones

MINNESOTA VIKINGS

THE SKINNY

The Vikings' offense is embarking on a transition after bidding farewell to QB Kirk Cousins. Rookie J.J. McCarthy projects as their long-term starter, but as it stands now, the plan is for veteran Sam Darnold to open training camp with the first team. So expect an offense geared toward Darnold to start off the season, one that focuses on downfield passing.

Over/Under: 207 touches for Aaron Jones. **Prediction: Over.** That works out to about 12 touches per game, which will be an easy mark to meet assuming Jones—the best running back on the roster—stays healthy. *-Kevin Seifert*

SCORE PROJECTIONS

WK	OPP	LOC	TM	OPP	WIN PROB
1	NYG	A	22.7	19.7	61%
2	SF	H	18.4	26.9	21%
3	HOU	H	21.6	25.1	38%
4	GB	A	20.5	25.0	34%
5	NYJ	H	18.6	26.3	24%
6					
7	DET	H	20.9	26.0	32%
8	LAR	A	22.7	25.5	40%
9	IND	H	22.0	22.7	47%
10	JAX	A	19.1	23.0	36%
11	TEN	A	22.3	21.1	54%
12	CHI	A	19.5	23.6	35%
13	ARI	H	24.4	21.3	61%
14	ATL	H	22.7	24.1	45%
15	CHI	H	20.6	22.5	43%
16	SEA	A	20.2	23.2	39%
17	GB	H	21.6	24.0	42%
18	DET	A	19.8	27.1	25%
			357	407	40%

Projected Wins: 6.8 (NFL Rank: 25)
Strength of Schedule Ranking: 24

FANTASY DEPTH CHART

QB
J.J. McCarthy
Sam Darnold

RB
Aaron Jones
Ty Chandler
Kene Nwangwu

WR
Justin Jefferson
Jordan Addison
Brandon Powell
Trent Sherfield
Jalen Nailor
Trishton Jackson

TE
T.J. Hockenson
Josh Oliver
Johnny Mundt

K
Will Reichard

USAGE PROJECTIONS

TARGET SHARES

Justin Jefferson	28%
Jordan Addison	19%
T.J. Hockenson	15%
Aaron Jones	10%
Brandon Powell	5%

CARRY SHARES

Aaron Jones	42%
Ty Chandler	40%
J.J. McCarthy	6%

TEAM SCORING FORECAST

Passing TD	Rushing TD	FG
23	13	28

NEW ENGLAND PATRIOTS

THE SKINNY

The plan is to have an open competition at QB, with veteran Jacoby Brissett likely holding the upper hand so Drake Maye isn't rushed onto the field. Wide-zone concepts will be featured, and drafting two WRs early should help open things up more than they have been the past two years.

Over/Under: 725 receiving yards for DeMario Douglas. **Prediction: Under.** In the old Josh McDaniels-type offense, projecting a high yardage total for a slot receiver was usually a sure bet. But that's more of a wild card until we see how coordinator Alex Van Pelt prioritizes that part of the offense. *-Mike Reiss*

SCORE PROJECTIONS

WK	OPP	LOC	TM	OPP	WIN PROB
1	CIN	A	17.8	25.4	24%
2	SEA	H	19.2	21.1	43%
3	NYJ	A	16.0	25.8	18%
4	SF	A	15.3	26.9	13%
5	MIA	H	17.4	22.9	31%
6	HOU	H	19.6	24.0	34%
7	JAX	A	17.6	21.4	37%
8	NYJ	H	17.1	24.7	24%
9	TEN	A	20.2	20.0	51%
10	CHI	A	17.4	22.5	32%
11	LAR	H	21.7	23.4	44%
12	MIA	A	16.4	24.0	24%
13	IND	H	19.9	21.7	44%
14					
15	ARI	A	21.3	21.3	50%
16	BUF	A	17.8	25.0	25%
17	LAC	H	21.0	21.9	47%
18	BUF	H	18.9	23.9	32%
			315	396	34%

Projected Wins: 5.7 (NFL Rank: 27)
Strength of Schedule Ranking: 32

FANTASY DEPTH CHART

QB
Drake Maye
Jacoby Brissett

RB
Rhamondre Stevenson
Antonio Gibson
Kevin Harris

WR
DeMario Douglas
Kendrick Bourne
Ja'Lynn Polk
JuJu Smith-Schuster
K.J. Osborn
Javon Baker

TE
Hunter Henry
Austin Hooper
Mitchell Wilcox

K
Chad Ryland

USAGE PROJECTIONS

TARGET SHARES

DeMario Douglas	16%
Kendrick Bourne	15%
Ja'Lynn Polk	15%
Hunter Henry	12%
Rhamondre Stevenson	11%

CARRY SHARES

Rhamondre Stevenson	49%
Antonio Gibson	32%
Drake Maye	7%

TEAM SCORING FORECAST

Passing TD	Rushing TD	FG
19	12	26

DeMario Douglas

Rashid Shaheed

NEW ORLEANS SAINTS

THE SKINNY

The Saints completely overhauled their offensive coaching staff with the idea to use more play-action, an area where they fell behind last season. The offense certainly felt more cohesive in the second half of Derek Carr's first season, and the Saints hope to see that trend continue in Year 2.

Over/Under: 54 receptions for Rashid Shaheed. **Prediction: Under.** In some seasons, 54 catches would be enough to lead the team. Shaheed will have to contend with both No. 1 WR Chris Olave and RB Alvin Kamara for receptions, among others. —*Katherine Terrell*

SCORE PROJECTIONS

WK	OPP	LOC	TM	OPP	WIN PROB
1	CAR	H	22.1	18.9	61%
2	DAL	A	17.9	24.0	29%
3	PHI	H	22.5	23.4	47%
4	ATL	A	21.4	23.1	44%
5	KC	A	19.6	26.6	26%
6	TB	H	22.1	19.9	58%
7	DEN	H	23.2	17.3	70%
8	LAC	A	21.8	21.9	49%
9	CAR	A	21.0	20.0	54%
10	ATL	H	22.5	22.0	52%
11	CLE	H	17.9	20.5	40%
12					
13	LAR	H	23.5	22.3	54%
14	NYG	A	22.5	17.5	67%
15	WAS	H	23.2	17.5	70%
16	GB	A	20.3	22.9	41%
17	LV	H	21.8	17.0	67%
18	TB	A	21.0	20.9	50%
			364	356	52%

Projected Wins: 8.8 (NFL Rank: 16)
Strength of Schedule Ranking: 4

FANTASY DEPTH CHART

QB
Derek Carr
Nathan Peterman

RB
Alvin Kamara
Jamaal Williams
Kendre Miller

WR
Chris Olave
Rashid Shaheed
Bub Means
Cedrick Wilson
A.T. Perry
Equanimeous St. Brown

TE
Juwan Johnson
Foster Moreau
Taysom Hill

K
Blake Grupe

USAGE PROJECTIONS

TARGET SHARES

Chris Olave	24%
Rashid Shaheed	15%
Alvin Kamara	14%
Juwan Johnson	12%
Taysom Hill	7%

CARRY SHARES

Alvin Kamara	43%
Jamaal Williams	20%
Kendre Miller	17%

TEAM SCORING FORECAST

Passing TD	Rushing TD	FG
25	13	27

NEW YORK GIANTS

THE SKINNY

Sure, the bar is incredibly low, but the Giants' offense looks better for the skill positions going into 2024. Not good, but better. They added a potential No. 1 receiver in Malik Nabers and spent a ton of resources in free agency on the offensive line, signing at least two projected starters—maybe three.

Over/Under: 1,032 receiving yards for Nabers. **Prediction: Over.** The Giants are going to scheme the ball into Nabers' hands. As long as the opportunities are there, so too will be the production. It almost doesn't matter who's at QB when it comes to standout rookie receivers. -*Jordan Raanan*

SCORE PROJECTIONS

WK	OPP	LOC	TM	OPP	WIN PROB
1	MIN	H	19.7	22.7	39%
2	WAS	A	19.6	22.1	41%
3	CLE	A	14.3	25.2	15%
4	DAL	H	16.5	26.5	17%
5	SEA	A	17.5	24.7	25%
6	CIN	H	18.2	26.8	21%
7	PHI	H	20.0	26.9	26%
8	PIT	A	15.4	23.2	24%
9	WAS	H	20.7	21.0	49%
10	CAR	A	19.1	23.0	36%
11					
12	TB	H	19.7	23.4	37%
13	DAL	A	15.4	27.6	12%
14	NO	H	17.5	22.5	33%
15	BAL	H	16.8	27.6	15%
16	ATL	A	18.9	26.6	24%
17	IND	H	19.3	24.2	33%
18	PHI	A	18.9	28.0	20%
			307	422	27%

Projected Wins: 4.7 (NFL Rank: 32)
Strength of Schedule Ranking: 18

FANTASY DEPTH CHART

QB
Daniel Jones
Drew Lock

RB
Devin Singletary
Tyrone Tracy Jr.
Eric Gray

WR
Malik Nabers
Darius Slayton
Wan'Dale Robinson
Jalin Hyatt
Allen Robinson II
Isaiah McKenzie

TE
Daniel Bellinger
Theo Johnson
Chris Manhertz

K
Graham Gano

USAGE PROJECTIONS

TARGET SHARES

Malik Nabers	22%
Wan'Dale Robinson	15%
Darius Slayton	14%
Jalin Hyatt	13%
Devin Singletary 8	8%

CARRY SHARES

Devin Singletary	49%
Tyrone Tracy Jr.	16%
Eric Gray	14%

TEAM SCORING FORECAST

Passing TD	Rushing TD	FG
17	12	28

Malik Nabers

Garrett Wilson

NEW YORK JETS

THE SKINNY

Anything is better than last season, when the Jets scored a league-low 18 touchdowns. A healthy Aaron Rodgers will make a dramatic difference. The offensive line is better and deeper than in 2023, which should result in even more production from Garrett Wilson and Breece Hall. Will a third weapon emerge? Can offensive coordinator Nathaniel Hackett galvanize the talent?

Over/Under: 1,139 receiving yards for Wilson. **Prediction:** **Over.** Wilson recorded 1,103 and 1,042 yards in his first two seasons—and he did that with six different QBs. Imagine what he can do with Rodgers. *–Rich Cimini*

SCORE PROJECTIONS

WK	OPP	LOC	TM	OPP	WIN PROB
1	SF	A	21.9	24.8	40%
2	TEN	A	26.8	17.9	80%
3	NE	H	25.8	16.0	82%
4	DEN	H	27.9	16.2	87%
5	MIN	A	26.3	18.6	76%
6	BUF	H	25.4	21.8	63%
7	PIT	A	22.6	18.5	64%
8	NE	A	24.7	17.1	76%
9	HOU	H	26.2	21.9	65%
10	ARI	A	27.9	19.2	79%
11	IND	H	26.5	19.5	74%
12					
13	SEA	H	25.8	19.0	74%
14	MIA	A	22.9	21.9	54%
15	JAX	A	23.6	19.8	64%
16	LAR	H	28.3	21.2	74%
17	BUF	A	24.4	22.8	55%
18	MIA	H	24.0	20.8	61%
			431	337	69%

Projected Wins: 11.7 (NFL Rank: 2)
Strength of Schedule Ranking: 9

FANTASY DEPTH CHART

QB
Aaron Rodgers
Tyrod Taylor

RB
Breece Hall
Braelon Allen
Isaiah Davis

WR
Garrett Wilson
Mike Williams
Malachi Corley
Xavier Gipson
Jason Brownlee
Allen Lazard

TE
Tyler Conklin
Jeremy Ruckert
Kenny Yeboah

K
Greg Zuerlein

USAGE PROJECTIONS

TARGET SHARES

Garrett Wilson	24%
Mike Williams	16%
Breece Hall	15%
Tyler Conklin	13%
Malachi Corley	10%

CARRY SHARES

Breece Hall	54%
Braelon Allen	18%
Isaiah David	15%

TEAM SCORING FORECAST

Passing TD	Rushing TD	FG
31	16	28

PHILADELPHIA EAGLES

THE SKINNY

Expect fireworks. The addition of Saquon Barkley in free agency gives QB Jalen Hurts yet another top-end skill-position player. With A.J. Brown and DeVonta Smith on the outside, tight end Dallas Goedert working the middle and Barkley coming out of the backfield, defenses will have a hard time accounting for everyone.

Over/Under: 1,400 total yards for Barkley. **Prediction:** **Under.** Health will be the determining factor here. Barkley has played more than 14 games in a season just once since 2020. *–Tim McManus*

SCORE PROJECTIONS

WK	OPP	LOC	TM	OPP	WIN PROB
1	GB	H	25.3	24.9	52%
2	ATL	H	27.0	24.5	59%
3	NO	A	23.4	22.5	53%
4	TB	A	25.5	23.4	57%
5					
6	CLE	H	22.3	23.0	47%
7	NYG	A	26.9	20.0	74%
8	CIN	A	24.1	26.8	40%
9	JAX	H	24.5	22.3	58%
10	DAL	A	22.3	26.5	35%
11	WAS	H	27.7	19.9	76%
12	LAR	A	26.9	25.9	54%
13	BAL	A	22.7	27.6	33%
14	CAR	H	26.6	21.4	68%
15	PIT	H	23.4	21.0	59%
16	WAS	A	26.6	21.0	69%
17	DAL	H	23.4	25.4	43%
18	NYG	H	28.0	18.9	80%
			426	395	56%

Projected Wins: 9.6 (NFL Rank: 10)
Strength of Schedule Ranking: 5

FANTASY DEPTH CHART

QB
Jalen Hurts
Kenny Pickett

RB
Saquon Barkley
Kenneth Gainwell
Will Shipley

WR
A.J. Brown
DeVonta Smith
Parris Campbell
Ainias Smith
Johnny Wilson
Britain Covey

TE
Dallas Goedert
C.J. Uzomah
Grant Calcaterra

K
Jake Elliott

USAGE PROJECTIONS

TARGET SHARES

A.J. Brown	27%
DeVonta Smith	23%
Dallas Goedert	17%
Saquon Barkley	12%
Parris Campbell	5%

CARRY SHARES

Saquon Barkley	58%
Jalen Hurts	18%
Kenneth Gainwell	14%

TEAM SCORING FORECAST

Passing TD	Rushing TD	FG
24	22	29

Saquon Barkley

PITTSBURGH STEELERS

THE SKINNY

It's a new day in Pittsburgh. Not only do the Steelers have a new offensive coordinator in Arthur Smith, but they've got a brand-new quarterback room led by Russell Wilson, with Justin Fields hot on his heels. But even with the new QBs, the Steelers' offensive line-heavy draft class further confirms the team's approach: ground and pound.

Over/Under: 4 starts for Justin Fields. **Prediction:** **Over.** If Wilson stumbles or gets hurt, Fields will be right there to take the reins—especially with the Steelers trying to determine his long-term viability. *–Brooke Pryor*

SCORE PROJECTIONS

WK	OPP	LOC	TM	OPP	WIN PROB
1	ATL	A	21.0	22.0	46%
2	DEN	A	21.7	17.3	65%
3	LAC	H	22.4	19.7	60%
4	IND	A	20.3	20.6	49%
5	DAL	H	18.5	21.9	38%
6	LV	A	20.3	17.0	62%
7	NYJ	H	18.5	22.6	36%
8	NYG	H	23.2	15.4	76%
9					
10	WAS	A	21.7	17.5	65%
11	BAL	H	18.9	23.0	36%
12	CLE	A	16.4	20.6	35%
13	CIN	A	19.2	23.3	36%
14	CLE	H	17.5	19.5	43%
15	PHI	A	21.0	23.4	41%
16	BAL	A	17.8	24.1	28%
17	KC	H	20.3	24.4	36%
18	CIN	H	20.3	22.2	43%
			339	354	47%

Projected Wins: 7.9 (NFL Rank: 21)
Strength of Schedule Ranking: 30

FANTASY DEPTH CHART

QB
Russell Wilson
Justin Fields

RB
Najee Harris
Jaylen Warren
Cordarrelle Patterson

WR
George Pickens
Van Jefferson
Roman Wilson
Calvin Austin III
Quez Watkins
Scotty Miller

TE
Pat Freiermuth
Connor Heyward
Darnell Washington

K
Chris Boswell

USAGE PROJECTIONS

TARGET SHARES

George Pickens	22%
Pat Freiermuth	16%
Jaylen Warren	13%
Van Jefferson	10%
Roman Wilson	9%

CARRY SHARES

Najee Harris	49%
Jaylen Warren	28%
Cordarrelle Patterson	7%

TEAM SCORING FORECAST

Passing TD	Rushing TD	FG
19	14	29

SAN FRANCISCO 49ERS

THE SKINNY

In 2023, the Niners shifted to a Christian McCaffrey–centric offense, spinning everything they do off his versatility. That won't change this season, as QB Brock Purdy has now settled into the starting role. Expect McCaffrey to be the focal point, with Purdy continuing to evolve in the dropback passing game and distributing the ball to other playmakers like Brandon Aiyuk, Deebo Samuel and George Kittle.

Over/Under: 91 touches for Samuel. **Prediction:** **Over.** Samuel had 97 touches in 2023 while appearing in 15 games. *–Nick Wagoner*

SCORE PROJECTIONS

WK	OPP	LOC	TM	OPP	WIN PROB
1	NYJ	H	24.8	21.9	60%
2	MIN	A	26.9	18.4	79%
3	LAR	A	28.3	21.6	73%
4	NE	H	26.9	15.3	87%
5	ARI	H	30.1	17.4	89%
6	SEA	A	25.8	19.3	72%
7	KC	H	26.6	23.7	60%
8	DAL	H	24.8	21.1	63%
9					
10	TB	A	26.9	19.2	76%
11	SEA	H	26.9	18.3	79%
12	GB	A	26.2	21.2	68%
13	BUF	A	25.5	22.1	62%
14	CHI	H	26.2	18.6	76%
15	LAR	H	29.4	20.5	80%
16	MIA	A	24.1	21.2	60%
17	DET	H	26.6	22.1	66%
18	ARI	A	29.0	18.5	84%
			455	340	73%

Projected Wins: 12.4 (NFL Rank: 1)
Strength of Schedule Ranking: 23

FANTASY DEPTH CHART

QB
Brock Purdy
Joshua Dobbs

RB
Christian McCaffrey
Elijah Mitchell
Jordan Mason

WR
Deebo Samuel
Brandon Aiyuk
Ricky Pearsall
Jauan Jennings
Jacob Cowing
Danny Gray

TE
George Kittle
Logan Thomas
Cameron Latu

K
Jake Moody

USAGE PROJECTIONS

TARGET SHARES

Brandon Aiyuk	22%
Deebo Samuel	18%
George Kittle	17%
Christian McCaffrey	16%
Ricky Pearsall	9%

CARRY SHARES

Christian McCaffrey	56%
Elijah Mitchell	17%
Jordan Mason	8%

TEAM SCORING FORECAST

Passing TD	Rushing TD	FG
28	24	27

Jaxon Smith-Njigba

SEATTLE SEAHAWKS

THE SKINNY

New coordinator Ryan Grubb oversaw one of college football's pass-heaviest offenses the past two seasons at Washington, but Mike Macdonald is a defensive-minded head coach who will undoubtedly want to focus more on the run game. The O-line has a chance to be noticeably better in 2024.

Over/Under: 72 receptions for Jaxon Smith-Njigba. **Prediction: Over.** He caught 63 passes last season despite the Seahawks running the fewest offensive plays of any team. Improvements on third down and on defense would put him in position for an increase in targets. *–Brady Henderson*

SCORE PROJECTIONS

WK	OPP	LOC	TM	OPP	WIN PROB
1	DEN	H	24.3	18.4	71%
2	NE	A	21.1	19.2	57%
3	MIA	H	20.4	22.9	41%
4	DET	A	20.7	26.0	32%
5	NYG	H	24.7	17.5	75%
6	SF	H	19.3	25.8	28%
7	ATL	A	22.5	24.2	44%
8	BUF	H	21.8	23.9	43%
9	LAR	H	24.7	23.4	55%
10					
11	SF	A	18.3	26.9	21%
12	ARI	H	25.4	20.2	68%
13	NYJ	A	19.0	25.8	26%
14	ARI	A	24.3	21.3	61%
15	GB	H	22.5	22.9	49%
16	MIN	H	23.2	20.2	61%
17	CHI	A	20.4	22.5	42%
18	LAR	A	23.6	24.4	47%
			376	386	48%

Projected Wins: 8.2 (NFL Rank: 19)
Strength of Schedule Ranking: 16

FANTASY DEPTH CHART

QB
Geno Smith
Sam Howell

RB
Kenneth Walker III
Zach Charbonnet
Kenny McIntosh

WR
DK Metcalf
Tyler Lockett
Jaxon Smith-Njigba
Jake Bobo
Laviska Shenault Jr.
D'Wayne Eskridge

TE
Noah Fant
Pharaoh Brown
A.J. Barner

K
Jason Myers

USAGE PROJECTIONS

TARGET SHARES

DK Metcalf	21%
Tyler Lockett	19%
Jaxon Smith-Njigba	19%
Noah Fant	11%
Zach Charbonnet	8%

CARRY SHARES

Kenneth Walker III	56%
Zach Charbonnet	28%
Kenny McIntosh	7%

TEAM SCORING FORECAST

Passing TD	Rushing TD	FG
24	15	28

TAMPA BAY BUCCANEERS

THE SKINNY

Baker Mayfield and Mike Evans are back, with a first-round draft pick devoted to the center position in Graham Barton and a third-round pick devoted to a receiver in Jalen McMillan, whom ESPN draft analyst Mel Kiper Jr. called a "steal." Expect the Bucs to carry the late-season momentum from last year into 2024.

Over/Under: 267 touches for Rachaad White. **Prediction: Over.** White got 336 touches last season. And his success in the passing game—549 receiving yards last season—will keep him on the field no matter what. *–Jenna Laine*

SCORE PROJECTIONS

WK	OPP	LOC	TM	OPP	WIN PROB
1	WAS	H	24.1	19.6	66%
2	DET	A	20.6	27.1	27%
3	DEN	H	24.1	19.4	67%
4	PHI	H	23.4	25.5	43%
5	ATL	A	22.3	25.2	40%
6	NO	A	19.9	22.1	42%
7	BAL	H	20.2	26.2	29%
8	ATL	H	23.4	24.1	47%
9	KC	A	20.6	28.7	22%
10	SF	H	19.2	26.9	24%
11					
12	NYG	A	23.4	19.7	63%
13	CAR	A	22.0	22.1	49%
14	LV	H	22.7	19.1	63%
15	LAC	A	22.7	24.0	45%
16	DAL	A	18.8	26.2	25%
17	CAR	H	23.1	21.0	57%
18	NO	H	20.9	21.0	50%
			371	398	45%

Projected Wins: 7.6 (NFL Rank: 23)
Strength of Schedule Ranking: 12

FANTASY DEPTH CHART

QB
Baker Mayfield
Kyle Trask

RB
Rachaad White
Bucky Irving
Chase Edmonds

WR
Mike Evans
Chris Godwin
Trey Palmer
Jalen McMillan
Rakim Jarrett
Ryan Miller

TE
Cade Otton
Payne Durham
Ko Kieft

K
Chase McLaughlin

USAGE PROJECTIONS

TARGET SHARES

Mike Evans	22%
Chris Godwin	21%
Rachaad White	11%
Cade Otton	11%
Trey Palmer	10%

CARRY SHARES

Rachaad White	55%
Bucky Irving	18%
Chase Edmonds	14%

TEAM SCORING FORECAST

Passing TD	Rushing TD	FG
27	12	29

Rachaad White

Tyjae Spears

TENNESSEE TITANS

THE SKINNY

The passing game will be more dynamic under new coach Brian Callahan. Adding Calvin Ridley to play alongside DeAndre Hopkins gives the Titans a chance to have their first pair of 1,000-yard WRs since 2004. The biggest boost comes from what should be an improved offensive line after signing free-agent center Lloyd Cushenberry and drafting tackle JC Latham.

Over/Under: 130 carries for Tyjae Spears. **Prediction:** **Over.** Spears had 100 carries as a rookie last season. The Titans will utilize a dual backfield, with Spears and Tony Pollard sharing duties. *–Turron Davenport*

SCORE PROJECTIONS

WK	OPP	LOC	TM	OPP	WIN PROB
1	CHI	A	18.2	24.6	28%
2	NYJ	H	17.9	26.8	20%
3	GB	H	20.4	25.0	34%
4	MIA	A	17.1	26.1	20%
5					
6	IND	H	20.7	23.8	39%
7	BUF	A	18.6	27.1	21%
8	DET	A	18.6	28.1	18%
9	NE	H	20.0	20.2	49%
10	LAC	A	20.7	25.1	34%
11	MIN	H	21.1	22.3	46%
12	HOU	A	19.3	27.3	23%
13	WAS	A	21.1	21.7	48%
14	JAX	H	18.9	23.0	36%
15	CIN	H	19.7	26.4	27%
16	IND	A	19.6	24.9	32%
17	JAX	A	17.8	24.0	28%
18	HOU	H	20.4	26.2	30%
			330	423	31%

Projected Wins: 5.3 (NFL Rank: 30)
Strength of Schedule Ranking: 26

FANTASY DEPTH CHART

QB
Will Levis
Mason Rudolph

RB
Tony Pollard
Tyjae Spears
Julius Chestnut

WR
DeAndre Hopkins
Calvin Ridley
Tyler Boyd
Treylon Burks
Nick Westbrook-Ikhine
Kyle Philips

TE
Chigoziem Okonkwo
Josh Whyle
Nick Vannett

K
Nick Folk

USAGE PROJECTIONS

TARGET SHARES

Calvin Ridley	21%
DeAndre Hopkins	21%
Tyler Boyd	14%
Chigoziem Okonkwo	12%
Tyjae Spears	11%

CARRY SHARES

Tony Pollard	45%
Tyjae Spears	34%
Julius Chestnut	8%

TEAM SCORING FORECAST

Passing TD	Rushing TD	FG
20	12	29

WASHINGTON COMMANDERS

THE SKINNY

Washington wants to reduce the pressure on rookie QB Jayden Daniels by relying more on the run game. In offensive coordinator Kliff Kingsbury's final three seasons as Arizona's head coach, the Cardinals ranked 11th in rush attempts. The Commanders love Daniels' ability to throw deep and provided him underneath targets in TE Zach Ertz and third-down back Austin Ekeler.

Over/Under: 161 touches for Ekeler. **Prediction:** **Under.** Ekeler will have a crucial role as a pass-catcher, but will he play in every game? That's tough for any running back, and it's why we'll hedge on the under. *–John Keim*

SCORE PROJECTIONS

WK	OPP	LOC	TM	OPP	WIN PROB
1	TB	A	19.6	24.1	34%
2	NYG	H	22.1	19.6	59%
3	CIN	A	18.2	27.5	19%
4	ARI	A	21.7	23.5	44%
5	CLE	H	16.4	23.8	25%
6	BAL	A	16.7	28.3	13%
7	CAR	H	20.7	22.1	45%
8	CHI	H	18.9	23.5	34%
9	NYG	A	21.0	20.7	51%
10	PIT	H	17.5	21.7	35%
11	PHI	A	19.9	27.7	24%
12	DAL	H	17.5	26.1	21%
13	TEN	H	21.7	21.1	52%
14					
15	NO	A	17.5	23.2	30%
16	PHI	H	21.0	26.6	31%
17	ATL	H	21.0	25.2	35%
18	DAL	A	16.4	27.2	15%
			328	412	33%

Projected Wins: 5.7 (NFL Rank: 28)
Strength of Schedule Ranking: 11

FANTASY DEPTH CHART

QB
Jayden Daniels
Marcus Mariota

RB
Brian Robinson Jr.
Austin Ekeler
Chris Rodriguez Jr.

WR
Terry McLaurin
Jahan Dotson
Luke McCaffrey
Jamison Crowder
Dyami Brown
Olamide Zaccheaus

TE
Zach Ertz
Ben Sinnott
John Bates

K
TBD

USAGE PROJECTIONS

TARGET SHARES

Terry McLaurin	21%
Jahan Dotson	15%
Austin Ekeler	12%
Luke McCaffrey	11%
Zach Ertz	9%

CARRY SHARES

Brian Robinson Jr.	49%
Austin Ekeler	27%
Jayden Daniels	14%

TEAM SCORING FORECAST

Passing TD	Rushing TD	FG
18	15	28

Austin Ekeler

THE OFFSEASON REPORT

The coaching hires, roster changes and rookie arrivals that will make the most impact in fantasy this year

BY LIZ LOZA

hange. It's inevitable. And in the NFL, it's constant. From roster shake-ups to coaching carousels to offensive overhauls, the churn is real. Here's a catch-up on the most significant fantasy news of the offseason, in no particular order.

NEW ERA IN NEW ENGLAND

Jerod Mayo will have an opportunity to redefine the "Patriot Way," replacing Bill Belichick as the team's head coach after 24 years. Mayo will look to new offensive coordinator Alex Van Pelt and No. 3 overall pick Drake Maye to reinvigorate the offense. New England's depth chart is far from stacked, though the aforementioned Maye and rookie WR Ja'Lynn Polk project as later-round investments and could provide fantasy value down the stretch.

Meanwhile, Rhamondre Stevenson remains the team's primary ball carrier. With Van Pelt likely to install a run-heavy scheme (similar to the one he ran in Cleveland), Stevenson figures to touch the ball 15 to 17 times per game, offering managers top-20 positional appeal.

(SEMI) SHAKE-UP IN SEATTLE

Pete Carroll served as the Seahawks' head coach for 14 seasons. In his stead, the organization tapped Mike Macdonald to captain the squad while calling up former Washington Huskies OC Ryan Grubb to design an offensive playbook. On the heels of such a substantial change, it was assumed the new regime would implement a number of roster tweaks. However, the fresh-faced coaching staff chose instead to run it back with many of Seattle's most-tenured players.

DK Metcalf returns as the most valuable fantasy asset, capable of delivering high-end WR2 numbers. Second-year receiver Jaxon Smith-Njigba presents with breakout appeal, though he'll compete for looks with Tyler Lockett and Noah Fant. JSN and Lockett figure to teeter on the WR3/WR4 bubble, with the younger player's upside being baked into his slightly higher ADP. Finally, Kenneth Walker III could cede touches to Zach Charbonnet but remains a decent RB2 option for fantasy purposes.

JIM HARBAUGH RECHARGES IN L.A.

Los Angeles hit the restart button at head coach for the fourth time in just over 10 years, signing Michigan head coach Harbaugh to a five-year contract worth an estimated $16 million annually. Upon coming to terms with Harbaugh, the Bolts cleaned house, forcing the exits of Keenan Allen, Mike Williams, Austin Ekeler and Gerald Everett.

The team spent an early second-round pick on WR Ladd McConkey while bolstering the backfield with the likes of J.K. Dobbins and Gus Edwards and adding depth at TE with Will Dissly and Hayden Hurst via free agency. L.A.'s revamped offensive line should help buy Justin Herbert time in the pocket. However, between a dearth of tested pass-catching options and OC Greg Roman's run-heavy approach, Herbert's days as a top-10 fantasy QB appear (momentarily) in the rearview.

Rhamondre Stevenson

BEARS FORCE A REBRAND

The "Monsters of the Midway" will always remain synonymous with Chicago. But Ryan Poles appears to be dragging the team into the future and attempting to "Push for the Pass." Promptly closing the book on the Justin Fields era, Chicago spent two early-first-round selections on QB Caleb Williams and WR Rome Odunze.

It's not the first time the Bears have used a first-round pick on a burgeoning signal-caller. It could be argued, however, that this is the first time (in a long time) the Bears have attempted to actually build around said QB. Prior to the draft, the organization traded for

The new coaching staff in Seattle will continue to rely on DK Metcalf.

Keenan Allen and also utilized the free-agency period to add D'Andre Swift and Gerald Everett. While the success of these efforts and additions has yet to be tested, at least on paper, the Bears are in possession of the team's most potent passing attack in 50-plus years.

If all goes well (and that is a big if, given the club's history), Williams could deliver top-15 fantasy numbers in his rookie campaign. DJ Moore figures to remain the corps' target leader, likely to deliver a second consecutive 1,000-yard receiving effort. Allen should draw a similar number of looks to Moore, potentially flirting with 80 grabs in his Windy City debut. Odunze will round out the trio of receivers, offering mid-round upside and oodles of flex potential. Swift's volume seems murkier, however, as he'll join Khalil Herbert and Roschon Johnson in the backfield. Coming off a career season, the former Eagle's numbers figure to regress, but Swift's ability as a pass-catcher keeps him on the RB2/3 bubble.

WASHINGTON'S COMMANDING OFFENSIVE CHANGES

The Commanders spent 2023 seeing what they had in Sam Howell... and decided it wasn't enough. After the team registered a 4–13 record, the fully transformed front office continued house cleaning, revamping the coaching staff and anointing a new face of the franchise. Rookie QB Jayden Daniels, whose playing style is similar to Kyler Murray's, is an intriguing fit for Kliff Kingsbury's offense. Expect the Commanders' OC to employ plenty of spread passing elements, which should help the 23-year-old's transition to the pros. With Terry McLaurin and Jahan Dotson leading the receiving corps and Austin Ekeler catching passes out of the backfield, Daniels slides into a sneaky-productive situation. Add in his elite rushing instincts, and the rookie could potentially thrive as a QB2 in superflex formats as early as Year 1.

While Daniels lands in a favorable situation, his surrounding talent may not be so lucky, at least initially. McLaurin has been saddled with instability under center for the bulk of his career. Regardless, he's cleared 1,000 receiving yards for four consecutive campaigns and should draw upwards of 130 looks again in 2024. Dotson is expected to function as the team's No. 2 WR and could manage the breakout he failed to post last season, but he is largely ranked outside of the top-60 fantasy wideouts. Ekeler and Brian Robinson Jr. figure to share snaps, working in a complementary fashion. Both backs offer managers high-end RB3 potential.

BUFFALO BIDS FAREWELL TO BIG NAMES

The Bills made a number of decisive moves this offseason, sometimes leaving fans a bit baffled. While Gabe Davis' departure and Damien Harris' retirement weren't terribly surprising, the Stefon Diggs trade created considerable consternation. The anxiety only seemed to increase after Buffalo traded down

Calvin Ridley

twice in the first round of April's draft, passing on buzzy receiving talent in the process. Ultimately, they selected WR Keon Coleman with the 33rd overall pick.

A former basketball standout who played briefly for Tom Izzo at Michigan State, Coleman is in possession of size (6-foot-3, 213 pounds) and hops. He has incredible ball skills, and he regularly climbed the ladder to make circus catches during his college career. An X receiver with downfield ability, Coleman figures to emerge as Josh Allen's primary target, likely drawing upwards of 100 targets in his first pro campaign.

Keon Coleman

KIRK COUSINS SET TO CAPTAIN A NEW OFFENSE—FOR NOW

Cousins averaged just north of 20 fantasy points per game during the first month of the 2023 season before Justin Jefferson was sidelined (hamstring). Cousins' productivity dipped slightly over the next four weeks (17.3 points per game) prior to tearing his Achilles in Week 8. The 36-year-old tested the free-agent market, ultimately securing a four-year deal worth an eye-popping $180 million with the Falcons. Cousins' celebration was cut short, however, when Atlanta reportedly "blindsided" the QB by selecting Michael Penix Jr. with the eighth overall pick in the draft.

Assuming a full recovery, Cousins remains atop the Falcons' depth chart and should start the season as the team's QB1. There exists considerable optimism that the four-time Pro Bowler—along with new offensive coordinator Zac Robinson, who gained experience under Sean McVay in Los Angeles—will unlock the first-round potential of Drake London and Kyle Pitts. Both pass-catchers project as low-end fantasy starters at their respective positions (WR14 and TE10). Bijan Robinson rounds out the trio of young stars and is expected to begin his sophomore season as a late-first-round pick in fantasy drafts.

DERRICK HENRY BRINGS CHARM TO A NEW CITY

Addressing Titans fans in early January, Henry was transparent about his relationship with the club and his plans for the future. Fantasy's favorite anomaly inked a two-year deal with Baltimore just two months later. While a player of Henry's stature doesn't normally fly, he absolutely could as a member of the Ravens Flock.

A perennial top-10 producer who has cleared at least 12 fantasy points per game every year since 2018, Henry has continued to evade tackles and rip off big runs. He's 30, and with more than 2,000 carries to his name, durability is an obvious concern. Still, Todd Monken's run-aggressive offense and the Ravens' solid O-Line should both work in the vet's favor. Assuming he stays healthy, Henry is in line for double-digit scores and top-12 RB consideration in Baltimore.

SAQUON BARKLEY BRINGS THE HURT(S) TO PHILLY'S BACKFIELD

Barkley served as the Giants' offensive engine, motoring his way to 1,489 total touches during his six seasons in New York. That volume buoyed his fantasy stock, as he managed nearly 16 fantasy points per game (RB13) despite averaging 3.9 yards per carry in 2023.

While the 27-year-old may be entering the twilight of his career, Barkley should continue to rip off long runs (he was tied for sixth among RBs with seven rushes of 20-plus yards in 2023) and evade tackles while working behind a much better offensive line in Philadelphia. With D'Andre Swift now in Chicago, Barkley's work in the passing game is likely to remain stable as he figures to (once again) average around three catches per contest. Any potential hit to Barkley's overall workload will be outweighed by an increase in efficiency, given the explosiveness of the Eagles' offense. He remains a solid RB1 for fantasy purposes in 2024.

CALVIN RIDLEY CASHES IN ON SHALLOW FREE-AGENT MARKET

Arguably the most sought-after wide receiver in this year's free-agent class, Ridley opted to leave Jacksonville, landing in Tennessee on a four-year deal reportedly worth $92 million. The 29-year-old, who returned to the field after missing the 2022 season due to a suspension, put together an up-and-down effort in 2023, managing six games of more than 20 fantasy points and nine outings below 10 fantasy points. Interestingly, two of his best showings (in which he recorded at least six catches and cleared 100 yards) came against his new team.

Ridley figures to work as a complement to DeAndre Hopkins, who is likely to find himself open more regularly next season. The new addition also puts a lid on the idea of a Treylon Burks breakout. The length and cost of Ridley's contract (along with the Tony Pollard signing) does, however, signal an investment in second-year QB Will Levis. Led by new head coach Brian Callahan, the new-look Titans appear to be taking an aerial approach to the offense. That should further work in Ridley's favor. He should be considered a low-end WR2 in fantasy with plenty of upside. ■

SHUNNING BACKS

Debating the merits of skipping RBs early in your draft

BY TRISTAN H. COCKCROFT AND ERIC KARABELL

Christian McCaffrey isn't just our top-ranked player entering 2024. He's also the poster boy for the risk and reward—and the mental anguish that goes with weighing either—when it comes to running backs.

Some backstory: McCaffrey has four of the 49 best single-season PPR fantasy point totals by running backs in NFL history, and four of the 12 best of the past decade. That level of production has made him a top-three selection overall in each of the past five seasons. Unfortunately, both times he was selected first overall (2020 and 2021), he missed more than half the season due to injuries and was labeled as one of those seasons' biggest busts.

McCaffrey isn't alone. Saquon Barkley, Le'Veon Bell (twice!), David Johnson, Eddie Lacy, Adrian Peterson (also twice!) and Jonathan Taylor are fellow running backs who have enjoyed historic peaks but also devastating follow-ups in seasons of lofty top-three ADPs, all within the past decade.

This collective running back volatility has caused many headaches over the years, to the extent that it even fueled a fantasy football strategy, "Zero-RB," which insists upon shunning running backs through at least the draft's first three rounds, and preferably as many as five to eight rounds, in order to first load up on top-shelf talent at wide receiver and quarterback.

But is this a wise—or, at its base, a viable—draft strategy?

Eric Karabell: I never go into a draft saying I *have* to do something extreme. Strategy, sure, that is a must. Always have a reasonable plan and be willing to tweak it on a moment's notice in whatever round, but I like to evaluate the best available choice with each pick, especially early, and then zig and zag later in the draft.

Tristan H. Cockcroft: I cannot *stand* forcing rigid draft strategies, and Zero-RB is just that when it's followed correctly. However, with all that's happened with running backs over the past half decade, I'm rethinking spending early picks on running backs.

Karabell: "Best available" is a strong strategy, and it stands the test of time. NFL GMs use it, too. Also, reasonable minds can disagree on who the best available is at any given point. I don't even follow my own rankings half the time. Which half, he wonders?

Cockcroft: I'd suggest the one that most resembles the 2023 Eagles' first half.

Karabell: Many would say I should have secured the No. 2 RB in this magazine's mock draft with the No. 4 overall pick. I didn't feel great about any RB after McCaffrey that early. I felt better about WR Ja'Marr Chase. Then I went WR with my next two picks as well, in part as a reaction to the available RBs and the likelihood of failure or injury. I felt the WRs were the best available. Is that really "shunning running backs"? No. I got RBs later. I didn't shun! I like them, too.

I know you have data proving that investing in RBs early is problematic, so why do fantasy managers still feel forced to invest?

Cockcroft: In the past five fantasy seasons, 35 running backs were selected in the first round, along with 13 wide receivers and TE Travis Kelce twice—2021 and 2023. Of those 35 RBs, nine finished the season outside the top 20 at the position in points scored. That's 26% of the pool that flat-out busted for their fantasy managers. Now, 26% might not sound like a lot, but these are supposed to be can't-miss players.

Those 35 backs averaged 13.7 games and 239.4 PPR fantasy points in those seasons. The wide receivers and Kelce, meanwhile, averaged 14.1 games and 265.5 points.

Karabell: That bust rate is egregious and recalls another popular fantasy football axiom: Teams cannot win their league with early picks, but they sure can lose them.

Clyde Edwards-Helaire

Worst first-round picks in past five seasons (2019–23)

The players on this list failed to finish within the top 20 in PPR fantasy points at their position in the given season.

Player	Pos.	Year	Overall ADP	Games Missed	Position Finish
Justin Jefferson	WR	2023	1	7	33
Austin Ekeler	RB	2023	4	3	26
Jonathan Taylor	RB	2022	1	6	33
Cooper Kupp	WR	2022	3	8	23
Christian McCaffrey	RB	2021	1	10	38
Derrick Henry	RB	2021	4	9	22
Saquon Barkley	RB	2021	6	4	30
Christian McCaffrey	RB	2020	1	13	54
Saquon Barkley	RB	2020	2	14	121
Michael Thomas	WR	2020	6	9	95
Clyde Edwards-Helaire	RB	2020	8	3	22
David Johnson	RB	2019	6	3	37
Davante Adams	WR	2019	10	4	22

Cockcroft: Bingo. And what if we've been wrong for years about the first round, and often rounds two and three, of our drafts? What if—and, yes, we all began to go in this direction last year, and then consensus No. 1 pick Justin Jefferson got hurt—it's the wide receivers who are the true lifeblood of fantasy football?

Karabell: Bingo! Hey, I can say it, too!

Cockcroft: Speaking of Jefferson, readers might notice that first-round wide receivers also had a high bust rate, four of 13 (31%) from the earlier list. So let's even out the playing field. Among those first-round running backs of the past five seasons, 17 of 35 (or 48.6%) delivered an average of 15-plus fantasy points per game while playing at least half their teams' games. If we take the top seven wide receivers in ADP in those same five seasons, 26 of 35 (or 74.3%) averaged 15-plus points while playing at least half their teams' games.

Karabell: Well, way to bury the lede! You could've opened with that. It supports the WR-early argument, if there deserves to be one. Why are we arguing, anyway?

Cockcroft: Now consider the reverse: What's available with those vital late-round picks? During those same five seasons, three running backs selected outside the top 160—the length of an ESPN standard draft—finished among the top-10 scorers at the position, and 10 managed top-20 seasons. Two more RBs selected in the final six rounds, picks 101 to 160, had top-10 positional totals. That's a *lot* of value left out there for the taking in-season. By comparison, only two wide receivers selected outside the top 160 finished in the top 10 at the position, one of whom was Puka Nacua in 2023, and five finished in the top 20. Jefferson was the only WR drafted in the final six rounds to finish top 10 at the position in 2020.

Karabell: My head is spinning.

Cockcroft: The deeper our league demands we dig into the player pool, and the closer our draft is to the start of the season—when we have the maximum information we can possibly have to make decisions—the greater the relevance of Zero-RB. I've got 12-team leagues that start three wide receivers and have benches of eight players or more. In those, I'll absolutely try it. In ESPN's standard format of 10 teams, seven bench spots, though? Hmm, that's a narrower margin of success, since fewer teams and fewer receiver spots means a greater need for running backs to fuel scoring. I say that, and yet there I am, picking Kyren Williams in the second, then Zamir White in the eighth in our magazine mock, and, um, hey, Eric, can you spare a running back? I simply didn't like the positional price points.

Karabell: I don't either. I'm not sure how anyone can. In a way, this is about shunning conventionality. Do that enough, and the past is no longer conventional. I know there are myriad wide receivers to trust—the numbers tell me so. After McCaffrey, why not treat the running backs like spaghetti against a wall? Throw a bunch on a team and see if they're cooked. Of course, we won't know whether they're cooked until around Week 6.

Cockcroft: Isn't that what NFL teams are doing nowadays anyway? See? Fantasy meets reality.

Karabell: Of course it does! Just look at this year's NFL draft. So many enticing running backs ended up on teams with other established starting running backs. Bummer! There is no Bijan Robinson this season, someone with elite skills in a perfect destination.

Cockcroft: And a perfect disaster of a coaching situation, which, sigh, did not go well in so many ways last season.

Karabell: NFL teams are telling us what to do. They treat running backs as easily replaceable, interchangeable parts, restocking them every few years when the stars show depreciation, determined to save money. There are so few high-volume options. Things have changed in the NFL, and fantasy reacts! We are only shunning the position because, in an obvious way, NFL teams are. ■

HOW TO WIN YOUR LEAGUE

The core principles are tried and true. Here's all you need to know to enjoy (and succeed at) fantasy football

BY FIELD YATES

ILLUSTRATION BY GLUEKIT

HURTS
1
17
BENGALS
LIONS
14
WCF
ATL
7
NKH
87

While there is a certain level of skill and attention that can influence your fantasy football fortunes, the reality of the game is that good luck can often overcome however many hours of lineup prep your league mates put in before each draft or each week during the season. You just need to know the essentials.

Vikings WR Justin Jefferson is once again a fantasy favorite.

THE BASICS

▶ **Joining a league:** Many people who play fantasy football get started via an invitation to a private league. A league that's full of office mates or high school friends typically makes for good banter. Your commissioner will send you an invite to join, and you're in. If you're looking to play and don't have a group to do it with, there are also public leagues available at fantasy.espn.com/football/welcome.

▶ **What type of league:** The two most basic elements that matter in your league are size and scoring type. A league of 10 teams is rather typical, but you can go smaller or bigger. Anything smaller than eight may feel a little light, while more than 16 leads to some roster crunches. As far as scoring goes, ESPN's default setting is Points Per Reception (PPR), in which a player receives a point for every catch he registers. Non-PPR is the other introductory option; you get no points for a catch, while the rest of the scoring stays the same.

▶ **Let's talk rules:** I'll use ESPN's most generic of settings as my template. Each week, you're setting a lineup that includes one quarterback, two running backs, two wide receivers, one tight end, one flex player (which can be any RB/WR/TE), one kicker and one defense and special teams unit (D/ST). You will also have seven players on your bench. Scoring in a basic PPR league: 1 point for every reception, 1 point for every 25 passing yards and 4 points for every passing TD, with 2 points lost for throwing an interception or losing a fumble. You get 1 point for every 10 rushing or receiving yards and 6 points for scoring a touchdown. You'll also get some points from your kicker and your defense, but the bulk of your scoring will come from yards and touchdowns.

BUILDING A TEAM

The draft is how you pick players for your team. You and your league mates agree upon a time to conduct a draft, either in person or online, or you can choose to have all teams be autodrafted by the computer. Let's discuss a handful of basic strategies for the draft.

▶ **Running backs and wide receivers are the most valuable:** If you spend a little time crunching some numbers with the scoring above, you may think quarterbacks are most valuable because they have the best chance to score the most points. While your QB is often your highest-scoring player, this is a supply-and-demand dynamic. Really good running backs are hard to find, while there is typically good depth at quarterback. Wide receivers are generally the second-most-valuable position on your roster.

▶ **Build depth:** It'll be tempting to fill out your starting lineup with your first eight picks, especially as you see your roster fleshed out in the draft room. Don't be overly concerned with that. Your depth at RB and WR is valuable, sometimes more valuable than your starting QB or TE, so don't be afraid to start filling up your bench.

▶ **When in doubt, trust the rankings:** ESPN analyst Mike Clay works extremely hard on his projections, and there's data backing up the practice of deferring to the projections when in doubt during the draft. The projections in the draft room are incredibly valuable.

▶ **Autodraft isn't advised, but:** All right, I'd prefer you take part in your draft actively. It's a ton of fun! But if you must, using the autodraft feature is OK. As mentioned above, the team you'll build through autodrafting will likely be a solid one, as the rankings in the draft room are updated to reflect the latest news and trends.

▶ **Wait to pick your kicker and defense:** In fact, you can wait until your final two picks. I'm telling you. Trust me and trust the math. Some custom leagues play without any defenses or kickers at all.

AFTER THE DRAFT

While a perfect draft can likely carry you far, any eventual championship team will require a bit of maintenance that can't be ignored. First and most important is setting your lineup. Your starting lineup will be made up of nine of your 16 players (QB, 2 RBs, 2 WRs, TE, Flex, K, D/ST), and only your lineup will accumulate points. Your bench players are held in reserve for future weeks.

Don't forget that each week during the season there is at least one game played on Thursday evening, so it's a good habit to go into your ESPN Fantasy app to set an initial lineup at some point before then.

▶ **Adjusting your lineup:** You can adjust your lineup up until a player's game kicks off. The deadline to make a deci-

Did you know that ESPN league managers can now adjust scoring settings on both the app and web, including new options like bonus wins and first downs?

The Colts' Jonathan Taylor has had inconsistent results, but he's still one of the top RBs in the league.

sion on a player is the moment his game begins, and not a second later. If you have a pair of players between whom you are deciding for your flex spot and both play in either the Sunday night or Monday night game, you have time on Sunday to deliberate.

▶ **When in doubt, trust the projections:** Mike Clay works tirelessly to account for many factors throughout the week (player, role, weather, opponent, injuries, specific matchups, etc.), so if you're stuck and can't decide which player to start, there's nothing wrong with following his lead.

▶ **Always look at the injury designations:** ESPN is constantly updating a player's health status during the week, which will be denoted by a small red letter next to his name. The three primary designations you'll see are Q for questionable, D for doubtful and O for out. Here's the important part—questionable can mean a lot of things. Basically, if a player is anything less than 100%, the team is required to list him as such, and that can lead to a Q next to his name. However, a player can be 50/50 to play in a game and also be listed as questionable; it's quite a wide-ranging scale to cover. You can always click on a player's name to see an in-depth explanation of just how severe—or not—the injury is. Another key: 90 minutes before every game, a team must designate up to seven players as inactive, which means you'll know by then if a player is able to go. Carve out some time each Sunday between 11:30 a.m. and 1 p.m. ET to make your final lineup decisions, as Mike will update his projections based on who is inactive that week.

▶ **Keep an eye out for bye weeks:** Every NFL team has one week off during the regular season, so make sure you're aware of the schedule for all your players. While starting Christian McCaffrey is a great idea 17 weeks of the season, it's not so smart during his bye week! Let him enjoy that well-deserved rest and find another running back option.

When it comes time to draft a QB, aim for dual threats like the Ravens' Lamar Jackson.

MANAGING YOUR ROSTER

▶ **Use the waiver wire:** Every player not on a roster in your league is on waivers and eligible to be added during the week, beginning with the initial waiver run overnight Tuesday into Wednesday. Waivers can be helpful to add players who are performing well, to replace struggling starters in your own lineup and to plug gaps when your usual starters are on a bye. Follow waivers weekly if you can—it makes a difference. The process works like this:

1. Every team can attempt to claim a player.

2. The team with the worst record has highest priority and will be awarded a player if multiple teams try to claim him. If your team is struggling, the waiver wire is here to help!

3. To enter a claim, you simply go to the "Players" tab, add a player of interest and submit a corresponding move you will be making in the event that you are awarded that player when waivers run. If you've got a player collecting dust on the end of your bench or a player who suffered an unfortunately serious injury, that's a prime candidate to drop. Early in the season, *do not* drop a star player who is struggling. We'll talk about trades next, but please do not act hastily with slumping stars you took early in the draft.

4. You can make multiple waiver claims. If there are five players of interest and you have five players not pulling their weight, feel free to make as many claims as possible.

5. By the time you wake up Wednesday morning, the first run of waivers will be complete. At that point, you can add any other player who is still available—first come, first served—until that respective player's game begins.

THE TRADE BLOCK

Trades are one of the great joys of playing fantasy football. The stakes are just slightly lower than doing something like trading four-time NFL MVP Aaron Rodgers, but trades produce an unmistakable adrenaline rush for both teams involved. We don't need to outline too many rules as they pertain to trades in fantasy football—it's no different than any negotiation in life—but here are a few suggestions to serve as a reminder.

The Lions' Sam LaPorta demonstrated the fantasy potential of tight ends last year.

1. Try your best to be fair: The worst kind of offers in fantasy football are the obvious low-ball offers. They're a waste of time more than anything. The conceit of a trade should be to help you and the other manager involved, not to fleece someone.

2. What you need may be different from what your league mates need: If you're well stocked at running back and other teams in your league are well stocked at wide receiver, that's an easy way to talk shop. It helps.

3. If you can't find middle ground, table it for later: Negotiations can be tough, so if you can't seem to bridge the gap, it's OK to press pause and agree to revisit later...or not revisit at all.

One last note on trades: There is a trade deadline in your league. Check in with your commissioner about when that deadline is so you know the final day to complete a deal.

CONSULT YOUR TOOLBOX

One of my favorite pieces of advice to share about fantasy football is a mere reminder: Your team is *your* team, so you always have the right to adjust your lineup and strategy as you see fit. But the beauty of our ESPN Fantasy platform and app is that we do our best to make the decisions as easy for you as possible.

Among the various tools you have at your disposal, I encourage you to consult these.

▶ **Preseason and weekly rankings:** Throughout the offseason, we are constantly tinkering with our rankings—both positional and overall—to prep you for drafts. During the season, we offer weekly rankings that are adjusted in perpetuity to account for injuries and other in-week dynamics. When in doubt, always check the ranks.

▶ **Projections:** These are the cousin of the rankings and another by-product of Mike Clay's meticulous work. If you are trying to decide between two players at different positions for your flex, projections are a great tiebreaker. They also help in same-position decision-making, functioning like the rankings do.

▶ **Weekly ESPN.com content:** Every week we are churning out tons of quality material. Among the staples are waiver-wire pickups by Eric Moody; matchup analysis by Mike Clay, Matt Bowen and Tristan H. Cockcroft; advice from Liz Loza and Eric Karabell; injury analysis from Stephania Bell; the Sunday morning inactives watch; and much more.

▶ **Player pages:** When you want or need a deeper dive on a player and his outlook, clicking on his name, either on the website or app, is a good way to get curated content, including the latest video analysis from our ESPN Fantasy team, game logs, projections, player news and injury info.

▶ ***Fantasy Focus* and *Fantasy Football Now*:** If you're interested in content to consume in audio or visual form, *Fantasy Focus* is our five-day-a-week podcast that also streams on basically all ESPN digital platforms, including the ESPN Fantasy app. *Fantasy Football Now* airs each Sunday at 10 a.m. ET on ESPN2, and we get you as ready as you can possibly be with the latest analysis prior to kickoff.

PLAYOFF ODDS AND (THE) ENDS

You'll continue to set a lineup each week of the regular season from Weeks 1 through 14, piling up a win-loss record based on how you fare. If you compile one of the best four records in your league, you'll advance to the fantasy playoffs. The semifinals run for a two-week period (Weeks 15 and 16), while the two-week championship runs during Weeks 17 and 18. (Note: This is the ESPN default setting. The number of teams that qualify for the playoffs and the start/finish date can be adjusted by your commissioner.)

There is nothing sweeter in fantasy football than a playoff run in your first time playing. Let me tell you that beginner's luck is real in this game: You can do this!

If I can leave you with one lasting message about fantasy football, it would be this: We humans are competitive by nature, and winning your league would be an unquestionably cool accomplishment, especially if this is your first time playing. But I will never hesitate in saying that my favorite part about fantasy football is the community it forms within a league.

Be it a league of high school friends, college buddies, coworkers and colleagues, family members, neighbors, a group of people who met by joining the same public league online or a group of people who met on social media, the community and bond formed by playing in a fantasy football league makes it all worth it, regardless of how your team performs on the field.

Let's have a great season! ■

THE PLAYBOOK

Evergreen tips from ESPN's fantasy prognosticator that will give you the edge in your league

BY MIKE CLAY

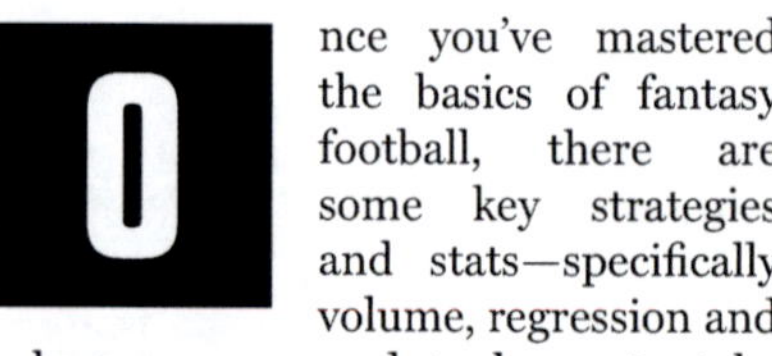

Once you've mastered the basics of fantasy football, there are some key strategies and stats—specifically volume, regression and schemes—you need to know to take your game to the next level.

VOLUME IS KING

Fantasy football has been around for a long time, yet the importance of volume remains grossly understated. Even the greatest player in the world can't accrue fantasy points if he's standing on the sideline or not touching the football, right? On the flip side, even a practice squad-level player can achieve fantasy viability simply because he has a significant role.

This is especially the case for running backs, who are less reliant on the splash plays we see often from quarterbacks and wide receivers. One easy way to see this in practice is by considering the value added by a big role in the passing game. For example, Raheem Mostert piled up 21 touchdowns (tied for the most among RBs), ran for 1,012 yards and averaged an impressive 4.8 yards per carry last season. Rachaad White, meanwhile, totaled nine TDs and 990 rushing yards while averaging 3.6 YPC.

Which of those two backs scored more fantasy points in 2023? Believe it or not, it was White. The Tampa Bay tailback had a 64-549-3 receiving line on 72 targets, compared with a 25-175-3 line on 33 targets for Mostert. That's a difference of 76.4 fantasy points, or 4.5 per game over 17 weeks.

Is that an extreme example? Sure, but there's a reason why superstar Nick Chubb has never finished a healthy season outside the top 10 in rushing yards but has yet to produce a top-five fantasy campaign. He's simply not much of a factor in the passing game, and that matters in fantasy football.

It's for that reason that we should be wary about the fantasy upside of players like Mostert (2.2 targets per game last season), David Montgomery (1.8) and Gus Edwards (0.8) but feel safer with the floors of players such as Alvin Kamara (6.7), Breece Hall (5.5) and Jaylen Warren (4.4).

I should point out that carry volume is important, too, but considering the average RB target is worth 2.5 times more fantasy points than the average RB carry, it's extremely important to not overlook each back's involvement in the passing game.

Similar logic applies to quarterbacks who do not add much value with their legs. Last season, Tua Tagovailoa led the NFL with 4,624 passing yards and tied for fifth with 29 pass TDs, so you'd think he must have been a good fantasy starter. But because he was held to a 35-74-0 rushing line, Tagovailoa finished 19th among QBs in fantasy PPG last season (minimum eight games played) and had zero weekly fantasy finishes better than ninth after Week 6.

Expect Bills tight end Dalton Kincaid to be more prolific in the touchdown department this season.

REGRESSION TO THE MEAN

The reason volume is king is because rate stats are so volatile and tough to predict. Some of the best evidence of that is in the touchdown department. Check this out: In last year's version of this article, 11 of the 12 players singled out as likely to score fewer TDs in 2023 did so (Jalen Hurts was the lone exception), with the group falling from a combined 139 scores in 2022 to 67 in 2023. Of the eight players identified as likely to see a boost in scoring, six did (Garrett Wilson and Pat Freiermuth were the exceptions).

When it comes to projecting football statistics, touchdown regression to the mean is about as close as you'll get to a sure thing.

So who are a few players likely to see a big swing in TD production in 2024? Wilson jumps off the page—and not only due to the obvious reason of having Aaron Rodgers under center. Wilson's 2023 TD total (3) was less than half his expected total (6.1) based on his usage. Since he was drafted in 2022, Wilson ranks fourth among WRs in targets (315), but tied for 45th in TDs (7). Dalton Kincaid is another good candidate, as he ranked top 10 at tight end in targets, receptions and yardage as a rookie but was held to two TDs.

A few other strong bets to score more TDs in 2024 include Chris Godwin, Drake London, DeMario Douglas, Aaron Jones, Jerry Jeudy, Zach Charbonnet, Zamir White and Darnell Mooney.

On the other hand, we have Miami RBs Mostert and De'Von Achane as the headliner candidates for a big dip in TDs this season. The 7.8 gap between Mostert's actual TD total (21) and his expected TD total (13.2) is 10th highest among all players since 2011. The nine players ahead of him on that list all scored fewer TDs the following season, and only two cleared 11. Achane's historical efficiency (7.7 YPC, 8.5 TD%) is nowhere close to sustainable. At wide receiver, Jayden Reed impressed with 10 TDs (fifth most at the position) as a rookie, but he ranked outside the top 25 in touches (75), yards (912) and expected TDs (5.2).

Others likely to score fewer TDs in 2024 include Christian McCaffrey, Jalen Hurts, Josh Allen, Kyren Williams, CeeDee Lamb, Travis Etienne Jr., Sam LaPorta, Deebo Samuel, Jordan Addison, Courtland Sutton, Jakobi Meyers and Gus Edwards.

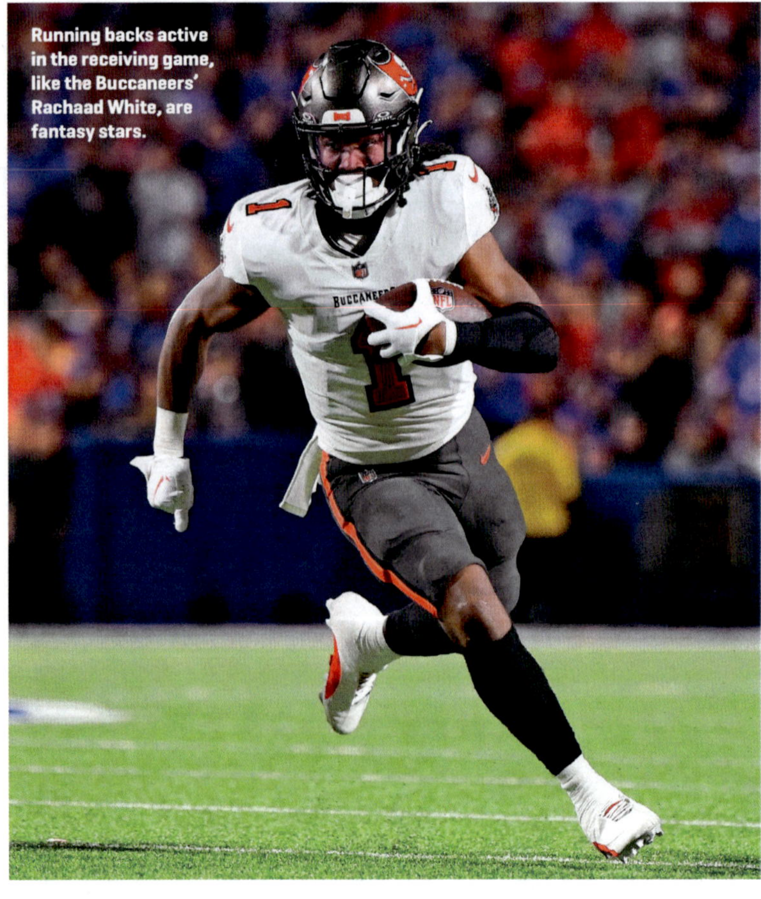

Running backs active in the receiving game, like the Buccaneers' Rachaad White, are fantasy stars.

THE SCHEME OF THINGS

This one is a little more in the weeds, but offensive schemes matter, and the head coach/playcaller turnover in this league is absurd. (Fun fact: Zero active offensive coordinators were hired to their post prior to 2022.) Keeping tabs on coaching changes is important because a scheme adjustment could cause a swing of hundreds of snaps (and, in turn, hundreds of fantasy points).

The Chargers and Falcons are two offenses likely to be severely impacted by scheme changes in 2024. Los Angeles ranks second in the NFL in pass attempts since Justin Herbert arrived in 2020 due to pass-heavy, fast-paced offenses. New coach Jim Harbaugh and playcaller Greg Roman, however, have generally operated conservative, run-first schemes, which figures to lead to a big dip in volume for Herbert and makes him a less appealing fantasy option. Atlanta, meanwhile, ranked 29th in pass attempts during the Arthur Smith era but could easily push for the top 10 (if not top five) with Zac Robinson calling the plays and Kirk Cousins under center in 2024. The likes of Drake London, Kyle Pitts and Bijan Robinson stand to benefit.

THE BOTTOM LINE

Fantasy football players are often tricked by big plays and short spurts of dominance (usually fueled by touchdowns), and that leads to poor decision-making. Sure, the occasional outlier sustains itself longer than expected, but the exception is not the rule. Understanding schemes and focusing your attention on players who consistently rack up carries and targets (raw totals and team shares), especially of the high-value nature, is step one in improving your team's odds for victory. ■

Did you know that if you play fantasy football with ESPN, any time a player is featured in an article, it will appear within your Roster News?

Watching player prop betting lines could help you decide on starting the Seahawks' Jaxon Smith-Njigba.

WHAT ARE THE ODDS?

How to factor sportsbook player props into your tough lineup decisions ***By Tyler Fulghum***

We've all been there. It's 12:55 p.m. ET on a Sunday in October. You're feverishly jiggling your knee up and down, and a bead of sweat drops from your brow onto your lap. Do you put Jaxon Smith-Njigba or Jahan Dotson in your flex spot? *Why is life so hard?*

If only there was some information you could lean on as a reliable tiebreaker for this type of gut-wrenching fantasy football decision!

Well, there is, and it's readily and easily accessible every day of the week, not just Sundays.

Turn to the sportsbooks. Specifically, the player prop markets. There you can compare what the market is expecting of the players in question. Perhaps Player A—let's use Smith-Njigba for this example—has the following player props: 3.5 receptions, 42.5 yards, +300 anytime TD. Player B, Dotson, has these props listed: 3.5 receptions, 38.5 yards, +250 anytime TD. Which player should earn that start in the flex spot?

Odds	Implied Probability
-200	66.7%
-190	65.5%
-180	64.3%
-170	63.0%
-160	61.5%
-150	60.0%
-140	58.3%
-130	56.5%
-120	54.5%
-110	52.4%
+100	50.0%
+110	47.6%
+120	45.5%
+130	43.5%
+140	41.7%
+150	40.0%
+160	38.5%
+170	37.0%
+180	35.7%
+190	34.5%
+200	33.3%

Well, the books are expecting Smith-Njigba to produce more yards in the game, while Dotson is the player more likely to score a touchdown. Both players are expected to make the same number of catches, so what do you do there? Look at the price.

For the purpose of this exercise, let's say Smith-Njigba is 3.5 receptions and the over is -150, while Dotson has a listed price of +120 for the over. In this scenario, the sportsbook is telling you with the price that Smith-Njigba is far more likely to catch at least four passes compared to Dotson. In fact, the implied probability of JSN making four catches is 60%, while the implied probability of Dotson doing so is just 45.5%.

So it's clear that Smith-Njigba is the player to start, right? He's expected to have more receiving yards and has a higher probability of eclipsing his reception total. This is an easy decision, isn't it?

Well, that depends. What kind of league are you playing in? What type of scoring are you using? If this is a PPR league, then yes, I would agree that the market is indicating you should start JSN. If you're playing in a non-PPR league, where scoring touchdowns is more valuable, the market is telling you Dotson is the better play, due to his anytime touchdown price indicating a 28.6% chance of a TD versus 25.0% for Smith-Njigba.

Of course, this is not a foolproof way to make a decision. Perhaps JSN has the game of his life, and Dotson gets hurt on the second play from scrimmage. That's fantasy football, baby. At a certain point, it's completely out of your control. However, you can start making better—or more +EV [expected value]—decisions for your fantasy lineup by looking at player props in the betting market for guidance with your lineup choices.

You can also use game totals [over/under] as a tiebreaker for your fantasy decisions. Smith-Njigba and the Seahawks are playing in a game with a total of 51.5, while Dotson and the Commanders are playing in a game with a total of 42.5. Clearly, one game environment is expected to produce more offense. It's never a bad idea to load up your roster with players from the game that's expected to produce the most points any given week. ■

THE INJURY REPORT

What to expect as these high-profile players recover from challenging setbacks

BY STEPHANIA BELL

Achilles tendon ruptures and ACL tears dominated the season-ending injury list in 2023, but there were also a few upper-extremity injuries that knocked out starting quarterbacks. As the new season approaches, it should come as no surprise that each situation comes with its own outlook.

ACHILLES REPAIR

Let's be honest: In the not-too-distant past, an Achilles rupture was considered a career-ender for most NFL players. Even those who managed to return to play (Texans RB Arian Foster, Colts RB Marlon Mack) often did so at less than their pre-injury level. Recently, however, players have not only returned more quickly (Rams RB Cam Akers); some have also returned to comparable or even superior performance levels over time (RB D'Onta Foreman while with the Panthers).

What we haven't seen since Dan Marino, Vinny Testaverde, Jim Miller and Trent Dilfer—a time period spanning more than two decades—is another starting quarterback who has suffered this injury. In 2023, we saw not one but two starters go down, and yet both are poised to return in 2024.

AARON RODGERS

QB, JETS

Four snaps and a pop. That's the sum of Rodgers' 2023 season, as he was on the field only briefly in the season opener before his left Achilles failed, leaving him sitting on the ground in disbelief. An aggressive rehab program and an optimistic outlook had Rodgers targeting a potential late-season return, but when it became apparent that the Jets' postseason aspirations had expired, the clock was reset to 2024. Still, his ability to return to practice before the season ended was evidence he would be ready to participate unrestricted this season. The additional time for tendon remodeling and strengthening only adds confidence to Rodgers' readiness, and his style of play should not be impacted.

KIRK COUSINS

QB, FALCONS

Cousins was having a strong first half of the season before it came to a crashing halt in Week 8 when he tore his right Achilles tendon. Although Cous-

Former Chargers WR Mike Williams, now with the Jets, is taking a cautious road back after a torn ACL last September.

ins' surgery and rehabilitation process has been less aggressive than Rodgers', he was never trying to get back within four months, given his late-October injury. All reports indicate his progression has gone smoothly, and the Falcons saw enough to make a guaranteed investment in his return. It is worth noting the injury is to Cousins' back leg when he throws, the one responsible for helping push the ball down the field. Any power deficit in the Achilles could show up in deeper throws, so this will be something to watch when Cousins retakes the field.

J.K. DOBBINS

RB, CHARGERS

Quarterbacks weren't the only victims of Achilles ruptures. Dobbins suffered a torn left Achilles in Week 1 of 2023, and as if the severity and timing of such an injury weren't painful enough, he had just returned the year prior from an ACL/LCL reconstruction on the same leg. It took Dobbins most of that 2022 season to regain his form, but heading into last season, he appeared poised to lead the backfield. He has played in only 24 games in his four NFL seasons, and he wants to turn his injury narrative around. During spring OTAs, he said he felt "100 percent" but acknowledged that the Chargers' staff will control his progression. It typically takes athletes a year of game action to regain explosiveness and power following an Achilles repair, elements critical to Dobbins' style of play. Even if he returns to action this fall, as it appears he will, it may be 2025 before Dobbins can realize his post-injury potential.

ACL RECONSTRUCTION

Return to play for NFL athletes following anterior cruciate ligament (ACL) reconstruction has become so successful that the expectation is to not only return the following season but also return to a pre-injury level of performance. It's important to remember that this remains a significant injury with a lengthy and intense recovery process, including highly variable individual parameters depending on the complexity of the injury (other ligament involvement, meniscus injury, cartilage damage), the timing (early in season vs. late, or even offseason), the demands of their position and style of play (mobile vs. pocket quarterback, power vs. speed/agility running back), to name a few. Consequently, each athlete's unique situation warrants consideration.

T.J. HOCKENSON

TE, VIKINGS

Perhaps the 2023 holidays were not the most fondly remembered for Hockenson, as he suffered a torn ACL and medial collateral ligament (MCL) in his right knee in Week 16 during a loss to his former team, no less. The upshot was that Hockenson had to wait several weeks for the MCL to heal before undergoing reconstructive surgery on his ACL in late January. While he has progressed well, the Vikings have made it clear that they will not rush to bring him back—nor should they, given his value to the team. When the season begins, Hockenson will be just over seven months removed from surgery. Even if he were to be cleared for football activities in training camp at six months post-op—as is sometimes the case to allow a player to progress via practice participation—it would not be too surprising if he were still delayed to start the season.

MIKE WILLIAMS

WR, JETS

In Week 3, the former Chargers receiver went down with a torn left ACL. Here's where the timing is the silver lining. After undergoing surgery in late October, Williams will be nine months post-op when training camp opens with his new team. He has already indicated that he expects to be ready to start the season, and if all continues smoothly, it's a reasonable expectation. Still, there is some acclimation to game action that will be necessary on his part, given his physical style and willingness to make contested catches, especially in the red zone. Moving past apprehension in a surgically repaired knee is a real thing athletes have to face, and just how confident Williams is in his knee early on could be telling when it comes to his involvement in the Jets' offense.

DANIEL JONES

QB, GIANTS

Jones tore his right ACL in a non-contact maneuver on the grass field at Allegiant Stadium in Week 9, the first game he had played in a month after missing time with a neck issue. The silver lining was that it was an isolated ACL tear—no other structural damage—and Jones underwent reconstructive surgery in late November. As of February, he was throwing, and by May, he was participating in spring practices, telling reporters he had introduced cutting alongside his running work and that his prior neck ailment is behind him. Jones' goal is to be ready for Week 1, and barring a setback, it appears he will meet that target. Given the nature of his recent injuries combined with his mobile style of play, there will be some apprehension about his durability at the outset.

Before his injury in December, Tank Dell had 47 receptions for 709 yards and seven TDs.

JONATHON BROOKS

RB, PANTHERS

Brooks is the only rookie to make this list. He comes into the league recovering from ACL surgery but has a pathway to playing time as soon as he is healthy enough to go. Brooks stepped into the Bijan Robinson role at the University of Texas and looked ready-made for the pros until he went down in November with a knee injury. At the NFL combine, Brooks reported he had begun running and hoped to be fully cleared for training camp. Of course, it remains to be seen what his new team will have to say about his progression. An NFL study published in 2019 found players who entered the combine post-ACL surgery had a 25% chance of suffering a second ACL injury (on either side) within 22 months (as compared to a 9% chance for those with no history of a prior ACL injury). It would stand to reason that even once he begins football activities, Brooks will be ramped up gradually as the Panthers protect their investment.

NICK CHUBB

RB, BROWNS

When Chubb's left knee encountered the helmet of Steelers safety Minkah Fitzpatrick, it looked as if it might be the end of his career. After all, this was the same knee Chubb had dislocated in 2015 while playing at the University of Georgia. Despite tearing his posterior cruciate ligament (PCL), lateral collateral ligament (LCL) and MCL in that injury, Chubb returned to post more than 1,000 yards rushing in each of the next two seasons, which led to him being drafted by the Browns. In 2023, that same knee sustained tears of the ACL, MCL and medial meniscus, requiring two separate surgeries (MCL and meniscus in September, ACL in November). The Browns have only gone so far as to say they hope to have Chubb return at some point in 2024, but given his specific knee history and the complexity of his injury, it is likely to be a very slow process.

EVERYTHING ELSE

JOE BURROW

QB, BENGALS (RIGHT WRIST)

Burrow struggled through the first six weeks of the 2023 season due to a calf injury sustained early in training camp. He finally rounded into form coming out of the team's Week 7 bye, only to suffer a season-ending right wrist injury four weeks later. Burrow underwent surgery in late November to repair a torn scapholunate ligament, which is critical for wrist stability and normal motion. The key to a successful outcome is balancing the stability required from surgical repair with the mobility necessary to preserve touch and accuracy as a thrower. Burrow was cleared to begin throwing the football during spring OTAs, but how he performs as the volume of work increases will be something to watch this summer.

Joe Burrow played in only 10 games last year before tearing a wrist ligament.

ANTHONY RICHARDSON

QB, COLTS (RIGHT SHOULDER)

Richardson began his rookie season by putting to rest many of the questions about whether he could execute at the pro level after starting a limited number of games in college. The injury concerns, whether fair or unfair, remained as he left early in three of the four games in which he played (bruised knee, concussion), with his third departure in Week 5 being for the remainder of the season. Richardson suffered an acromioclavicular joint (AC) separation severe enough to warrant surgery, which, at the time, presented some unknowns for how he would enter his second season. AC injuries are common in quarterbacks as a result of frequently being taken to the ground and landing on the point of the shoulder; surgeries to repair them are not, as most are less severe than Richardson's. The good news is that the early videos that surfaced of Richardson throwing, combined with his spring practices, should inspire confidence about his progress. As of now, he appears well on his way to starting the season without limitation.

TANK DELL

WR, TEXANS (FIBULA FRACTURE)

Dell was somewhat of a revelation in the upstart Texans' offense, proving he could line up anywhere on the field and have success. In Week 13, however, he suffered a fibula fracture, bringing his strong rookie campaign to a premature end. He was determined to participate at the start of spring OTAs and appeared on his way to doing so, as he was running full speed in March. Unfortunately, he was wounded in a shooting in April, and although the injuries were reportedly minor, it appeared he might be delayed in his return to football. But he was on the field with his teammates in May, running routes and moving well. His unrestricted return indicates he'll be a full participant in training camp and on track to start the season.

DESHAUN WATSON

QB, BROWNS (RIGHT SHOULDER)

Watson had problems with his right (throwing) shoulder for several weeks following a reported rotator cuff contusion in Week 3. He later sustained a fractured glenoid (socket of the shoulder) and a torn labrum, which ended his season. He underwent surgery in November to repair the fracture and the labrum and was projected to be ready to start the 2024 campaign, a lofty but not impossible goal. He resumed a progressive throwing program in March and had no setbacks up to spring OTAs. While there is still work to be done to increase his work volume and throwing distance, it appears Watson is on track to start the season. ■

RATING THE ROOKIES

A scouting report on the newcomers who can help you right away—and in the future

BY MATT BOWEN

Every year, the NFL draft brings new talent into the league, providing fantasy football managers new names to speculate on. The potential these players possess and when they are expected to receive the opportunity to produce is what separates the rookies you should consider drafting from those you will need to be more patient with. This year's draft was unlike any other, as six quarterbacks were selected in the top 12 picks. It was also loaded with wide receiver talent. Here are the top players who could be factors in redraft leagues of varying sizes, followed by those best viewed as dynasty targets.

Bears QB Caleb Williams, the 2022 Heisman Trophy winner at USC, was the No. 1 overall draft pick this year.

BEARS
Advocate
18

QUARTERBACKS

CALEB WILLIAMS

BEARS

A natural creator with the ability to produce difference-making plays, Williams has the dual-threat traits to generate viable fantasy production as a rookie. Keeping him on schedule as a pocket thrower will be a priority in Chicago, but with a proven pair of veteran pass-catchers (DJ Moore and Keenan Allen) plus dynamic rookie Rome Odunze, Williams has the highest ceiling of any quarterback in the 2024 class. He should be targeted in redraft leagues as a high-end QB2 who can provide immediate returns in superflex formats, with the talent to jump into the lower-tier QB1 mix as the season progresses.

JAYDEN DANIELS

COMMANDERS

Daniels is an electric, dual-threat talent with the field vision and throwing efficiency to deliver the ball from the pocket. Under new offensive coordinator Kliff Kingsbury, the Commanders can set Daniels up with a mix of pro and spread concepts, maximizing his ability to anticipate windows while scheming for him as a situational runner on designed carries. Plus, with his ability to escape pressure, Daniels can put up rushing numbers, and explosive plays, on scramble attempts. He can slice through defensive angles in the open field. With a true No. 1 target in Terry McLaurin, you can draft Daniels as an upside QB2 who has the ability to produce early in Year 1.

DRAKE MAYE

PATRIOTS

At 6-foot-4 and 223 pounds, Maye has the physical tools to create fantasy production in his rookie season. While he'll have to show more consistent accuracy and anticipation in the NFL, he is a high-velocity thrower to the middle of the field, and he has the arm talent to rip the ball to the third level. As a runner, Maye can be schemed on designed carries inside the red zone, and he has the movement qualities to extend plays. The Patriots signed veteran Jacoby Brissett in the offseason, so a camp battle looms. If Maye wins the No. 1 job, however, he elevates into the QB2 mix as a potential starter in superflex formats.

J.J. MCCARTHY

VIKINGS

McCarthy landed in an ideal scheme fit with Kevin O'Connell's offense in Minnesota. Here, McCarthy can work the middle of the field, making defined throws off play-action, plus the Vikings can get him on the edges using boot concepts. He possesses excellent pocket mobility and the second-reaction skills to create as a both a runner and thrower. McCarthy will battle with veteran Sam Darnold in training camp. If the rookie wins the spot, he heads into the season

Jayden Daniels

in an offense that should facilitate production, with superstar wide receiver Justin Jefferson as his top target. You can draft McCarthy as a lower-tier QB2 who can serve as a superflex starter.

BO NIX

BRONCOS

A rhythm thrower with the movement skills to escape pressure and create as a runner, Nix is a really solid fit for Sean Payton's pass game. In Denver, Nix will operate as a point guard, distributing the ball at multiple levels of the field, using his quick release to hit timing routes on schemed concepts. Nix's decision-making late as the play extends will have to improve as a pro, but he has a top target in Courtland Sutton and a big-play threat in Marvin Mims Jr. Nix will likely have to use his legs to generate enough weekly fantasy production to stay in the QB2 discussion as a deeper superflex option.

RUNNING BACKS

JONATHON BROOKS

PANTHERS

Brooks suffered an ACL injury in November, so we need to monitor his progress this summer. If he's cleared to play, however, Brooks has the three-down traits to create an immediate fantasy impact. He's a slasher with great vision, and he has the second-level elusiveness to win in the open field. Plus, Brooks has the receiving skills to create positive matchups on backfield releases. He's an upgrade over Chuba Hubbard and Miles Sanders in Carolina and should be targeted as a flex/RB2.

TREY BENSON

CARDINALS

Benson has the pro frame (6 feet, 216 pounds) and the contact balance to thrive as a downhill runner in Arizona. With his 4.39 speed, he can hit home runs, too. As a receiver, he can work the underneath levels and produce as a screen target. Benson is a smart insurance play behind starter James Conner, who missed four games in each of his past two seasons. Benson will play a rotational role as a rookie and is worth a late-round pick in redraft leagues.

Trey Benson

BLAKE CORUM

RAMS

Corum has excellent vision and contact balance, which fits Sean McVay's run game in L.A. And as he showed at Michigan, Corum is a grinder who can handle a high volume of touches from week to week, including as an underneath outlet in the pass game. With Kyren Williams leading the way for the Rams' backfield, Corum's ceiling is limited as a rookie. But he should be targeted late in drafts as an insurance back who would elevate to RB2 status if Williams sustained an injury.

MARSHAWN LLOYD

PACKERS

With Josh Jacobs and AJ Dillon in the Packers' running back room, Lloyd faces a tough test to earn consistent rushing volume as a rookie. However, he has the pass-catching abilities to carve out a role as a third-down back. He's a sudden mover after the catch and has the open-field juice to shake defenders. If you play in a deeper PPR league, keep Lloyd on your radar as a potential late-round flier.

RAY DAVIS

BILLS

Davis will compete to earn the No. 2 role behind James Cook in Buffalo's backfield. He runs with a low pad level, finishes on contact and can set up blockers to create his own daylight. Davis also has the receiving ability to develop into a three-down player, which creates some fantasy upside if he emerges from camp as the primary backup in the Bills' explosive offense. He should be targeted only as a deeper-league insurance back as a rookie.

BUCKY IRVING

BUCCANEERS

Irving is a very decisive runner with high-end contact balance and the ability to slip tacklers at the point of attack. If Irving wins the backup spot behind Rachaad White in Tampa, he brings value as an insurance back, with some upside in deeper PPR formats due to his ability to produce after the catch.

RATING THE ROOKIES

WIDE RECEIVERS

MARVIN HARRISON JR.

CARDINALS

Harrison reminds me of DeAndre Hopkins. He has the route-running savvy, coverage awareness and body control/ball skills to produce immediate fantasy results. As Kyler Murray's No. 1 option in Arizona, Harrison will get plenty of volume, and he has the ability to isolate in scoring position. Considering the anticipated targets and his pro-ready traits, Harrison should be drafted as a fringe WR1.

MALIK NABERS

GIANTS

Nabers is an extremely explosive mover in the route tree. He can roll past defenders on vertical concepts from slot or boundary alignments, plus he has the physical catch-and-run skills to produce in open grass. In New York, Nabers will be schemed as a big-play, three-level target in Brian Daboll's offense. Yes, the Giants will need to see a higher level of play from quarterback Daniel Jones this season, but there's no question that Nabers can elevate the pass game. He should be drafted as a WR3, with the ability to produce lower-end WR2 numbers.

ROME ODUNZE

BEARS

With the physical profile at 6-foot-3 and 212 pounds, Odunze fits as the boundary X in a Bears offense that will major in three-wide receiver sets. He can go get it as a vertical target and make plays on contested throws. Plus, he is instinctive after the catch, and he has the ability to develop quickly as a top red zone option for rookie quarterback Caleb Williams. With veteran receivers DJ Moore and Keenan Allen demanding targets in this offense, Odunze enters a crowded wide receiver room, but he has the potential to produce WR3 weeks this season.

BRIAN THOMAS JR.

JAGUARS

Thomas joins the Jaguars as the replacement for Zay Jones, giving quarterback Trevor Lawrence that vertical element in the pass game. Thomas has excellent ball-tracking skills, plus the proven ability to separate at the third level of the field. In Doug Pederson's system, Thomas can also be schemed to attack interior voids on the underneath levels. You can draft Thomas as a WR3 who has the ability to produce breakout weeks due to his big-play ability.

Ja'Lynn Polk

LADD MCCONKEY

CHARGERS

McConkey can operate as a prime target for quarterback Justin Herbert in L.A. this season. With heavy play-action elements in Jim Harbaugh's offense, which will open middle-of-the-field voids, McConkey can live between the numbers on catch-and-run targets. Plus, we know he has the quickness and savvy route skills to uncover in one-on-one matchups. McConkey, who checked in with a 4.39 40 at the combine, fits here as a volume WR3/flex.

XAVIER WORTHY

CHIEFS

An electric mover with ridiculous 4.21 speed, Worthy can stretch defenses vertically or run away from coverage on crossers and over routes. In Andy Reid's offense, look for Worthy to be deployed as a multilevel target for quarterback Patrick Mahomes. The Chiefs have some depth at wide receiver now, and tight end Travis Kelce remains the No. 1 option for Mahomes. However, given Worthy's speed and big-play chops, he should be drafted as a late-round WR3, with potentially more upside in non-PPR formats.

KEON COLEMAN

BILLS

At 6-foot-3 and 213 pounds and possessing the leaping ability to play well above the rim, Coleman can make plays at the third level for quarterback Josh Allen. He's a physical, middle-of-the-field target who can drop his pads after the catch. With both Stefon Diggs and Gabe Davis no longer in Buffalo, the door is wide open here for Coleman to play as a multilevel, boundary target. He should be drafted in all formats as a WR3.

XAVIER LEGETTE

PANTHERS

Legette has the straight-line juice and power to make plays down the field, and he brings a physical element after the catch. He can shift gears and go on underneath throws, which can facilitate more production for second-year quarterback Bryce Young. Legette will work opposite veterans Diontae Johnson and Adam Thielen, so he could see volume limitations early in the season, which puts him in the WR3 mix for 12-team leagues.

ADONAI MITCHELL

COLTS

A sudden mover at the release and at the top of the route, Mitchell could emerge as a vertical threat for quarterback Anthony Richardson. He'll have competition for targets in Indianapolis with Michael Pittman Jr. and slot man Josh Downs. However, if you play in a deeper league and want to take a shot on a rookie with playmaking upside and elite ball skills, then Mitchell is your guy.

JA'LYNN POLK

PATRIOTS

The Patriots lacked difference-makers on the offensive perimeter last season, so look for Polk to jump into the mix as a starting receiver. I don't see big-time speed on his tape, but he is willing to make plays in traffic and has the body control to separate. Put him in your draft queue as a potential volume target this season.

RICKY PEARSALL

49ERS

Pearsall can get down the field to use his 4.41 speed, but he also has the ability to work out of the slot in Kyle Shanahan's offense. While the 49ers already have Brandon Aiyuk and Deebo Samuel, there's upside here due to Pearsall's ability to uncover. He could play a defined role in a system that creates open voids and catch-and-run opportunities. Pearsall might start the season as a bench stash, but he's worth a shot as a late-round flier.

MALACHI CORLEY

JETS

Corley will work out of the slot for Aaron Rodgers, bringing high-end catch-and-run ability to the Jets offense. He's a physical mover with the ball carrier vision to create positive open-field angles. Garrett Wilson is the No. 1 in New York, and the club signed veteran free agent Mike Williams this offseason. But don't sleep on Corley as a rookie, given his strengths and Rodgers' ability to throw perfectly to the middle of the field. Corley should be targeted as a potential WR3 in 12-team leagues.

ROMAN WILSON

STEELERS

Wilson is an inside target who has the 4.39 speed to stress defenses on deep over routes and vertical concepts. He should man the slot for the Steelers in their three-wide receiver sets. He'll work the underneath levels, too, but I really like the idea of Pittsburgh offensive coordinator Arthur Smith

Adonai Mitchell

scheming up play-action targets for Wilson to create big-play opportunities. Considering the expected volume for George Pickens and Smith's run-heavy approach, Wilson can be considered a WR3 target in deeper leagues only.

TIGHT ENDS

BROCK BOWERS

RAIDERS

The unquestioned top TE prospect in the 2024 class, Bowers has the route-running capabilities to uncover versus safeties and linebackers and the ability to stretch the seams. Plus, he's a skilled and rugged mover after the catch. While Vegas drafted TE Michael Mayer in the second round last year, Bowers is the Raiders tight end you want to roster in fantasy. He'll be a fringe TE1 as a rookie with the ability to produce breakout games.

DYNASTY TARGETS

JALEN MCMILLAN

WR, BUCCANEERS

McMillan has playmaking ability from the slot. He can get vertical, create in space and turn underneath throws into big gains. His route running is pro-ready, too. He faces strong competition for targets in Tampa with established veterans Mike Evans and Chris Godwin, which lowers his projected totals. While McMillan has real value in dynasty formats, Baker Mayfield's aggressive throwing mentality opens the door for fantasy managers to use a late-round flier on him.

LUKE MCCAFFREY

WR, COMMANDERS

The younger brother of Christian McCaffrey boosted his draft profile by running a 4.46 40-yard dash at the combine. He's a taller slot target (6-foot-2) who is willing to work the dirty areas of the field, and he has the savvy route skills to manipulate coverage and get open. He faces tough competition for targets with Terry McLaurin and Jahan Dotson, making him a late-round option only.

Jalen McMillan

MICHAEL PENIX JR.

QB, FALCONS

With veteran Kirk Cousins entrenched atop the Falcons' depth chart, Penix is strictly a dynasty option at this point. He's a pocket thrower with the arm talent and deep-ball accuracy to create big-play opportunities. In Atlanta, he can develop as a rhythm passer in a system that will use play-action elements to open intermediate windows.

JAYLEN WRIGHT

RB, DOLPHINS

A big-play runner with 4.38 speed and the pass-catching skills to see an increase in target volume as a pro, Wright is an easy fit for Mike McDaniel's play-calling in Miami. The Dolphins feature a crowded running back room, so the volume might not click for Wright as a rookie, but he has future upside in this offensive system.

JERMAINE BURTON

WR, BENGALS

Burton will compete for the No. 3 job in the Bengals' pass-heavy offense. He has the strength to play through contact at multiple levels of the field and the ability to separate over the top, and he is a natural hands-catcher on the boundary. With Tee Higgins slated to play this season on the franchise tag, Burton should be on your list as a dynasty target.

BEN SINNOTT

TE, COMMANDERS

With the route skills to work the middle of the field or stretch defenses at the third level, Sinnott is an easy mover from multiple alignments. He can rumble after the catch, too. He offers potential streaming value in Kliff Kingsbury's offense and should be a priority dynasty target with 33-year-old Zach Ertz ahead of him on the depth chart.

TROY FRANKLIN

WR, BRONCOS

Franklin will get a shot to compete for early playing time as a rookie in Denver, but he also carries dynasty value as a vertical target in Sean Payton's system. Franklin is a glider who can float past the top of the secondary, and he's elusive after the catch.

ISAAC GUERENDO

RB, 49ERS

A powerful runner at 6 feet and 221 pounds, Guerendo dropped a blistering 4.33 40-yard dash time at the combine that highlighted his explosive ability. He'll start the season behind Christian McCaffrey and Elijah Mitchell, but Guerendo has the potential to be a productive back in Kyle Shanahan's heavily schemed offense.

Isaac Guerendo

JARED WILEY

TE, CHIEFS

Travis Kelce is still the No. 1 target for Patrick Mahomes in Kansas City, but the veteran tight end will turn 35 in October. Wiley is a physical target who can climb the ladder at the catch point and use his 4.62 speed to separate on seams and crossers. That's a fit for Andy Reid's system.

DYLAN LAUBE

RB, RAIDERS

Keep an eye on Laube out in Vegas during camp. The FCS product (New Hampshire) has upper-level receiving skills on backfield releases, and he showed his ability to separate from slot alignments. There's potential here to develop a role as a third-down back with PPR upside.

JAVON BAKER

WR, PATRIOTS

Baker has the ball-tracking skills and leaping ability to work down the field, and his route running is improving. As a boundary receiver, his skill set fits with the arm talent of quarterback Drake Maye.

TYRONE TRACY JR.

RB, GIANTS

Tracy Jr. started his college career at wide receiver before making the move to running back. He'll compete for the No. 2 role behind Devin Singletary this summer in camp. Keep Tracy on your dynasty radar as a versatile back with perimeter speed, contact balance and pass-catching traits.

JA'TAVION SANDERS

TE, PANTHERS

A pass-catching tight end with the frame (6-foot-4, 245 pounds) and straight-line speed to separate, Sanders has NFL upside as a big-body target in the middle of the field. He's a player to keep on the radar as a potential streaming option, too.

BRAELON ALLEN

RB, JETS

Allen will compete for the No. 2 role in New York behind Breece Hall, so there's limited value for him in redraft leagues this season. However, with his size (6-foot-1, 235 pounds) and downhill power, Allen can be targeted in deeper dynasty formats as a potential rotational back with the ability to handle goal line carries.

KIMANI VIDAL

RB, CHARGERS

Vidal will start his pro career behind J.K. Dobbins and Gus Edwards on the depth chart in Los Angeles, but he has the traits to play a future role in Jim Harbaugh's run-centered system. At 5-foot-8 and 213 pounds, Vidal has a compact and strong frame, with the ability to run through contact. And he displays the short-area burst to pull away from underneath coverage as a receiver as well.

CADE STOVER

TE, TEXANS

Stover has the play speed and open-field vision to move the sticks after the catch, and he can separate late when running seams and corner routes. Landing in Houston, where he'll play behind veteran Dalton Schultz (who clicked with the offense in his first season with the Texans last year), definitely puts a hit on Stover's immediate fantasy value.

THEO JOHNSON

TE, GIANTS

Johnson ran a 4.57 40-yard-dash at the combine this winter, which translates to working the seams in an NFL offense. Plus, at 6-foot-6 and 259 pounds, Johnson can use his frame to shield defenders at the catch point, creating one-on-one potential. Johnson is a dynasty target whose value is rising following the retirement of Darren Waller. ■

ON THE REBOUND

Can these star players recapture their former fantasy greatness?

BY ERIC KARABELL

The record books will say that future Hall of Fame quarterback Aaron Rodgers threw one pass in his first season with the New York Jets. While reasonable minds could debate whether Rodgers—one of the best QBs to ever play the sport—would have finished as a QB1 in his age-39 season, we will never know. Rodgers tore his left Achilles tendon on the fourth play of his 19th NFL season, scoring nary a fantasy point, just like you and me. (Hopefully, you stayed healthy.)

Of course, Rodgers is now 40 and presumably ready to bounce back to some level of NFL prominence—and there is a whole lot of prominence, including recently. In the 2022 season, his final campaign with the Green Bay Packers, Rodgers finished outside the top 10 quarterbacks in fantasy scoring, but not by much. He wasn't bad. He just wasn't the typical Aaron Rodgers, the one who was a top-five fantasy QB in 2020, 2021 (NFL MVP both years!) and seven other times in a legendary career that isn't over yet.

Injury often gets in the way of a positive, noteworthy story, and Rodgers typified this theme more than anyone in 2023, with his season ending mere minutes into his Jets debut. As we highlight the NFL players aiming to bounce back from a disappointing 2023 season—whether due to injury or simply poor performance—to prior statistical glory or expectations thereof, all eyes will be on Rodgers. As we pondered one year ago at this time, his performance should be interesting and fantasy relevant.

After all, Rodgers threw for 3,695 passing yards and 26 touchdowns in his final season with the Packers, despite an alarming lack of exceptional targets once Davante Adams left town. Jets wide receiver Garrett Wilson is an exciting playmaker, one who surpassed 1,000 receiving yards in each of his first two NFL seasons despite shoddy (to say the least) quarterback play. The Jets coveted Rodgers, hoping the four-time league MVP would deliver a Super Bowl run. Perhaps that can still happen. He and Wilson could become one of the top QB/WR tandems in the league.

Rodgers was not an early pick in most fantasy drafts because, well, investors wisely focus on running backs and wide receivers early on. They should. Quarterback is a deep fantasy position in standard formats. Still, there was no shortage of running backs and wide receivers who statistically underachieved during the 2023 season, as well as QBs not named Rodgers and tight ends.

What follows is a list of bounce-back

Can Aaron Rodgers have the success this year that the Jets were hoping for in 2023?

NFL
NFL

candidates heading into the 2024 season. Expectations were high a year ago, and they are likely lower today, fair or not. Let's go position by position.

QUARTERBACK

▶ **Joe Burrow, Bengals:** Burrow threw for more than 9,000 yards and 69 touchdowns over his second and third NFL seasons, rising into the positional top five for fantasy purposes. A strained right calf thwarted him early last season, and soon after the big numbers finally arrived a month later, he suffered a season-ending wrist injury in Week 11. He may not come at a discount in drafts, but he should be worth it.

▶ **Justin Herbert, Chargers:** Herbert played through a fractured middle finger on his left (non-throwing) hand early in the season and delivered solid numbers for three months, but he could not overcome a fractured right index finger in Week 14. Reliable quarterbacks succumbing to injury was an unfortunate theme in 2023. Unlike Burrow, Herbert will find many new faces on his offense, with Keenan Allen, Mike Williams and Austin Ekeler no longer in L.A., and he also has a new head coach in Jim Harbaugh.

▶ **Kirk Cousins, Falcons:** Cousins got off to a fantastic start last season, pacing toward career bests in passing yards and touchdown passes before tearing his right Achilles tendon in Week 8. Now a Falcon after six seasons with the Vikings, Cousins will have ample playmakers surrounding him. But unlike Burrow and Herbert, he must overcome a debilitating lower-leg injury, one suffered months after Rodgers was carted away. Betting against Cousins in the past hasn't worked out, though, so expect him to overachieve again. If he doesn't, top-10 draft pick Michael Penix Jr. is there for a reason.

▶ **Anthony Richardson, Colts:** Richardson, the No. 4 pick in the 2023 NFL draft, started in Week 1 and looked like a fantasy star when we saw him. He rushed for four touchdowns in his first three games, but he left early in Week 2 with a concussion. His season ended with a serious shoulder injury in Week 5, leading fantasy managers to wonder about his ability to stay on the field. Richardson has an elite size/speed combination for a quarterback, but there are doubts about his passing accuracy and, now, his durability.

▶ **Deshaun Watson, Browns:** Watson made this list last year after struggling in his much-awaited Browns debut, which came in Week 13 after a long suspension. Much was expected from him in his first full season in Cleveland, but it didn't come to fruition. Watson again played in only six games, this time due to a season-ending shoulder injury that may hamper him in the season ahead, with moribund statistics that look nothing like his Houston days. Fantasy managers may not be quick to invest after three lost seasons.

▶ **Russell Wilson, Steelers:** Wilson's two-year run as a Bronco went quite poorly, but the Steelers were eager to add him to their roster. As with Watson, Wilson has looked nothing like a QB1 option over the past three seasons, including during his final run with the Seahawks, and it remains to be seen how much Pittsburgh coach Mike Tomlin wants to throw the football. Oh, and the Steelers acquired former Bears first-rounder Justin Fields just to make things more interesting.

▶ **Daniel Jones, Giants:** Jones was a top-10 fantasy quarterback during the 2022 season (no, really, it's actually true!), thanks mostly to rushing for 708 yards and seven touchdowns. But last season was a nightmare. He played poorly in September, dealt with a neck injury and then suffered a right ACL tear in Week 9. Jones figures to start when healthy, thanks to his exorbitant contract, but fantasy managers should be wary.

Nick Chubb

RUNNING BACK

▶ **Nick Chubb, Browns:** Chubb had finished among the top 10 in rushing yards for five consecutive seasons, but he suffered injuries to his left ACL, MCL and meniscus in Week 2, prematurely ending his season and placing doubt on whether he will be ready for the start of this one. Many will question if he will ever return to prior levels.

▶ **Austin Ekeler, Commanders:** Ekeler was the league's preeminent fantasy running back during the 2021 and '22 seasons for the Chargers—he scored a silly 38 touchdowns. His 2023 campaign was silly for other reasons. Ekeler injured an ankle in Week 1 (while scoring 26.4 fantasy points), missed three games and scored double-digit fantasy points only seven times after that. The Commanders will likely have him focus on catching the football.

▶ **Josh Jacobs, Packers:** The league's

leading rusher in 2022 with 1,653 yards, Jacobs rushed for less than half that total in his follow-up for the Raiders, albeit over only 13 games. He enjoyed massive volume in 2022, and it predictably decreased last season. The Packers may be inclined to return Jacobs to extensive volume, though the drafting of MarShawn Lloyd could make things interesting.

▶ **Aaron Jones, Vikings:** The former Packers star left for Green Bay's NFC North rivals after suffering through an injury-plagued season that saw him average only 12.3 fantasy points per game, far below his massive 2022 season. Jones is older than Jacobs and unlikely to see the same volume, but fantasy managers fondly recall his consistency and ability to find the end zone.

▶ **Jonathan Taylor, Colts:** Taylor rushed for 1,811 yards and 18 touchdowns in 2021. Since then, he has rushed for 1,602 yards and 11 touchdowns over 21 games, been frustrated by repeated ankle injuries, as well as a thumb injury, and even requested a trade in July 2023. He enters his fifth NFL season presumably healthy and motivated to return to statistical greatness.

▶ **Rhamondre Stevenson, Patriots:** A strong RB2 option during the 2022 season when he totaled more than 1,400 total yards and caught 69 passes, he struggled last season, as many Patriots did. He didn't hit the 100-yard rushing mark in any games and then missed the final five contests with an ankle injury. He remains atop the team's depth chart.

Christian Kirk

WIDE RECEIVER

▶ **Cooper Kupp, Rams:** Much like Colts RB Taylor, Kupp was one of the top fantasy picks entering 2022, and things haven't been the same since. Kupp registered 1,947 receiving yards and 16 touchdowns in 2021. He has 1,549 receiving yards and 11 touchdowns since then. Unlike Taylor, Kupp no longer leads his team's depth chart, as the surprising Puka Nacua has become a star.

▶ **Tee Higgins, Bengals:** Higgins eclipsed 1,000 receiving yards during the 2021 and 2022 seasons, and fantasy managers enjoyed high-WR2 production, but things went differently last season. It started with a contract dispute; then came multiple injuries and general inefficiency during a frustrating season. Higgins caught only 42 passes in 12 games, and the drafting of Jermaine Burton may complicate things.

▶ **Mike Williams, Jets:** A longtime Charger who had his best season in 2021, Williams tore the ACL in his left knee in Week 3 last season. Now he's a Jet, in a prime position to succeed with Aaron Rodgers and Garrett Wilson, but we must remember Williams' history of inconsistent performance and staying healthy.

▶ **Marquise Brown, Chiefs:** Only one of Brown's first five NFL seasons resulted in WR2 production, but things are looking up now that he has joined Patrick Mahomes and the two-time defending Super Bowl champions. Lower-leg injuries cost Brown eight games over his two seasons with the Cardinals. If he's healthy, the 2024 season could be his best yet.

▶ **Christian Kirk, Jaguars:** The underrated Kirk was a solid WR2 performer in 2022, surpassing 1,000 receiving yards for the first time and scoring eight touchdowns, and he was pacing well last season before a groin injury in Week 13 ended things. With Calvin Ridley leaving town, Kirk again leads the depth chart. The Jaguars spent a first-round pick on LSU's Brian Thomas Jr., though he and Kirk should work well together.

TIGHT END

▶ **Mark Andrews, Ravens:** Andrews was pacing below his extraordinary 2021 numbers when his regular season ended with a Week 11 ankle injury. He was physically compromised when he returned for the AFC Championship Game. Andrews averaged 13.5 fantasy points per game, a mark bettered by only three tight ends. Expectations remain high this season. ■

THE VALUE OF CONSISTENCY

Avoid a boom-or-bust scenario by drafting players who are dependable performers week after week

BY TRISTAN H. COCKCROFT

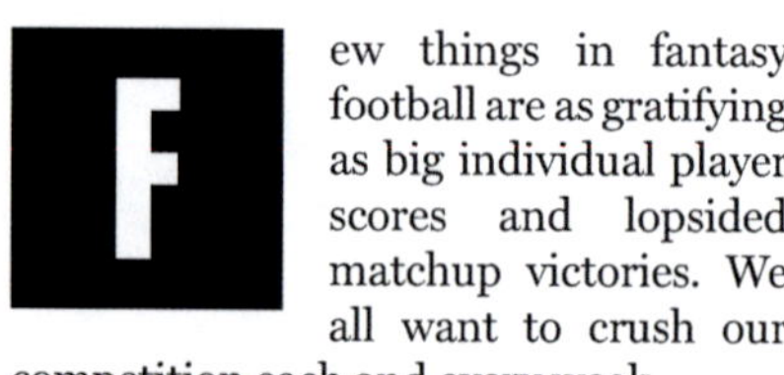

Few things in fantasy football are as gratifying as big individual player scores and lopsided matchup victories. We all want to crush our competition each and every week.

But here's the harsh reality: Scoring records are great and all, but it's the steady teams that typically advance to the fantasy playoffs. Be competitive every week, and don't risk being a team that runs hot or cold.

In short: Consistency matters.

It's great when your player goes off for 50-plus fantasy points to almost single-handedly win your playoff-week matchup, but remember that you have to *make* the playoffs to reap the rewards of that performance. Chasing such players might pad your seasonal point total, but it can lead to too many heartbreaking losses.

If the above playoff hero sounds familiar, he should. He's Amari Cooper, who scored 51.5 points in Week 16 of last season. He finished 2023 with 227.0 points, 20th best at his position, and had career highs with 1,250 receiving yards and 17.4 yards per catch. The magnifying glass, however, amplifies that Cooper scored 54% of his fantasy points in four games (Weeks 3, 9, 15 and 16) and was near-silent in many other weeks. He was held beneath 10 points six times and missed another two contests. In 2023, he earned your fantasy start only 35% of the time, and he was a complete stiff in 27% of the games he played. This season, he'll have Jerry Jeudy in town to consume more of his portion of the Browns' proverbial target pie.

The charts below identify the most consistent fantasy players over the past three seasons combined (2021–23).

▶ **Start%:** The percentage of weeks that the player "earned your start," meaning they were a top-10 quarterback or tight end or top-25 running back or wide receiver in PPR fantasy points in a given week. Those thresholds reflect the number of available lineup spots in a standard ESPN league. Players get penalized for games missed, but not bye weeks, since fantasy managers can draft accounting for the latter but not always for the former.

▶ **Stiff%:** The percentage of the player's games played—differing from Start%, as you'd know to bench an injured player—in which his PPR fantasy point total was significantly beneath those thresholds (outside the top 20 quarterbacks or tight ends or top 50 running backs or wide receivers).

This is not to say successful fantasy football rosters are entirely comprised of consistency kings. Far from it. The best teams blend a mix of reliable performers and picks with upside.

Here are two of fantasy football's most consistent players:

MICHAEL PITTMAN JR.

WR, COLTS

One of the game's most underrated receivers, Pittman has averaged 14.4 PPR

Basic Consistency Ratings from 2021–23

Quarterbacks	Start%	Stiff%
Josh Allen	74.0%	8.0% [4/50]
Jalen Hurts	66.7%	10.6% [5/47]
Patrick Mahomes	58.8%	8.0% [4/50]
Justin Herbert	49.0%	25.5% [12/47]
Dak Prescott	43.1%	20.0% [9/45]
Kirk Cousins	39.2%	24.4% [10/41]
Lamar Jackson	39.2%	17.5% [7/40]
Joe Burrow	38.0%	19.0% [8/42]
Derek Carr	37.3%	36.7% [18/49]

Running Backs	Start%	Stiff%
Bijan Robinson	82.4%	11.8% [2/17]
Austin Ekeler	70.6%	2.1% [1/47]
Christian McCaffrey	70.6%	2.5% [1/40]
Joe Mixon	66.0%	0.0% [0/47]
Najee Harris	64.7%	3.9% [2/51]
Josh Jacobs	64.7%	0.0% [0/45]
Jahmyr Gibbs	64.7%	0.0% [0/15]
Alvin Kamara	58.8%	0.0% [0/41]
Jonathan Taylor	58.8%	5.3% [2/38]
Rachaad White	58.8%	11.8% [4/34]
David Montgomery	56.9%	4.7% [2/43]
Derrick Henry	56.9%	4.9% [2/41]
Breece Hall	55.9%	12.5% [3/24]
Ezekiel Elliott	54.9%	10.2% [5/49]
Saquon Barkley	52.9%	7.0% [3/43]
D'Andre Swift	52.9%	7.0% [3/43]
James Conner	52.9%	2.4% [1/41]
Kenneth Walker III	52.9%	16.7% [5/30]
Leonard Fournette	51.2%	9.4% [3/32]

Our complete Consistency Ratings can be found at espn.com/fantasy/football (under the More tab), and both the single-season and three-year data sets are updated weekly throughout the season.

Michael Pittman Jr.

fantasy points per game the past three seasons, scored within five points of that number in 26 of 49 games (53%) and outscored it by five-plus points in 12 additional contests. Pittman is the top receiver for up-and-coming QB Anthony Richardson, and he saw at least 10 targets plus a 25% target share in nine of 16 games in 2023.

JOE MIXON

RB, TEXANS

We think of the Texans as pass-oriented, but Mixon's consistency makes him a sneaky-good pick there. His 16.9 fantasy points per game the past three seasons is fourth best among running backs, and only once did he finish outside his position's top 40 in scoring for the week. And apropos to his role, Mixon led all running backs in goal-line carries (34) and scores (17) in this span.

Besides Cooper, here's another frustratingly inconsistent player:

RAHEEM MOSTERT

RB, DOLPHINS

We all remember that 70-20 drubbing of the Broncos, in which Mostert and De'Von Achane exploded for huge PPR fantasy point totals (45.2 and 51.3), but Achane's presence affects Mostert's workload and inconsistency. Mostert scored 48% of his 2023 points in four games (Weeks 2, 3, 6 and 14) and has been held beneath 12 points in 15 of his 31 games with the Dolphins over the past two seasons. ■

Tony Pollard	51.0%	8.3% (4/48)
Aaron Jones	49.0%	9.3% (4/43)
Rhamondre Stevenson	47.1%	19.5% (8/41)
Isiah Pacheco	47.1%	12.9% (4/31)
Devin Singletary	46.0%	18.0% (9/50)
Travis Etienne Jr.	43.1%	5.9% (2/34)
Nick Chubb	43.1%	0.0% (0/33)

Wide Receivers	Start%	Stiff%
Tyreek Hill	66.7%	12.0% (6/50)
Justin Jefferson	64.7%	13.6% (6/44)
CeeDee Lamb	62.7%	14.0% (7/50)
Stefon Diggs	62.0%	14.0% (7/50)
Puka Nacua	58.8%	23.5% (4/17)
Davante Adams	56.9%	16.0% (8/50)
Cooper Kupp	56.9%	13.2% (5/38)
Amon-Ra St. Brown	52.9%	20.4% (10/49)
Mike Evans	51.0%	20.8% (10/48)
A.J. Brown	51.0%	21.3% (10/47)
DeVonta Smith	49.0%	34.0% (17/50)
Keenan Allen	49.0%	5.1% (2/39)
Michael Pittman Jr.	47.1%	16.3% (8/49)
Deebo Samuel	47.1%	13.6% (6/44)
Chris Olave	47.1%	12.9% (4/31)
Jayden Reed	47.1%	12.5% (2/16)
DK Metcalf	45.1%	26.0% (13/50)
Tyler Lockett	45.1%	30.6% (15/49)
Garrett Wilson	44.1%	29.4% (10/34)
DJ Moore	41.2%	27.5% (14/51)
Jaylen Waddle	41.2%	21.3% (10/47)
Diontae Johnson	41.2%	13.0% (6/46)
Rashee Rice	41.2%	12.5% (2/16)
Zay Flowers	41.2%	25.0% (4/16)
Ja'Marr Chase	40.0%	15.6% (7/45)
Tee Higgins	40.0%	28.6% (12/42)

Tight Ends	Start%	Stiff%
Travis Kelce	68.6%	12.5% (6/48)
Sam LaPorta	64.7%	11.8% (2/17)
George Kittle	47.1%	35.6% (16/45)
Evan Engram	45.1%	36.7% (18/49)
T.J. Hockenson	45.1%	15.9% (7/44)
Mark Andrews	45.1%	16.7% (7/42)
Dalton Schultz	43.1%	34.0% (16/47)
Dalton Kincaid	41.2%	37.5% (6/16)
Dallas Goedert	35.3%	31.7% (13/41)

PLAYING FOR KEEPS

A keeper league gives you the flexibility to hold on to a few promising players while also drafting new talent each year

BY ERIC MOODY

Fantasy football leagues are like an ice cream shop with lots of flavors and toppings to choose from. You can customize the scoring systems, league depth and number of quarterbacks you can have in your starting lineup. You can even have a league without kickers or defenses. Anything your heart desires is at your disposal.

Ever wonder about those leagues where you're not just picking players for a single season, but you're investing in their long-term success? You've probably heard the terms "dynasty" and "keeper" floating around, and you're itching to know more, right? Let me give you the lowdown, because these formats are where the real fun begins. Essentially, you're building an empire for years to come. Here's a rundown of each format and why diving into one or the other could be the fantasy football adventure you've been waiting for.

DYNASTY LEAGUES

This format is the ultimate test of team management skills. Instead of starting fresh every August, as you do in redraft leagues, you get to hold on to most, or even all, of your players from year to year. It's like building a dynasty—hence the name.

Your rookie draft in dynasty leagues begins right after the NFL draft. The top pick can shape your team's future, just as it does in the big leagues. You shouldn't expect smooth sailing; the wrong move or a stroke of bad luck can ruin your season. You're on a roller coaster of highs and lows with this format.

KEEPER LEAGUES

Dynasty leagues require continuous roster management and long-term planning, while redraft leagues focus on drafting new teams every season with a "win now" attitude. You get the best of both worlds in keeper leagues. There's still something to play for even if your team isn't a contender one season, because you're allowed to carry over a few players from year to year.

Keeper leagues are flexible. They can have different restrictions on keeping players, the length of time they can be kept and the cost of keeping them.

Here's some advice on getting started with a keeper league:

▶ **The success of your league is based largely on how great the commissioner is.** He or she must be on top of everything in your league and communicate things clearly to everyone. The commissioner's first job should be to create a league constitution, which will lay out the format and the rules and clearly define what is and isn't acceptable in the league. A good constitution is a commissioner's best friend, helping everyone avoid surprises, impasses and, above all, the appearance

Rams WR Puka Nacua is a wise fantasy investment for now—and for the future.

of a conflict of interest.

▶ **So, who else should be in your league?** Those who consistently field competitive teams in your redraft league and spend time and energy on draft strategies are the best managers for keeper formats. Twelve managers is a good number, since too few can lead to teams full of superstars, which takes away some of the skill involved in managing a roster. If you're up to a real challenge, you can expand to up to 16 managers, but be aware this means there won't be much on the waiver wire from week to week, and a bit of bad luck or one key injury can totally tank your season. That said, in a keeper league, there's always next year to play for.

▶ **Three keepers is the ideal amount for each team.** It's easier to manage, and your drafts will still have plenty of good talent available. A limit on keepers makes total dominance much more difficult for one team to achieve. League parity is a good thing most of the time. If you want a few more keepers, consider no more than six, which is basically a starting lineup. Anything more than that and you're squarely in dynasty territory.

▶ **"Keeper by round" is the most common system to use when determining the cost of keeping a player.** A player who was drafted in the fifth round the previous season counts as your fourth-round pick this year. The more players you are allowed to keep, the steeper the price should be to keep them for the long term. Another way to keep the pool fresh is to limit how long managers are allowed to keep players before having to return them to the draft pool. Three years is a good length. This creates parity in the league, and remember, it's a keeper league, not a dynasty.

▶ **Salary cap drafts add an extra dimension of strategy, with each keeper's "salary" carrying over but escalating every time they're kept.** For example, It could be an extra $3 the first year you keep a player, an additional $6 the second year and $9 in the third, for a total of $18. This mirrors the salary cap choices NFL teams have to make all the time; you can't keep all your best players and stay under the cap if they cost too much.

Bringing this all together, a keeper league combines player value, opportunity and upside while considering long-term implications. Balance immediate production with planning for future seasons. You should target young, high-upside players, but don't overextend. Be proactive on the waiver wire, as the next Puka Nacua might be out there. Make trades and monitor player news; a savvy pickup at the end of this season could pay huge dividends for next season.

Take note of these tips. Some of my best fantasy football memories have come in keeper leagues. If you give it a try, the same could happen for you. ■

DEFYING EXPECTATIONS

Receiver tracking metrics can help fine-tune your rankings to identify overachievers (and underachievers)

BY SETH WALDER

Let's beat the wideout fantasy market with ESPN's receiver tracking metrics (RTMs). Last year in this space we showed off "open score," which measures a receiver's ability to get open on every route—regardless of whether they are targeted—relative to expectations using NFL Next Gen Stats data. But the question I came back to this year was: Do the RTMs actually help us beat average draft position (ADP)? It turns out some of them do! But, critically, not all.

There are three components to the receiver tracking metrics: the aforementioned open score, and then catch score and YAC score, which measure a receiver's ability to make the catch and generate yards after the catch—again, relative to expectations based on factors such as the route run, defensive coverage and the positioning, speed and direction of all 22 players on the field.

All three RTM categories are on a 0 to 99 scale, with 50 being roughly average.

From 2018 to 2023, a simple out-of-sample model using ADP, prior-season open score and prior-season catch score outperformed a model of ADP alone in terms of predicting wide receiver fantasy rank. This is great news! It means the RTMs have information that has not been fully baked into the market—and we can use that to our advantage. Notably, the YAC score did not improve the model.

Knowing the market underrates players who perform well in open score and catch score relative to their ADP, we can identify players who appear either underrated or overrated relative to their market. A benefit of this approach is that, by incorporating ADP into the model, we are able to partially bake in factors outside of last season's on-field performance—such as a player's age or changes in opportunity, teammates or scheme—and just focus on where the RTMs nudge us in one direction or another.

Using ESPN's current default rankings as a stand-in for ADP, let's use our simple model of ADP, open score and catch score to identify players who look like values and fades. The full list of RTMs can be found at espnanalytics.com/rtm.

2023 RTM LEADERS (WRs)

Open Score		Catch Score	
1. Keenan Allen	91	1. Brandon Aiyuk	97
2. CeeDee Lamb	85	2. DJ Moore	93
3. Kalif Raymond	84	3. Nico Collins	91
4. Tyreek Hill	83	4. A.J. Brown	90
T5. Garrett Wilson	82	5. Adam Thielen	87
T5. DeAndre Hopkins	82	6. Michael Wilson	80
T5. A.J. Brown	82	7. Romeo Doubs	77
T8. Tank Dell	81	T8. Jakobi Meyers	75
T8. Brandon Aiyuk	81	T8. CeeDee Lamb	75
10. Courtland Sutton	79	T10. Amari Cooper	74
		T10. Justin Jefferson	74

DRAFT 'EM

BRANDON AIYUK

49ERS

WR RANK: 17 MODEL RANK: 3

The RTMs have no greater love than Aiyuk, who smashed in the categories we care about for this exercise: open score (81) and catch score (97). Aiyuk's volume (1,342 receiving yards) was stymied by the 49ers jumping out to leads and no longer needing to throw, but on a down-to-down basis, the skill was all there. He's an elite receiver in an elite offense, and if the RTMs are screaming one thing, it is this: Aiyuk is going to be underrated by fantasy managers. The difference between WR rank and model rank is jarring here, so I want to be clear: I'm not advocating Aiyuk be selected third among WRs—consider this a simple model to push us directionally one way or another off of ADP, not as a replacement for draft ranks.

Brandon Aiyuk

KEENAN ALLEN
BEARS
WR RANK: 29 MODEL RANK: 9

Allen had arguably his best season in his final campaign as a Charger. His 2.5 yards per route run was nearly a career high and indicated he was still playing at an exceptional level. So did the RTMs, as Allen recorded a 91 open score (and 61 catch score) at age 31. Open score is the most important RTM here, both in terms of predicting future yardage and in terms of performance relative to ADP, so he's another player to buy. Lots of factors have changed with Allen—he's getting older and is now playing on a new team, with rookie QB Caleb Williams—but we're relying on the market to handle that information and using the RTMs to tell us that he's still got it.

TANK DELL
TEXANS
WR RANK: 28 MODEL RANK: 18

Dell's rookie season was cut short by a fractured fibula, but make no mistake: He showed plenty in the 11 games he did play, recording 709 receiving yards and 2.4 yards per route run. In terms of the RTMs, Dell shined in open score with an 81 (tied for eighth among wideouts, along with Aiyuk). In other words, Dell flashed No. 1 ability as a rookie, but he may still be available at a discount relative to his talent.

DIONTAE JOHNSON
PANTHERS
WR RANK: 35 MODEL RANK: 20

We highlighted Johnson in our open score story a year ago as a player to target, and while I wouldn't call that a success based on the baseline numbers he put up last season—717 receiving yards and five touchdowns in 13 games—his 2.1 yards per route run were a career high. His open score dropped from 99 in 2022 to 78 in 2023, but that still ranked him 12th among wide receivers. There are new complications (or potential upsides!) with his new home in Carolina, but the RTMs remain firm on Johnson: He still looks like a player underrated by the market.

FADE 'EM

DEEBO SAMUEL
49ERS
WR RANK: 18 MODEL RANK: 39

Though we mentioned that YAC score offered no additional value to ADP, that doesn't mean it's bad (obviously). It just means that YAC skills, and how they predict future performance, are fully baked into the market. The issue for Samuel is that he is *all* YAC. Over the past four seasons, his open and catch scores have both been below 50 in every season. He is incredible at generating YAC—he has three of the top five YAC scores in the history of the metric, which dates back to 2017. But his profile suggests he will be overrated in fantasy markets.

NFL player tracking, also known as Next Gen Stats, is the capture of real-time location data, speed and acceleration for every player, every play, on every inch of the field. Sensors throughout the stadium track tags placed on players' shoulder pads, charting individual movements within inches.

AMON-RA ST. BROWN
LIONS
WR RANK: 4 MODEL RANK: 17

The Lions' outrageously productive No. 1 wide receiver just scored a huge new contract, but the RTMs are skeptical that St. Brown is the top-five wideout and top-10 player our fantasy rankings currently reflect, due to a surprising 58/51 open/catch score combination. That isn't to say he's average—ADP is the most important variable in predicting future success, and we should respect the market—but rather that ADP is perhaps just too bullish at this juncture.

PUKA NACUA
RAMS
WR RANK: 7 MODEL RANK: 19

Though Nacua's rookie season was certifiably outrageous, the RTMs cooled on him as the year went along. Particularly so for our exercise, because YAC was his best category. The Rams wideout recorded an open/catch/YAC triple-slash of 53/57/64, and that's going to be hard to justify as the No. 7 wide receiver selected, as Nacua is currently.

DRAKE LONDON
FALCONS
WR RANK: 14 MODEL RANK: 21

There is hype for London, coming off a successful campaign and an incoming quarterback upgrade. But has it gone too far? The RTMs think yes. London ranks 14th among wide receivers, and the simple model believes that's high for a player who recorded a 54/60 open/catch score in 2023. Good numbers? Yes. Great? Not quite. ■

Chiefs QB Patrick Mahomes has passed for over 4,000 yards in each of the past six seasons.

THE EXPERTS' MOCK DRAFT

When it comes to coming out on top of your draft, practice makes perfect

BY DANIEL DOPP

The offseason flew by, and here we are in fantasy football draft season again! The Chiefs have had their moment in the spotlight after winning back-to-back Super Bowls; free agency sent guys like Kirk Cousins, Saquon Barkley, Josh Jacobs and Derrick Henry to new destinations; and the NFL draft saw a bunch of young talent come into the league to help jump-start their teams' path to success. It might not be September, but we've got everything we need to start our fantasy prep. And trust me, there will be prep.

You can't just walk into a draft and build a championship roster by winging it. You need to do research, or at a minimum, let someone else do the research for you. Do you think Howie Roseman casually walks into the NFL draft and asks Jerry Jones for an extra cheat sheet because he accidentally left his at home? It's a rookie mistake to just waltz into your league's draft without preparing and practicing different draft strategies. And yes, I just said you need to practice drafting. It's not because you don't know how to draft—the drafting part is easy. But adhering to a draft strategy requires focus.

Every year, things change in the league that alter a potential strategy. Last year, we talked about taking Travis Kelce in the first round because of how big the gap was between him and the rest of the tight end position. Then Sam LaPorta and Evan Engram put on a clinic, unexpectedly finishing as TE1 and TE2, ahead of Kelce. And it didn't stop there, as T.J. Hockenson, George Kittle, David Njoku and Trey McBride also put up stellar seasons. Because the landscape has changed so much, not only is Kelce not the first tight end on our board this year, but we don't need to consider a tight end in the first round anymore, either. Instead, we'll mock a different strategy: drafting a tight end in the second or third round to ensure we get one of the top three. Like I said, every year we make tweaks, because no two seasons are alike.

The idea is to get comfortable with the draft board breaking in a fairly consistent fashion based on each strategy, so when something unexpected happens, you'll be able to easily pivot in another direction. For example, if a player falls to you a round past their mock draft ADP, it's an easy decision to move them up in your queue and consider them, since they're normally not available at this point. Or vice versa: Maybe someone snipes you on the player you really wanted. It happens to all of us, but with a strategy in place, you won't make a panic pick because you're flustered and upset at your leaguemate. Instead, you can pivot to the next-best player on your board and confidently take him, knowing he's the best choice for your squad. Know what I'm saying? It's OK to get a little emotional about football—just not until *after* the draft.

This year, I have four takeaways that will impact my strategies while doing mock drafts this summer. There are a ton of different strategies and thought exercises I don't have time to get into in this column, so please don't consider this an exhaustive list. At a minimum, I hope it gets you thinking about how you want to build *your* team. Good luck!

▶ **Rookies are not guaranteed fantasy points.** It's exciting to draft a rookie for your fantasy squad because of the excitement around his unrealized potential, but for now, that's all it is—unrealized. And more often than not, rookies don't perform quite as high as the (often unrealistic) expectations placed upon them heading into the season. Guys like Puka Nacua and Sam LaPorta are the exceptions, not the rule. It's particularly easy to see QBs drafted by teams with good pass-catching options, such as Caleb Williams and J.J. McCarthy, being overvalued, especially considering the depth at the position. This isn't to say rookies can't have great seasons; I'm just saying don't get too invested and impulse-buy a one-way ticket on the next rookie hype train.

▶ **QB runs deep this year, so practice multiple scenarios.** This is the deepest I remember the QB position being in fantasy football. Not only is the league throwing more than ever, but there are more dual-threat quarterbacks than ever, and those rushing QBs are a cheat code in fantasy. Last season, we saw eight quarterbacks finish with at least 70 carries, and it likely would've been 10 had Daniel Jones and Kyler Murray stayed healthy. Considering how deep the position is, try drafting a QB in different parts of the draft. Start in the early rounds with one of the top three. Then wait until the middle rounds to grab your guy and see how different your team looks. Then do a few more mocks waiting until the end of the draft to see if you can be OK with a lower-end QB1 as your starter. (We call this last one "the Karabell," since it's one of Eric Karabell's favorite ways to draft.) With how deep the position is, give each scenario a try and decide which strategy is giving you the best team overall. Then move forward with your prep, knowing where you want to grab your QB.

▶ **TE runs deep too!** This is the deepest I remember the tight end position being in fantasy football, as well. Not only is

The Jets' Breece Hall was one of the top RBs last year, and his usage as a receiver—along with the return of Aaron Rodgers—make him a hot commodity in any 2024 fantasy draft.

this league throwing to tight ends more than ever, but the NFL has more pass-catching specialists at the position than ever before, and those pass-catching TEs are another cheat code in fantasy. There are some similarities in depth at both tight end and quarterback. There were 11 tight ends that averaged double-digit fantasy points per game last season. Eleven! And that list doesn't include Dalton Kincaid, Kyle Pitts or Dallas Goedert. All three of those guys are fringe TE1s in 2024. With how deep the position is, don't feel like you need to grab a guy early to lock in a quality starter. Stay patient and let the draft come to you.

▶ **Draft with conviction.** When it's your turn to make a pick, don't be afraid to go after the player you want. You're the one who put in the work, did the prep, conducted countless mock drafts and listened to fantasy podcasts (such as ESPN's *Fantasy Focus Football*, my personal favorite). It's OK if your board doesn't look like everyone else's. That's actually a *good* thing: If everyone shows up to your draft with the same cheat sheet, then you're just drafting by consensus. You don't want to draft based on what other people think; you want to draft based on what *you* think. I'm going to draft players I've researched and feel strongly about, not just because they're the guys with the highest numbers next to their names. It's about valuing personal conviction in your decisions over the perception of what groupthink would say. "Conviction over perception" will always be my motto when it comes to drafting.

And with all of that out of the way, let's take a look at a few interesting nuggets from the first ESPN Fantasy Mock Draft of 2024.

THE EXPERTS

STEPHANIA BELL
Injury and Fantasy Analyst

MATT BOWEN
NFL and Fantasy Analyst

MIKE CLAY
NFL and Fantasy Analyst

TRISTAN H. COCKCROFT
Fantasy Analyst

DANIEL DOPP
Fantasy Analyst

TYLER FULGHUM
Sports Betting Analyst

ERIC KARABELL
Fantasy Analyst

LIZ LOZA
Fantasy Analyst

ERIC MOODY
Fantasy Analyst

FIELD YATES
NFL Insider and Fantasy Analyst

TEAM ANALYSIS

By Daniel Dopp
in order of draft selection

DANIEL DOPP
I had the luck of drawing the top pick, which meant Christian McCaffrey would anchor my "hero-RB" squad. I went hard at WR with this strategy, and I think I drafted the deepest group of wideouts in the league. I especially liked the value of grabbing Ladd McConkey [10th round] and Quentin Johnston [14th] so late in the draft, since one of them will emerge as Herbert's main target. My RBs are extremely thin behind CMC, which means I'll have to make some trades with one of the RB-heavy teams to balance things out for a championship run.

FIELD YATES
With the opportunity to take anyone other than CMC, Field chose CeeDee Lamb. It's tough to argue with that, given Lamb's breakout 2023 season. Pairing him with Michael Pittman Jr. and Stefon Diggs gives the entire starting WR corps a super-high floor, while Calvin Ridley, Christian Watson and Xavier Legette are solid, high-upside bench guys. Getting Patrick Mahomes in the fifth round is great value, but I didn't love taking T.J. Hockenson in Round 8, since he could miss as much as half the season with his ACL rehab. But that would be the first position Field fills in free agency, with Hock on IR. Another great draft from Field.

LIZ LOZA
Liz paired Tyreek Hill with Marvin Harrison Jr., and I love the move. If you're going to grab the rookie as your WR2 knowing there may be some ups and downs, make sure you have a surefire rock star as your WR1. Getting Lamar Jackson in the fifth and George Kittle in the seventh both felt like nice values, and I like the dart throw on J.K. Dobbins, a supremely talented back with an unfortunate injury history, as an RB4, too.

ERIC KARABELL
Karabell hammered WR early, and I love how his team turned out. Going Ja'Marr Chase, Davante Adams and Mike Evans gives him an incredibly high floor at the position each week. Alvin Kamara is the obvious lead back here, with a lot of smart dart throws to fill the RB2 slot. Eric's team is really balanced, with high-end starters and depth at every position. This is one of my favorite teams in the entire draft.

MIKE CLAY
Mike hates fun and your favorite NFL team. He also doesn't care for WRs, since he started this draft RB-RB-RB. What is this, 1985? Was Mike Clay Sr. behind the keyboard of this mock draft? Honestly, it's hard to argue starting with Breece Hall and Jahmyr Gibbs. I didn't love Rachaad White in the third—not because he doesn't belong there, I just don't like locking in a RB to my flex in most weeks. Still, Deebo Samuel, Jaylen Waddle, Rashee Rice and Trey McBride give him a solid group of pass-catchers. He also has Jordan Love [Round 8] *and* Justin Herbert [Round 13], which may give him some QB trade bait later on in the season.

TYLER FULGHUM
Tyler knew I was writing this recap, so he naturally took Amon-Ra St. Brown in the first round, thinking it would sway my analysis. Well, it did...until Round 2, when he took Isiah Pacheco. I would've doubled up on Lions and taken Jahmyr Gibbs, but maybe I'm biased. I think Diontae Johnson in the eighth and Marquise Brown in the 10th were great values, but I question using a roster spot on Justin Fields as a backup QB in a league of this size when he doesn't have a starting job.

TRISTAN H. COCKCROFT
If you can start a draft from the seven spot and get Justin Jefferson with your first pick, it usually means things are going to work out. Tristan also grabbed a top-five RB in Kyren Williams and was the first to take a tight end with Travis Kelce [!] in the third. His "hero-RB" approach worked out great with low-end starters Zamir White and Gus Edwards picked late as options to fill his RB2 slot. Super-solid draft, as always.

ERIC MOODY
Moody is going to ride the youth train to a fantasy championship in this one! Bijan Robinson, Garrett Wilson, Sam LaPorta and De'Von Achane are the things dynasty dreams are made of. Even in a redraft league, that's a heckuva start to a fantasy draft. I really liked Moody's selection of Kyler Murray in the ninth, as the 10th QB off the board, and Xavier Worthy as a 12th-round dart throw, since he's an NFL first-rounder with Mahomes throwing him the ball. Temper expectations on Worthy, but in the 12th round, that upside is dynamite!

MATT BOWEN
Matt's start of Saquon Barkley and Puka Nacua gives him a legit superstar at each position. Drafting a guy like Joe Burrow in the sixth round [No. 7 QB off the board] is great value. This was another RB-heavy approach, with four drafted in the first nine rounds, so WR depth is a little bit of a concern, but the upside of Malik Nabers is exciting here. This team is loaded with talent and could be wheeling and dealing as the season progresses with its RB depth.

STEPHANIA BELL
Starphania's crew is littered with talent at every position. Jonathan Taylor and Josh Jacobs at RB? That sounds awesome. A.J. Brown and Nico Collins at WR? Yes, please. Plus C.J. Stroud in a loaded offense and Kyle Pitts with a real quarterback? I've already said yes twice—why even keep asking? Seriously, though, my only concern is the WR depth. There's a lot of potential talent on the bench, and as long as one of them hits, this team is set to contend for a title.

ROUND 1

1	DOPP	**CHRISTIAN MCCAFFREY**, SF	RB1
2	YATES	**CEEDEE LAMB**, DAL	WR1
3	LOZA	**TYREEK HILL**, MIA	WR2
4	KARABELL	**JA'MARR CHASE**, CIN	WR3
5	CLAY	**BREECE HALL**, NYJ	RB2
6	FULGHUM	**AMON-RA ST. BROWN**, DET	WR4
7	COCKCROFT	**JUSTIN JEFFERSON**, MIN	WR5
8	MOODY	**BIJAN ROBINSON**, ATL	RB3
9	BOWEN	**SAQUON BARKLEY**, PHI	RB4
10	BELL	**JONATHAN TAYLOR**, IND	RB5

Justin Jefferson

ROUND 2

1	BELL	**A.J. BROWN**, PHI	WR6
2	BOWEN	**PUKA NACUA**, LAR	WR7
3	MOODY	**GARRETT WILSON**, NYJ	WR8
4	COCKCROFT	**KYREN WILLIAMS**, LAR	RB6
5	FULGHUM	**ISIAH PACHECO**, KC	RB7
6	CLAY	**JAHMYR GIBBS**, DET	RB8
7	KARABELL	**DAVANTE ADAMS**, LV	WR9
8	LOZA	**TRAVIS ETIENNE JR.**, JAX	RB9
9	YATES	**DERRICK HENRY**, BAL	RB10
10	DOPP	**CHRIS OLAVE**, NO	WR10

ROUND 3

1	DOPP	**DRAKE LONDON**, ATL	WR11
2	YATES	**MICHAEL PITTMAN JR.**, IND	WR12
3	LOZA	**MARVIN HARRISON JR.**, ARI	WR13
4	KARABELL	**MIKE EVANS**, TB	WR14
5	CLAY	**RACHAAD WHITE**, TB	RB11
6	FULGHUM	**JAMES COOK**, BUF	RB12
7	COCKCROFT	**TRAVIS KELCE**, KC	TE1
8	MOODY	**SAM LAPORTA**, DET	TE2
9	BOWEN	**JOE MIXON**, HOU	RB13
10	BELL	**NICO COLLINS**, HOU	WR15

ROUND 4

1	BELL	**JOSH JACOBS**, GB	RB14
2	BOWEN	**DK METCALF**, SEA	WR16
3	MOODY	**DE'VON ACHANE**, MIA	RB15
4	COCKCROFT	**JOSH ALLEN**, BUF	QB1
5	FULGHUM	**BRANDON AIYUK**, SF	WR17
6	CLAY	**DEEBO SAMUEL**, SF	WR18
7	KARABELL	**ALVIN KAMARA**, NO	RB16
8	LOZA	**AARON JONES**, MIN	RB17
9	YATES	**STEFON DIGGS**, HOU	WR19
10	DOPP	**DEVONTA SMITH**, PHI	WR20

ROUND 5

1	DOPP	**JALEN HURTS**, PHI	QB2
2	YATES	**PATRICK MAHOMES**, KC	QB3
3	LOZA	**LAMAR JACKSON**, BAL	QB4
4	KARABELL	**MARK ANDREWS**, BAL	TE3
5	CLAY	**JAYLEN WADDLE**, MIA	WR21
6	FULGHUM	**ANTHONY RICHARDSON**, IND	QB5
7	COCKCROFT	**DJ MOORE**, CHI	WR22
8	MOODY	**COOPER KUPP**, LAR	WR23
9	BOWEN	**MALIK NABERS**, NYG	WR24
10	BELL	**C.J. STROUD**, HOU	QB6

ROUND 6

1	BELL	**KEON COLEMAN**, BUF	WR25
2	BOWEN	**JOE BURROW**, CIN	QB7
3	MOODY	**KENNETH WALKER III**, SEA	RB18
4	COCKCROFT	**ZAY FLOWERS**, BAL	WR26
5	FULGHUM	**DALTON KINCAID**, BUF	TE4
6	CLAY	**TREY MCBRIDE**, ARI	TE5
7	KARABELL	**JONATHON BROOKS**, CAR	RB19
8	LOZA	**CHRIS GODWIN**, TB	WR27
9	YATES	**RHAMONDRE STEVENSON**, NE	RB20
10	DOPP	**TANK DELL**, HOU	WR28

ROUND 7

1	DOPP	**EVAN ENGRAM**, JAX	TE6
2	YATES	**CALVIN RIDLEY**, TEN	WR29
3	LOZA	**GEORGE KITTLE**, SF	TE7
4	KARABELL	**DAK PRESCOTT**, DAL	QB8
5	CLAY	**RASHEE RICE**, KC	WR30
6	FULGHUM	**DAVID MONTGOMERY**, DET	RB21
7	COCKCROFT	**TEE HIGGINS**, CIN	WR31
8	MOODY	**KEENAN ALLEN**, CHI	WR32
9	BOWEN	**D'ANDRE SWIFT**, CHI	RB22
10	BELL	**BRIAN ROBINSON JR.**, WAS	RB23

ROUND 8

1	BELL	**KYLE PITTS**, ATL	TE8
2	BOWEN	**DAVID NJOKU**, CLE	TE9
3	MOODY	**GEORGE PICKENS**, PIT	WR33
4	COCKCROFT	**ZAMIR WHITE**, LV	RB24
5	FULGHUM	**DIONTAE JOHNSON**, CAR	WR34
6	CLAY	**JORDAN LOVE**, GB	QB9
7	KARABELL	**JAMES CONNER**, ARI	RB25
8	LOZA	**TERRY MCLAURIN**, WAS	WR35
9	YATES	**T.J. HOCKENSON**, MIN	TE10
10	DOPP	**JAYLEN WARREN**, PIT	RB26

ROUND 9

1	DOPP	**JAYDEN REED**, GB	WR36
2	YATES	**CHRISTIAN WATSON**, GB	WR37
3	LOZA	**JAVONTE WILLIAMS**, DEN	RB27
4	KARABELL	**NICK CHUBB**, CLE	RB28
5	CLAY	**TYJAE SPEARS**, TEN	RB29
6	FULGHUM	**TONY POLLARD**, TEN	RB30
7	COCKCROFT	**JORDAN ADDISON**, MIN	WR38
8	MOODY	**KYLER MURRAY**, ARI	QB10
9	BOWEN	**NAJEE HARRIS**, PIT	RB31
10	BELL	**ZACK MOSS**, CIN	RB32

George Kittle

ROUND 10

1	BELL	**DEVIN SINGLETARY**, NYG	RB33
2	BOWEN	**CHRISTIAN KIRK**, JAX	WR39
3	MOODY	**AUSTIN EKELER**, WAS	RB34
4	COCKCROFT	**GUS EDWARDS**, LAC	RB35
5	FULGHUM	**MARQUISE BROWN**, KC	WR40
6	CLAY	**JAXON SMITH-NJIGBA**, SEA	WR41
7	KARABELL	**DEANDRE HOPKINS**, TEN	WR42
8	LOZA	**AMARI COOPER**, CLE	WR43
9	YATES	**JAKOBI MEYERS**, LV	WR44
10	DOPP	**LADD MCCONKEY**, LAC	WR45

Did you know that you can now conduct a practice draft based on your specific ESPN league settings, including keepers and draft pick trades?

ROUND 11

1	DOPP	**ZACH CHARBONNET**, SEA	RB36
2	YATES	**RAHEEM MOSTERT**, MIA	RB37
3	LOZA	**J.K. DOBBINS**, LAC	RB38
4	KARABELL	**EZEKIEL ELLIOTT**, DAL	RB39
5	CLAY	**ROME ODUNZE**, CHI	WR46
6	FULGHUM	**CURTIS SAMUEL**, BUF	WR47
7	COCKCROFT	**COURTLAND SUTTON**, DEN	WR48
8	MOODY	**TY CHANDLER**, MIN	RB40
9	BOWEN	**TYLER LOCKETT**, SEA	WR49
10	BELL	**JAMESON WILLIAMS**, DET	WR50

ROUND 12

1	BELL	**BROCK BOWERS**, LV	TE11
2	BOWEN	**TREY BENSON**, ARI	RB41
3	MOODY	**XAVIER WORTHY**, KC	WR51
4	COCKCROFT	**KIRK COUSINS**, ATL	QB11
5	FULGHUM	**ADONAI MITCHELL**, IND	WR52
6	CLAY	**JAKE FERGUSON**, DAL	TE12
7	KARABELL	**JAYDEN DANIELS**, WAS	QB12
8	LOZA	**BRIAN THOMAS JR.**, JAX	WR53
9	YATES	**XAVIER LEGETTE**, CAR	WR54
10	DOPP	**JEROME FORD**, CLE	RB42

ROUND 13

1	DOPP	**CHASE BROWN**, CIN	RB43
2	YATES	**TYRONE TRACY JR.**, NYG	RB44
3	LOZA	**DARNELL MOONEY**, ATL	WR55
4	KARABELL	**ADAM THIELEN**, CAR	WR56
5	CLAY	**JUSTIN HERBERT**, LAC	QB13
6	FULGHUM	**BLAKE CORUM**, LAR	RB45
7	COCKCROFT	**KENDRE MILLER**, NO	RB46
8	MOODY	**MIKE WILLIAMS**, NYJ	WR57
9	BOWEN	**CALEB WILLIAMS**, CHI	QB14
10	BELL	**GABE DAVIS**, JAX	WR58

ROUND 14

1	BELL	**RASHID SHAHEED**, NO	WR59
2	BOWEN	**JERRY JEUDY**, CLE	WR60
3	MOODY	**JAYLEN WRIGHT**, MIA	RB47
4	COCKCROFT	**BRANDON AUBREY**, DAL	K1
5	FULGHUM	**JUSTIN FIELDS**, PIT	QB15
6	CLAY	**CHUBA HUBBARD**, CAR	RB48
7	KARABELL	**49ERS D/ST**, SF	D/ST1
8	LOZA	**AARON RODGERS**, NYJ	QB16
9	YATES	**KHALIL SHAKIR**, BUF	WR61
10	DOPP	**QUENTIN JOHNSTON**, LAC	WR62

ROUND 15

1	DOPP	**HARRISON BUTKER**, KC	K2
2	YATES	**BROWNS D/ST**, CLE	D/ST2
3	LOZA	**COWBOYS D/ST**, DAL	D/ST3
4	KARABELL	**DALLAS GOEDERT**, PHI	TE13
5	CLAY	**JETS D/ST**, NYJ	D/ST4
6	FULGHUM	**GREG ZUERLEIN**, NYJ	K3
7	COCKCROFT	**RAVENS D/ST**, BAL	D/ST5
8	MOODY	**STEELERS D/ST**, PIT	D/ST6
9	BOWEN	**JUSTIN TUCKER**, BAL	K4
10	BELL	**BENGALS D/ST**, CIN	D/ST7

ROUND 16

1	BELL	**JAKE ELLIOTT**, PHI	K5
2	BOWEN	**CHIEFS D/ST**, KC	D/ST8
3	MOODY	**KA'IMI FAIRBAIRN**, HOU	K6
4	COCKCROFT	**KIMANI VIDAL**, LAC	RB49
5	FULGHUM	**BEARS D/ST**, CLE	D/ST9
6	CLAY	**EVAN MCPHERSON**, CIN	K7
7	KARABELL	**YOUNGHOE KOO**, ATL	K8
8	LOZA	**JAKE MOODY**, SF	K9
9	YATES	**DUSTIN HOPKINS**, CLE	K10
10	DOPP	**LIONS D/ST**, DET	D/ST10

CHEAT SHEETS

Players on this cheat sheet are ranked by overall draft position, with a suggested value for 10-team salary cap drafts that have a $200 budget. Bye weeks and positional ranking are also included.

PPR TOP 200

RK	NAME	TM	POS RK	BYE	$$
1	CHRISTIAN MCCAFFREY	SF	RB1	9	57
2	BREECE HALL	NYJ	RB2	12	56
3	BIJAN ROBINSON	ATL	RB3	12	55
4	CEEDEE LAMB	DAL	WR1	7	55
5	TYREEK HILL	MIA	WR2	6	54
6	JA'MARR CHASE	CIN	WR3	12	53
7	AMON-RA ST. BROWN	DET	WR4	5	53
8	JUSTIN JEFFERSON	MIN	WR5	6	52
9	JONATHAN TAYLOR	IND	RB4	14	51
10	SAQUON BARKLEY	PHI	RB5	5	50
11	KYREN WILLIAMS	LAR	RB6	6	48
12	A.J. BROWN	PHI	WR6	5	46
13	PUKA NACUA	LAR	WR7	6	45
14	GARRETT WILSON	NYJ	WR8	12	43
15	JAHMYR GIBBS	DET	RB7	5	42
16	ISIAH PACHECO	KC	RB8	6	40
17	DAVANTE ADAMS	LV	WR9	10	38
18	CHRIS OLAVE	NO	WR10	12	37
19	MICHAEL PITTMAN JR.	IND	WR11	14	36
20	MIKE EVANS	TB	WR12	11	35
21	TRAVIS ETIENNE JR.	JAX	RB9	12	34
22	DERRICK HENRY	BAL	RB10	14	33
23	ALVIN KAMARA	NO	RB11	12	32
24	JOE MIXON	HOU	RB12	14	32
25	RACHAAD WHITE	TB	RB13	11	31
26	JAMES COOK	BUF	RB14	12	30
27	SAM LAPORTA	DET	TE1	5	30
28	TRAVIS KELCE	KC	TE2	6	29
29	JOSH ALLEN	BUF	QB1	12	28
30	JALEN HURTS	PHI	QB2	5	27
31	JOSH JACOBS	GB	RB15	10	26
32	KENNETH WALKER III	SEA	RB16	10	25
33	DE'VON ACHANE	MIA	RB17	6	24
34	MARVIN HARRISON JR.	ARI	WR13	11	23
35	DRAKE LONDON	ATL	WR14	12	22
36	NICO COLLINS	HOU	WR15	14	22
37	DK METCALF	SEA	WR16	10	22
38	BRANDON AIYUK	SF	WR17	9	21
39	DEEBO SAMUEL	SF	WR18	9	21
40	STEFON DIGGS	HOU	WR19	14	20
41	DJ MOORE	CHI	WR20	7	19
42	DEVONTA SMITH	PHI	WR21	5	19
43	JAYLEN WADDLE	MIA	WR22	6	18
44	LAMAR JACKSON	BAL	QB3	14	17
45	PATRICK MAHOMES	KC	QB4	6	17
46	COOPER KUPP	LAR	WR23	6	15
47	ZAY FLOWERS	BAL	WR24	14	15
48	CALVIN RIDLEY	TEN	WR25	5	14
49	MALIK NABERS	NYG	WR26	11	13
50	TEE HIGGINS	CIN	WR27	12	13
51	MARK ANDREWS	BAL	TE3	14	12
52	TANK DELL	HOU	WR28	14	11
53	KEENAN ALLEN	CHI	WR29	7	11
54	CHRIS GODWIN	TB	WR30	11	10
55	AMARI COOPER	CLE	WR31	10	10
56	GEORGE PICKENS	PIT	WR32	9	10
57	DEANDRE HOPKINS	TEN	WR33	5	10
58	RASHEE RICE	KC	WR34	6	9
59	EVAN ENGRAM	JAX	TE4	12	9
60	TREY MCBRIDE	ARI	TE5	11	9
61	JOE BURROW	CIN	QB5	12	8
62	C.J. STROUD	HOU	QB6	14	8
63	ANTHONY RICHARDSON	IND	QB7	14	8
64	DAK PRESCOTT	DAL	QB8	7	7
65	RHAMONDRE STEVENSON	NE	RB18	14	7
66	JONATHON BROOKS	CAR	RB19	11	7
67	AARON JONES	MIN	RB20	6	7
68	GEORGE KITTLE	SF	TE6	9	6
69	DAVID NJOKU	CLE	TE7	10	6
70	DALTON KINCAID	BUF	TE8	12	6
71	D'ANDRE SWIFT	CHI	RB21	7	6
72	JAMES CONNER	ARI	RB22	11	6
73	BRIAN ROBINSON JR.	WAS	RB23	14	6
74	DAVID MONTGOMERY	DET	RB24	5	5
75	NAJEE HARRIS	PIT	RB25	9	5
76	JAYLEN WARREN	PIT	RB26	9	5
77	ZAMIR WHITE	LV	RB27	10	5
78	JORDAN LOVE	GB	QB9	10	4
79	KYLER MURRAY	ARI	QB10	11	4
80	BROCK PURDY	SF	QB11	9	4
81	AARON RODGERS	NYJ	QB12	12	4
82	DIONTAE JOHNSON	CAR	WR35	11	4
83	TERRY MCLAURIN	WAS	WR36	14	4
84	CHRISTIAN KIRK	JAX	WR37	12	4
85	JORDAN ADDISON	MIN	WR38	6	4
86	COURTLAND SUTTON	DEN	WR39	14	4
87	JAKE FERGUSON	DAL	TE9	7	3
88	KYLE PITTS	ATL	TE10	12	3
89	DALLAS GOEDERT	PHI	TE11	5	3
90	T.J. HOCKENSON	MIN	TE12	6	3
91	CHRISTIAN WATSON	GB	WR40	10	3
92	JAYDEN REED	GB	WR41	10	3
93	JAXON SMITH-NJIGBA	SEA	WR42	10	3
94	MIKE WILLIAMS	NYJ	WR43	12	3
95	TYLER LOCKETT	SEA	WR44	10	3
96	JAVONTE WILLIAMS	DEN	RB28	14	2
97	TYJAE SPEARS	TEN	RB29	5	2
98	TONY POLLARD	TEN	RB30	5	2
99	ZACK MOSS	CIN	RB31	12	2
100	AUSTIN EKELER	WAS	RB32	14	2
101	DEVIN SINGLETARY	NYG	RB33	11	2
102	EZEKIEL ELLIOTT	DAL	RB34	7	2
103	RAHEEM MOSTERT	MIA	RB35	6	2
104	MARQUISE BROWN	KC	WR45	6	2
105	ROME ODUNZE	CHI	WR46	7	2
106	XAVIER WORTHY	KC	WR47	6	2
107	LADD MCCONKEY	LAC	WR48	5	2
108	KEON COLEMAN	BUF	WR49	12	2
109	BRIAN THOMAS JR.	JAX	WR50	12	2
110	JUSTIN HERBERT	LAC	QB13	5	2
111	JAYDEN DANIELS	WAS	QB14	14	2
112	KIRK COUSINS	ATL	QB15	12	2
113	CALEB WILLIAMS	CHI	QB16	7	2
114	GUS EDWARDS	LAC	RB36	5	2
115	NICK CHUBB	CLE	RB37	10	2
116	J.K. DOBBINS	LAC	RB38	5	2
117	ZACH CHARBONNET	SEA	RB39	10	2
118	ANTONIO GIBSON	NE	RB40	14	2
119	TYLER ALLGEIER	ATL	RB41	12	2
120	JEROME FORD	CLE	RB42	10	2
121	TY CHANDLER	MIN	RB43	6	1
122	CHASE BROWN	CIN	RB44	12	1
123	DARNELL MOONEY	ATL	WR51	12	1
124	JAKOBI MEYERS	LV	WR52	10	1
125	JERRY JEUDY	CLE	WR53	10	1
126	ADAM THIELEN	CAR	WR54	11	1
127	CURTIS SAMUEL	BUF	WR55	12	1
128	JAMESON WILLIAMS	DET	WR56	5	1
129	XAVIER LEGETTE	CAR	WR57	11	1
130	GABE DAVIS	JAX	WR58	12	1
131	BROCK BOWERS	LV	TE13	10	1
132	DALTON SCHULTZ	HOU	TE14	14	1
133	PAT FREIERMUTH	PIT	TE15	9	1
134	COLE KMET	CHI	TE16	7	1
135	DESHAUN WATSON	CLE	QB17	10	1
136	TREVOR LAWRENCE	JAX	QB18	12	1
137	TREY BENSON	ARI	RB45	11	1
138	BLAKE CORUM	LAR	RB46	6	1
139	TYLER CONKLIN	NYJ	TE17	12	1
140	RASHID SHAHEED	NO	WR59	12	1
141	CLEVELAND BROWNS	CLE	DST1	10	1
142	DALLAS COWBOYS	DAL	DST2	7	1
143	NEW YORK JETS	NYJ	DST3	12	1
144	BALTIMORE RAVENS	BAL	DST4	14	1
145	SAN FRANCISCO 49ERS	SF	DST5	9	1
146	PITTSBURGH STEELERS	PIT	DST6	9	1
147	MIAMI DOLPHINS	MIA	DST7	6	1
148	JACKSONVILLE JAGUARS	JAX	DST8	12	1
149	NEW ORLEANS SAINTS	NO	DST9	12	1
150	CINCINNATI BENGALS	CIN	DST10	12	1
151	HARRISON BUTKER	KC	K1	6	1
152	BRANDON AUBREY	DAL	K2	7	1
153	JUSTIN TUCKER	BAL	K3	14	1
154	JAKE ELLIOTT	PHI	K4	5	1
155	GREG ZUERLEIN	NYJ	K5	12	1
156	KA'IMI FAIRBAIRN	HOU	K6	14	1
157	EVAN MCPHERSON	CIN	K7	12	1
158	JAKE MOODY	SF	K8	9	1
159	CAMERON DICKER	LAC	K9	5	1
160	CAIRO SANTOS	CHI	K10	7	1
161	TUA TAGOVAILOA	MIA	QB19	6	0
162	MATTHEW STAFFORD	LAR	QB20	6	0
163	KENDRE MILLER	NO	RB47	12	0
164	JALEEL MCLAUGHLIN	DEN	RB48	14	0
165	MARSHAWN LLOYD	GB	RB49	10	0
166	ALEXANDER MATTISON	LV	RB50	10	0
167	CHUBA HUBBARD	CAR	RB51	11	0
168	MILES SANDERS	CAR	RB52	11	0
169	RICO DOWDLE	DAL	RB53	7	0
170	KEATON MITCHELL	BAL	RB54	14	0
171	KHALIL HERBERT	CHI	RB55	7	0
172	CLYDE EDWARDS-HELAIRE	KC	RB56	6	0
173	RAY DAVIS	BUF	RB57	12	0
174	DEMARIO DOUGLAS	NE	WR60	14	0
175	ROMEO DOUBS	GB	WR61	10	0
176	JA'LYNN POLK	NE	WR62	14	0
177	ADONAI MITCHELL	IND	WR63	14	0
178	QUENTIN JOHNSTON	LAC	WR64	5	0
179	JOSHUA PALMER	LAC	WR65	5	0
180	BRANDIN COOKS	DAL	WR66	7	0
181	KENDRICK BOURNE	NE	WR67	14	0
182	MARVIN MIMS JR.	DEN	WR68	14	0
183	KHALIL SHAKIR	BUF	WR69	12	0
184	JOSH DOWNS	IND	WR70	14	0
185	TAYSOM HILL	NO	TE18	12	0
186	JUWAN JOHNSON	NO	TE19	12	0
187	CHIGOZIEM OKONKWO	TEN	TE20	5	0
188	HUNTER HENRY	NE	TE21	14	0
189	KANSAS CITY CHIEFS	KC	DST11	6	0
190	DETROIT LIONS	DET	DST12	5	0
191	YOUNGHOE KOO	ATL	K11	12	0
192	MICHAEL BADGLEY	DET	K12	5	0
193	JAHAN DOTSON	WAS	WR71	14	0
194	RICKY PEARSALL	SF	WR72	9	0
195	ROSCHON JOHNSON	CHI	RB58	7	0
196	JAYLEN WRIGHT	MIA	RB59	6	0
197	JARED GOFF	DET	QB21	5	0
198	BRYCE YOUNG	CAR	QB22	11	0
199	DRAKE MAYE	NE	QB23	14	0
200	J.J. MCCARTHY	MIN	QB24	6	0

Josh Allen

1 JOSH ALLEN BUF · $28 · AGE 28 · BYE 12

Allen is back for his seventh season with the Bills. The dual-threat quarterback has been a fantasy dynamo over the past three seasons, averaging 24.7 fantasy points per game (best among QBs). Allen lost Stefon Diggs and Gabe Davis this offseason, which is notable because he averaged only 253.3 passing yards per game last season (his lowest since 2019), and he rushed for his fewest yards since 2020. He more than made up for the rushing decline with 15 rush TDs, which will be tough to repeat. It will be difficult to replace Diggs, but the team did add Curtis Samuel in free agency and Keon Coleman with the No. 33 pick in the draft. Allen is still firmly on the QB1 radar, but managers shouldn't be surprised if we see some regression in 2024.

	G	COM	ATT	YDS	TD	INT	C%	YPA	CAR	YDS	TD	FPTS
2023	17	385	579	4306	29	18	66%	7.4	111	524	15	393
PROJ	15	342	518	3701	23	12	66%	7.1	95	498	9	312

2 JALEN HURTS PHI · $27 · AGE 26 · BYE 5

Hurts comes off his best NFL season, thanks mainly to 15 rushing touchdowns, tying Josh Allen for the most among QBs. In fact, no other QBs reached seven rushing scores. Hurts finished behind only Allen in fantasy points at the position, despite playing the final months with a knee injury as the Eagles collapsed down the stretch. Don't blame Hurts—he averaged 21.5 fantasy points from Weeks 15 through 17 before sitting out most of the finale. Center Jason Kelce retired, but the Eagles' offensive line and wide receiver options remain top-notch, and the controversial "tush push" play Hurts feasts on remains legal. Expect another fantastic statistical season and a legitimate chance to finish as fantasy's top scorer.

	G	COM	ATT	YDS	TD	INT	C%	YPA	CAR	YDS	TD	FPTS
2023	17	352	538	3858	23	15	65%	7.2	157	605	15	357
PROJ	15	319	495	3632	21	11	64%	7.3	125	537	10	315

3 LAMAR JACKSON BAL · $17 · AGE 27 · BYE 14

The reigning NFL MVP enters his seventh pro season as one of the league's most dynamic players at the position. In 2023, working under new offensive coordinator Todd Monken, Jackson played in 16 games, posting a career high in pass yards while leading all quarterbacks in rushing. He averaged 20.7 fantasy points per game, finishing as QB4 in total points. With a strong supporting cast in Baltimore led by tight end Mark Andrews, wide receiver Zay Flowers and running back Derrick Henry, plus a system that maximizes his elite dual-threat ability, Jackson should once again produce top-tier fantasy numbers.

	G	COM	ATT	YDS	TD	INT	C%	YPA	CAR	YDS	TD	FPTS
2023	16	307	457	3678	24	7	67%	8.0	148	821	5	331
PROJ	15	299	459	3386	22	11	65%	7.4	124	736	6	305

4 PATRICK MAHOMES KC · $17 · AGE 28 · BYE 6

Though Mahomes' 2023 saw him post his worst yards per attempt (7.0), aDOT (6.2), touchdown (4.5%) and interception (2.3%) rates of his six seasons as an NFL regular, consider the context: He was working with his weakest set of receivers in any of those years. The Chiefs were worst in the league in drops (38) and had the second-worst catch rate on throws 20-plus yards downfield (27.4%) after having been seventh best in that department the season before. Mahomes made it work—he led the team to a Super Bowl title, after all. The additions of Marquise Brown and Xavier Worthy, coupled with Rashee Rice's late-season emergence, should give Mahomes the weapons necessary to rebound as a top-five positional pick and early-round selection.

	G	COM	ATT	YDS	TD	INT	C%	YPA	CAR	YDS	TD	FPTS
2023	16	401	597	4183	27	14	67%	7.0	75	389	0	280
PROJ	15	363	549	4030	33	11	66%	7.3	62	337	1	307

5 JOE BURROW CIN · $8 · AGE 27 · BYE 12

Heading into his fifth pro season, Burrow looks to rebound after an injury-plagued 2023 that limited his production and availability. A calf injury during training camp forced him to miss practice time, while a wrist injury in Week 11 shut him down for the season. From Weeks 1 through 4, with Burrow clearly still impacted by the calf injury, he averaged only 7.9 fantasy points per game. However, from Weeks 5 through 10, he posted three games of 22 or more points, with an average of 21.4 points during that stretch. With two big-play receivers in Ja'Marr Chase and Tee Higgins, a healthy Burrow should be in the mix to produce top-five quarterback numbers in the Bengals' pass-heavy offense.

	G	COM	ATT	YDS	TD	INT	C%	YPA	CAR	YDS	TD	FPTS
2023	10	244	365	2309	15	6	67%	6.3	31	88	0	147
PROJ	15	369	554	4118	27	11	67%	7.4	53	173	3	278

6 C.J. STROUD HOU · $8 · AGE 22 · BYE 14

The former Buckeye looks to build on a momentous first season that included becoming just the fifth rookie quarterback ever to throw for at least 4,000 yards. Without much rushing volume or success in either his collegiate or professional profile, Stroud's fantasy production will be defined by his proficiency from the pocket. He finished eighth in per-game fantasy output last season, and another prolific passing season could unfold, given the presence of a trio of talented receivers—Nico Collins, Stefon Diggs and Tank Dell—each of whom brings special route trees and skill sets to the field. Securing Stroud in the middle rounds is a sound strategy for those who wait a bit at the position.

	G	COM	ATT	YDS	TD	INT	C%	YPA	CAR	YDS	TD	FPTS
2023	15	319	499	4108	23	5	64%	8.2	39	167	3	276
PROJ	15	349	542	4051	27	11	64%	7.5	45	182	3	276

C.J. Stroud

23 DRAKE MAYE NE · $- · AGE 22 · BYE 14

Maye was drafted No. 3 overall out of North Carolina in April and is projected to start over veteran Jacoby Brissett right out of the gate. With his arm strength, Maye can attack all three levels of the field and can add value with his legs. Given his shaky group of offensive playmakers in New England, it would be wise for fantasy managers to temper their expectations. They should keep him on their radar as a QB3 in superflex formats due to his rushing ability.

	G	COM	ATT	YDS	TD	INT	C%	YPA	CAR	YDS	TD	FPTS
2023	0	0	0	0	0	0	0%	0.0	0	0	0	0
PROJ	15	324	512	3370	17	13	63%	6.6	66	329	3	216

24 J.J. MCCARTHY MIN · $- · AGE 21 · BYE 6

McCarthy joins the Vikings after being selected with the 10th overall pick of the 2024 NFL draft. He was 27-1 as a starter at Michigan and enters an incredible situation in Minnesota with Justin Jefferson, Jordan Addison and T.J. Hockenson leading the receiving corps. He won't be mistaken for a running QB, but McCarthy has the ability to scramble and use his legs effectively to extend plays and keep drives alive. Even if he starts out behind Sam Darnold, that shouldn't last very long, though McCarthy figures to require some development and won't be worth drafting in most formats in 2024.

	G	COM	ATT	YDS	TD	INT	C%	YPA	CAR	YDS	TD	FPTS
2023	0	0	0	0	0	0	0%	0.0	0	0	0	0
PROJ	14	325	514	3513	19	13	63%	6.8	45	196	2	218

25 DANIEL JONES NYG · $- · AGE 27 · BYE 11

Jones was a surprise top-10 fantasy QB in 2022, thanks mostly to health and running prowess (seven TDs). The 2023 season hardly went as well. Jones tossed six interceptions in the first four games—one more than he had the prior year over 16 games—and then things got worse. He missed three games due to a neck injury, only to return briefly in Week 9 and tear his right ACL. Jones accounted for three touchdowns in six games, and the New York offense played better without him. He expects to be fully cleared for training camp, and his contract all but guarantees playing time. Fantasy managers should be mighty wary, even in superflex formats, and consider choosing at least 20 other quarterbacks first.

	G	COM	ATT	YDS	TD	INT	C%	YPA	CAR	YDS	TD	FPTS
2023	6	108	160	909	2	6	68%	5.7	40	206	1	57
PROJ	14	317	490	3263	14	11	65%	6.7	92	486	3	224

26 BAKER MAYFIELD TB · $- · AGE 29 · BYE 11

Mayfield enjoyed a resurgence in 2023, appearing in all 17 of the Buccaneers' games and finishing no lower than 10th in pass attempts, completions, yards, TDs and fantasy points. The latter includes some survivor bias (he was 17th on a per-game basis), which was due to limited rushing production (outside the top 20 in both rushing yards and touchdowns). Mayfield has never been a rushing factor, and his supporting cast in Tampa Bay remains roughly the same as it was last season, so especially considering he's never finished better than 17th in PPG, he's best viewed as a low-ceiling QB2.

	G	COM	ATT	YDS	TD	INT	C%	YPA	CAR	YDS	TD	FPTS
2023	17	364	566	4044	28	10	64%	7.1	62	163	1	274
PROJ	15	342	540	3899	24	12	63%	7.2	51	162	1	245

27 GENO SMITH SEA · $- · AGE 33 · BYE 10

Author of one of the greatest script flips of the 2022 season, Smith was met with cautious optimism by fantasy managers who were unsure of his ability to duplicate a top-five fantasy finish at QB again in 2023. As expected, Smith's numbers regressed. Most disappointing was his dip in scoring, as the 33-year-old passed for just 20 TDs last season (down from 30). Smith finished the season just inside the top 20 fantasy producers at the position, averaging a little more than 15 fantasy points per game. He figures to rebound slightly with new offensive coordinator Ryan Grubb bringing an uptempo approach and further integration of Jaxon Smith-Njigba to the team, but he remains best utilized as a QB2.

	G	COM	ATT	YDS	TD	INT	C%	YPA	CAR	YDS	TD	FPTS
2023	15	323	499	3624	20	9	65%	7.3	37	155	1	227
PROJ	14	321	484	3540	20	10	66%	7.3	48	226	1	228

28 WILL LEVIS TEN · $- · AGE 25 · BYE 5

Levis is the incumbent starter for Tennessee heading into his second season. The front office spent the offseason seeking to support its young quarterback with a scaffolding built on proven veteran skill players. Levis topped 15 rushing yards just once in nine starts last year, and without much of a rushing resume in college, most of the fantasy value he develops will have to come from the pocket. A retooled offensive line and improved receiving corps work in his favor, but expectations remain tempered, given his inexperience and a shaky first go in the NFL. This all reads like Levis makes for a fun, boom-or-bust late-round investment for fantasy managers in deeper leagues.

	G	COM	ATT	YDS	TD	INT	C%	YPA	CAR	YDS	TD	FPTS
2023	9	149	255	1808	8	4	58%	7.1	25	57	1	102
PROJ	15	348	549	3811	18	13	63%	6.9	49	161	2	219

29 DEREK CARR NO · $- · AGE 33 · BYE 12

Carr is back for his second season as the Saints' starting QB. The 33-year-old did his usual bit, soaking up plenty of passing volume (he finished 14th or better in passing yardage and TDs for the fourth straight season) but not producing as a rusher (career-low 40 rush yards and zero TDs for the third straight season). The limited rushing led to a 16th-place finish in total fantasy points (24th in PPG), and he's yet to produce a top-10 fantasy campign in his career. Carr's supporting cast isn't overly impressive outside of Chris Olave and Alvin Kamara, so a big leap forward in passing production is unlikely. He's a low-ceiling QB2.

	G	COM	ATT	YDS	TD	INT	C%	YPA	CAR	YDS	TD	FPTS
2023	17	375	548	3878	25	8	68%	7.1	32	40	0	241
PROJ	15	346	522	3816	22	11	66%	7.3	31	84	1	224

30 RUSSELL WILSON PIT · $- · AGE 35 · BYE 9

Wilson is entering his 13th season in the league, and he signed a one-year deal in free agency with the Steelers. He is a very instinctual thrower who finished as QB14 in fantasy last season. Wilson will compete with Justin Fields for the starting job in a pass game under new offensive coordinator Arthur Smith that will be play action-based. Last season in Denver, Wilson completed 67.3% of his play-action passes, including 11 touchdowns. However, given his declining play speed outside of the pocket and the expected run-heavy approach in Pittsburgh, Wilson's fantasy ceiling is limited to the lower-tier QB2 range if he sticks as Pittsburgh's starter this season.

	G	COM	ATT	YDS	TD	INT	C%	YPA	CAR	YDS	TD	FPTS
2023	15	297	447	3070	26	8	66%	6.9	80	341	3	257
PROJ	13	263	412	2901	15	9	64%	7.0	58	269	2	191

31 BO NIX DEN · $- · AGE 24 · BYE 14

Selected 12th overall by the Broncos, Nix stands a good chance at capturing the starting role after coach Sean Payton raved about the rookie's potential. Nix is an extensively experienced college quarterback, having started in 61 games and attempted 1,936 passes across three seasons at Auburn and two at Oregon. He finished with a stellar 2023 in which he completed an FBS record 77.4% of his pass attempts, with 45 touchdowns compared to three interceptions. Though that came in an exceedingly pass-friendly offense, his ability to make quick reads and sharp throws should serve him well as he adapts to NFL play. Nix should be drafted only in superflex formats.

	G	COM	ATT	YDS	TD	INT	C%	YPA	CAR	YDS	TD	FPTS
2023	0	0	0	0	0	0	0%	0.0	0	0	0	0
PROJ	14	304	489	3161	16	13	62%	6.5	44	189	2	190

32 GARDNER MINSHEW II LV · $- · AGE 28 · BYE 10

One of the game's better backup quarterbacks over the course of his five-year career, Minshew signed for a surprisingly large guarantee in March, signaling his probable Week 1 starter status ahead of sophomore Aidan O'Connell. Minshew's advanced metrics are unexceptional—his career 17.8% off-target rate, 50.8 Total QBR and minus-1.6% completion percentage over expected were all noticeably beneath league average—yet he has averaged 16.1 fantasy points and scored 20-plus points in 10 of his 37 starts. With a star pass-catcher in Davante Adams and capable receivers in Jakobi Meyers and rookie TE Brock Bowers, Minshew could serve as a matchups-oriented quarterback in deeper leagues.

	G	COM	ATT	YDS	TD	INT	C%	YPA	CAR	YDS	TD	FPTS
2023	16	305	490	3305	15	9	62%	6.7	34	100	3	196
PROJ	9	199	312	2155	9	7	64%	6.9	27	100	2	125

33 AIDAN O'CONNELL LV · $- · AGE 26 · BYE 10

Though O'Connell performed admirably in a nine-start audition as a rookie under coach Antonio Pierce to conclude last season, he'll be tasked with competing for a job in 2024. O'Connell scored 17-plus fantasy points in three of his final four games, hinting at fantasy matchups value, but for the season had well-below-average 1.7 TD/INT and 16.7% off-target rates. That caused the Raiders to bring in veteran Gardner Minshew as competition. O'Connell would need to impress the coaching staff, either in the preseason or the season's early weeks, to be worth a fantasy add.

	G	COM	ATT	YDS	TD	INT	C%	YPA	CAR	YDS	TD	FPTS
2023	11	213	343	2218	12	7	62%	6.5	17	11	1	126
PROJ	8	178	279	1927	9	6	64%	6.9	25	74	1	111

34 JUSTIN FIELDS PIT · $- · AGE 25 · BYE 9

After spending his first three seasons with Chicago, Fields was traded to Pittsburgh, where he will compete with Russell Wilson for the starting job. Fields, who finished as QB7 in 2022, posted a career high in passing yards last season, but his rushing totals declined, as he dropped from 7.1 yards per carry to 5.3. Fields possesses the high-level arm talent to attack vertically and the physical tools to create big plays as a runner, which give him breakout-game potential. He's worth drafting only if he wins the starting job, though.

	G	COM	ATT	YDS	TD	INT	C%	YPA	CAR	YDS	TD	FPTS
2023	13	227	370	2562	16	9	61%	6.9	124	657	4	230
PROJ	4	77	124	846	5	3	62%	6.8	39	216	1	72

Michael Penix Jr.

35 SAM DARNOLD MIN · $- · AGE 27 · BYE 6

Darnold signed with the Vikings this offseason, his fourth team in five years, after backing up Brock Purdy in San Francisco last year. At best, he'll be a bridge starter in Minnesota, with the Vikings trading up to draft J.J. McCarthy in this year's NFL draft. In his six seasons in the league, Darnold has never finished higher than QB28, and he is not worth drafting in standard ESPN leagues.

	G	COM	ATT	YDS	TD	INT	C%	YPA	CAR	YDS	TD	FPTS
2023	10	28	46	297	2	1	61%	6.5	21	15	1	23
PROJ	3	68	110	719	4	3	62%	6.6	11	41	1	44

36 MICHAEL PENIX JR. ATL · $- · AGE 24 · BYE 12

Much to the shock of most of the football world, Penix was selected by Atlanta with the No. 8 pick in the draft out of Washington. Falcons coach Raheem Morris simply fell in love with Penix and took his guy, despite the Falcons having signed Kirk Cousins to a four-year, $180 million contract in March. The plan is still for the Falcons to start Cousins, meaning Penix will serve as a backup for the next couple of seasons as long as Cousins can stay on the field. Penix is on the "old" side for a rookie, has two right ACL surgeries on his résumé, adds little with his legs and won't play any time soon. He should be drafted in dynasty formats only.

	G	COM	ATT	YDS	TD	INT	C%	YPA	CAR	YDS	TD	FPTS
2023	0	0	0	0	0	0	0%	0.0	0	0	0	0
PROJ	2	42	69	472	4	2	61%	6.8	5	15	0	31

37 SAM HOWELL SEA · $- · AGE 23 · BYE 10

Howell was traded to Seattle in March and is set to work as Geno Smith's backup in 2024. Washington gave Howell a shot to be the team's starter, and while the North Carolina product flashed at times, he mostly flopped. Blunders were the hallmark of Howell's 2023 campaign, as he registered 21 passing scores and 21 interceptions (with 12 of those INTs occurring the final seven games of the season). His mobility was a bright spot for fantasy purposes, however, as his five rushing scores padded his overall stat line and allowed for a top-15 positional finish. The 23-year-old could (once again) provide streaming value if Smith were to be sidelined for an extended period.

	G	COM	ATT	YDS	TD	INT	C%	YPA	CAR	YDS	TD	FPTS
2023	17	388	612	3946	21	21	63%	6.4	48	263	5	258
PROJ	3	66	102	719	4	3	65%	7.0	11	57	1	50

38 TYROD TAYLOR NYJ · $- · AGE 35 · BYE 12

Taylor signed with the Jets and will operate as Aaron Rodgers' backup. He has made 58 starts and has thrown for 65 touchdowns and 29 interceptions in his career. He's been a backup over the past six seasons, though he showed well in four full games with the Giants last season, producing at least 17 fantasy points three times. Taylor provides the Jets with a reliable backup, and he would find himself on the QB2 radar if Rodgers misses time.

	G	COM	ATT	YDS	TD	INT	C%	YPA	CAR	YDS	TD	FPTS
2023	11	116	180	1341	5	3	64%	7.5	38	197	0	87
PROJ	2	42	68	443	3	2	62%	6.6	7	39	0	32

39 JOE FLACCO IND · $- · AGE 39 · BYE 14

Flacco signed with the Colts as the primary backup to Anthony Richardson. It's another new landing spot for Flacco after an impressive comeback effort in 2023, in which he tossed 13 TDs and eight INTs in five regular-season games with the Browns. Flacco produced 16-plus fantasy points in all five games, thanks to an aggressive style of play (9.3 aDOT). That led to plenty of turnovers and didn't work well in the playoff loss, however, and he remained a nonfactor with his legs (2 yards on nine carries). Flacco is 39 years old, and even if Richardson misses time, the veteran QB will be no more than a back-end QB2.

	G	COM	ATT	YDS	TD	INT	C%	YPA	CAR	YDS	TD	FPTS
2023	5	123	204	1616	13	8	60%	7.9	9	2	0	101
PROJ	2	40	65	434	2	2	62%	6.7	5	18	0	25

40 JAKE BROWNING CIN · $- · AGE 28 · BYE 12

The 28-year-old started the final seven games in relief of the injured Joe Burrow. During that time, Browning averaged 16.0 fantasy points per game, with three games of more than 21. A ball distributor who can play outside of structure when necessary, Browning's fantasy relevance this season is tied to Burrow's health. As the projected No. 2 to start the season, Browning is strictly a potential waiver pickup if Burrow misses time again.

	G	COM	ATT	YDS	TD	INT	C%	YPA	CAR	YDS	TD	FPTS
2023	9	171	243	1936	12	7	70%	8.0	27	127	3	144
PROJ	2	45	72	497	4	2	63%	6.9	8	35	1	37

41 JAMEIS WINSTON CLE · $- · AGE 30 · BYE 10

The first overall draft pick in 2015, Winston enters his 10th pro season—and first in Cleveland—as the backup to Deshaun Watson. Winston started three games over the past two seasons with the Saints, all in 2022, when he averaged 14.6 points per game while throwing four touchdowns and five interceptions. Winston's aggressive throwing mentality, along with his ability to create outside of structure, does provide some fantasy intrigue, but his questionable decision-making can lead to turnovers and missed opportunities. Keep Winston on the fantasy radar this season, given Watson's availability concerns, but he is not worth drafting at this point.

	G	COM	ATT	YDS	TD	INT	C%	YPA	CAR	YDS	TD	FPTS
2023	7	25	47	264	2	3	53%	5.6	5	-6	0	12
PROJ	2	42	69	476	2	2	60%	6.9	8	26	0	28

42 JARRETT STIDHAM DEN · $- · AGE 28 · BYE 14

It didn't bode well for Stidham's 2024 that the Broncos acquired Zach Wilson in the days leading up to the NFL draft and then added rookie Bo Nix with the 12th overall pick. Stidham delivered a pair of serviceable starts to conclude the 2023 season, his second straight year as a play-out-the-string fill-in, and he's averaged a serviceable 7.9 yards per attempt, a 8.9 aDOT and a 63% completion percentage in his four career starts, all of which paint the picture of a clear backup. For these reason, Stidham is well off the fantasy radar.

	G	COM	ATT	YDS	TD	INT	C%	YPA	CAR	YDS	TD	FPTS
2023	3	40	66	496	2	1	61%	7.5	9	8	0	27
PROJ	3	66	105	708	4	3	63%	6.7	11	44	0	42

43 JACOBY BRISSETT NE · $- · AGE 31 · BYE 14

Brissett signed a one-year, $8 million deal with the Patriots this offseason, and the veteran is expected to back up No. 3 overall draft pick Drake Maye. It's a homecoming for Brissett after he was drafted by New England in the third round in 2016. Brissett played in just three games with the Commanders last season and threw just 23 passes. That's a small sample size, but he did throw three touchdowns. Brissett should be rostered only if Maye misses time, and even then, only in superflex formats.

	G	COM	ATT	YDS	TD	INT	C%	YPA	CAR	YDS	TD	FPTS
2023	3	18	23	224	3	0	78%	9.7	3	19	0	23
PROJ	2	44	69	451	3	2	64%	6.6	8	32	0	30

44 DREW LOCK NYG · $- · AGE 27 · BYE 11

Lock signed with the Giants in March after playing one season with the Seahawks, in which he started two games and performed competently. He has started 23 games over four seasons with the Seahawks and Broncos, and the former second-round pick failed to distinguish himself. Presumed Giants starter Daniel Jones is on the mend from a torn ACL and has had neck problems the past few seasons, so it is no, um, lock that he stays healthy. But even if Lock gets a chance, the talent surrounding him in this offense pales in comparison to what he had in Seattle, making him easy to ignore in fantasy.

	G	COM	ATT	YDS	TD	INT	C%	YPA	CAR	YDS	TD	FPTS
2023	4	48	76	543	3	3	63%	7.1	5	14	0	29
PROJ	3	70	111	781	3	3	63%	7.0	10	41	1	45

RUNNING BACKS

RBs may not dominate the early rounds like they used to, but you still need a plan of attack to address the position

BY ERIC MOODY
PLAYER PROJECTIONS BY MIKE CLAY

ONCE UPON A TIME, NFL offenses relied heavily on running backs the way cars needed gasoline. But times have changed, and we now have hybrid cars, pass-happy NFL offenses and backfield committees. Last season, in a stark contrast to previous decades, only four running backs who played at least 10 games saw 20 or more touches per game. Back in 2013, it was eight, and in 2003, it was 17 (seven of whom averaged 25-plus touches). The game has shifted gears, and, if it hasn't already, so should your fantasy draft strategy. While snagging an every-down back at the top of the draft is still a win, it's no longer the norm for running backs to dominate the early rounds.

At one end of the fantasy football drafting spectrum, you've got your "Robust RB" fans, who load up on running backs early. At the other end, you've got the "Zero RB" crew, who accumulate wide receivers and tight ends early and often.

Both strategies have their success stories. Last season's ADP data backs this up. Robust RB drafters point to running backs like Christian McCaffrey (RB1 in fantasy points), Travis Etienne Jr. (RB3), Joe Mixon (RB6) and Derrick Henry (RB8) as shining stars from the early rounds. However, there were also backs drafted early who fizzled out and underperformed, including Najee Harris (RB23), Austin Ekeler (RB26) and Josh Jacobs (RB28). On the flip side, the Zero RB believers highlight the likes of Raheem Mostert (RB5), Kyren Williams (RB7) and David Montgomery (RB17), who soared above expectations after being selected in the latter half of drafts.

TIERED RANKINGS

Tiers allow you to identify players you should value similarly at various points of your draft.

RANK	PLAYER, TEAM	ROUND
1	CHRISTIAN MCCAFFREY, SF	1
2	BREECE HALL, NYJ	1
3	BIJAN ROBINSON, ATL	1
4	JONATHAN TAYLOR, IND	1/2
5	SAQUON BARKLEY, PHI	1/2
6	KYREN WILLIAMS, LAR	1/2
7	JAHMYR GIBBS, DET	2
8	ISIAH PACHECO, KC	2
9	TRAVIS ETIENNE JR., JAX	2/3
10	DERRICK HENRY, BAL	2/3
11	ALVIN KAMARA, NO	3
12	JOE MIXON, HOU	3
13	RACHAAD WHITE, TB	3
14	JAMES COOK, BUF	3
15	JOSH JACOBS, GB	3/4
16	KENNETH WALKER III, SEA	3/4
17	DE'VON ACHANE, MIA	4
18	RHAMONDRE STEVENSON, NE	7
19	JONATHON BROOKS, CAR	7
20	AARON JONES, MIN	7

Whether you employ one of these two approaches or something in between, don't sleep on the mid-tier running backs—those in timeshares or backups in good offenses—who may not get 200 rushing attempts but are still valuable additions to your fantasy team. It's all about value, folks. So relax, let the draft unfold and trust your instincts as you unearth some gems at the position in the middle rounds.

What about endgame roster strategy? You've locked in your starters and built up some depth, but what about those final few roster spots? Think upside. Consider drafting a rookie with potential or a veteran returning from injury, even if they are buried on the depth chart. If there is an obvious backup to one of your starting backs—or the backup to someone else's early-round RB—this is the time to pounce. Sleepers come in all shapes and sizes, so cast a wide net. You want players who, given the right circumstances, could become start-worthy. When in doubt at this stage of the draft, prioritize talent over expected playing time. It's all about maximizing your chances to strike gold.

So, when you're drafting your fantasy team, make sure to prioritize grabbing one of the top running backs early on, ideally within the first two rounds. But don't panic if you can't snag one right away. Depth is key, so aim to have at least two solid running backs by the sixth round. By the time you're done drafting, plan to have five to seven backs on your roster: five or six if your top two backs are every-week NFL starters, seven if you didn't prioritize the position and require less depth at other positions.

ABOUT OUR PROJECTIONS: All are for a 17-game season, with some degree of player maintenance and injury risk factored in and then rounded up or down as appropriate. Player ages are as of Sept. 5, 2024.

Christian McCaffrey

1 CHRISTIAN MCCAFFREY SF · $57 · AGE 28 · BYE 9

McCaffrey recorded the most fantasy points per game (24.5) and the third-most fantasy points overall (391) among all players last season. He ranked inside the top three fantasy producers at the position in nearly every statistical category—from rushing yards (1,459, RB1) and receiving yards (564, RB2) to evaded tackles (77, RB1) and total TDs (21, RB1)—and the 28-year-old stayed healthy for a second straight season. McCaffrey is the centerpiece of the 49ers' explosive offense, and he deserves to be at the top of draft boards this summer.

	G	CAR	YDS	TD	YPC	TGT	REC	YDS	TD	YPT	FPTS
2023	16	272	1459	14	5.4	83	67	564	7	6.8	391
PROJ	14	263	1242	12	4.7	83	67	527	4	6.3	338

2 BREECE HALL NYJ · $56 · AGE 23 · BYE 12

Hall appeared fully recovered from his ACL tear by the end of the 2023 season. He was one of the few bright spots in a struggling Jets offense that was without future Hall of Fame quarterback Aaron Rodgers. From Week 5 on, Hall was no longer on a snap count, and his usage increased significantly, as he averaged 20.2 touches and 20.0 fantasy points per game over the final 13 games. Despite the Jets' offense ranking 29th in run block win rate, Hall consistently produced and also led all running backs in targets, receptions and receiving yards. His potential is even greater with Rodgers hopefully under center for the entire 2024 season. Fantasy managers should feel confident drafting him as the second running back off the board behind Christian McCaffrey.

	G	CAR	YDS	TD	YPC	TGT	REC	YDS	TD	YPT	FPTS
2023	17	223	994	5	4.5	94	76	591	4	6.3	291
PROJ	14	235	1047	8	4.5	85	67	546	3	6.4	287

3 BIJAN ROBINSON ATL · $55 · AGE 22 · BYE 12

Robinson's rookie season was a mixed bag that included limited rushing contributions (15th or lower in carries, yards and TDs) but excellent receiving production (top five among RBs in routes, targets, yards and TDs), as well as terrific efficiency. His season felt underwhelming, considering his early-first-round pedigree, but he finished fifth among RBs in snaps, sixth in yards and ninth in fantasy points. With Kirk Cousins now under center and Zac Robinson replacing run-heavy Arthur Smith as the team's playcaller, a leap forward for Robinson seems likely in his second campaign. That will especially be the case if he manages more work near the goal line (only two carries inside the 5-yard line in 2023). Robinson should be one of the first RBs off the board on draft day.

	G	CAR	YDS	TD	YPC	TGT	REC	YDS	TD	YPT	FPTS
2023	17	214	976	4	4.6	87	58	487	4	5.6	246
PROJ	14	213	956	7	4.5	88	65	570	4	6.5	284

4 JONATHAN TAYLOR IND · $51 · AGE 25 · BYE 14

An appraisal of Taylor's four-year career thus far shows his epic All-Pro 2021 effort as an outlier of sorts. His other three seasons include rushing outcomes between 74.1 and 78.3 yards per game and a total of 24 scores in 36 games, painting a picture of a strong RB1 candidate, just not the RB1 overall. It's worth noting that we've yet to see Taylor take handoffs from Anthony Richardson, a reality that presents a blend of mystery and upside ahead of this season. With an unproven collection of backs behind him on the depth chart and the potential for a league-leading touch tally, Taylor remains a worthy early-round fantasy pick, even if that 2021 opus isn't the appropriate expectation.

	G	CAR	YDS	TD	YPC	TGT	REC	YDS	TD	YPT	FPTS
2023	10	169	741	7	4.4	23	19	153	1	6.7	156
PROJ	14	262	1176	10	4.5	53	41	318	1	6.0	255

5 SAQUON BARKLEY PHI · $50 · AGE 27 · BYE 5

Barkley left the rival Giants for the superior offense down the New Jersey Turnpike, one stacked with elite options at quarterback, wide receiver and, perhaps most important, along the still-dominant offensive line. Barkley's 2023 numbers may appear average, but blame the underwhelming New York offense, from the players to its direction. Still blessed with elite skills, a mostly healthy Barkley finished ninth among running backs at 15.9 fantasy points per game, and he may return to his 2022 numbers (1,312 rushing yards, 57 catches) in this top offense. He is a first-round fantasy pick and potential top-three fantasy RB provided health (one never knows) and volume (no problems there).

	G	CAR	YDS	TD	YPC	TGT	REC	YDS	TD	YPT	FPTS
2023	14	247	962	6	3.9	59	41	280	4	4.7	223
PROJ	14	253	1045	9	4.1	64	46	360	2	5.6	253

6 KYREN WILLIAMS LAR · $48 · AGE 24 · BYE 6

After injuries kept Williams off the field in 2022, he entered his sophomore effort barely drafted by fantasy managers (14th-round ADP in 12-team PPR leagues). That quickly changed as he emerged as the Rams' undisputed RB1, averaging nearly 22 touches per contest in his 12 games played. A creative runner with receiving chops and an uncanny nose for the end zone (15 total TDs, third among RBs), he turned on the jets down the stretch, posting nearly 24 fantasy points per game from Weeks 12 through 17. He did break his hand during the team's wild-card game in Detroit, but he should be healed up in time for training camp. Fantasy managers will want to keep an eye on rookie Blake Corum's potential ascent, but Williams remains the lead back and is a solid RB1 target.

	G	CAR	YDS	TD	YPC	TGT	REC	YDS	TD	YPT	FPTS
2023	12	228	1144	12	5.0	48	32	206	3	4.3	255
PROJ	14	242	1127	10	4.7	48	35	285	2	6.0	249

7 JAHMYR GIBBS DET · $42 · AGE 22 · BYE 5

Gibbs dispelled any draft-day doubts by finishing as fantasy's RB10 in his rookie season. The 12th overall pick in 2023 showcased his explosiveness in a Lions offense that had the second-most RB rushing yards and attempts. He had six weeks inside the top three at RB, finished second in yards before first contact and was fifth in fantasy points per touch. Despite being in a committee with David Montgomery, Gibbs was also 12th in scrimmage yards, ninth in total touchdowns and top 10 in targets and receptions. All this while ranking 25th among RBs in touches. He won't have the workload of a feature back, but at just 22 years old, Gibbs is already a superstar and should be viewed as a clear top-10 RB.

	G	CAR	YDS	TD	YPC	TGT	REC	YDS	TD	YPT	FPTS
2023	15	182	945	10	5.2	72	52	316	1	4.4	242
PROJ	14	186	858	8	4.6	68	51	375	2	5.5	236

8 ISIAH PACHECO KC · $40 · AGE 25 · BYE 6

If Pacheco's rookie campaign was the one that put him on the fantasy map, his sophomore year was the one that earned him star status. His 15.3 fantasy points per game were nearly double his 2022 number (7.9), and he surged late in the season, scoring 20-plus points in three of his final four regular-season games before totaling 373 yards and three touchdowns on 93 touches during the Chiefs' Super Bowl championship run. Most important, Pacheco handled seven of the team's 10 goal line RB carries and 16 of 23 carries in goal-to-go situations, establishing himself as the clear primary rusher. He's a fantasy RB1 and should settle in as a near-universal second-round pick.

	G	CAR	YDS	TD	YPC	TGT	REC	YDS	TD	YPT	FPTS
2023	14	205	935	7	4.6	52	44	244	2	4.7	214
PROJ	14	220	978	8	4.4	54	46	289	2	5.4	232

23 BRIAN ROBINSON JR. WAS · $6 · AGE 25 · BYE 14

Robinson returns as Washington's lead rusher. He started 15 games for the Commanders in 2023, averaging 13.2 fantasy points per game, the same figure as his new backfield competition, veteran Austin Ekeler. One man's emergence can equal another's downfall. Adding Ekeler hardly means Robinson loses all fantasy value, though. At 6-foot-2, 230 pounds, the bruising Robinson may see extensive early down work and cede pass-catching responsibilities, offering similar value. Even with Ekeler around, Robinson is talented enough to be a midround sleeper pick and RB3 choice.

	G	CAR	YDS	TD	YPC	TGT	REC	YDS	TD	YPT	FPTS
2023	15	178	733	5	4.1	43	36	368	4	8.6	198
PROJ	14	201	846	5	4.2	45	35	281	1	6.3	181

24 DAVID MONTGOMERY DET · $5 · AGE 27 · BYE 5

Montgomery signed with the Lions in 2023 and quickly put together the most efficient season of his young career. In a committee with Jahmyr Gibbs, Monty was a solid RB2 for fantasy managers, providing a steady dose of rushing yards and touchdowns. He was ninth in rushing yards, third in rushing touchdowns and handled the third-most carries inside the 5 last season. He lacks passing-game upside (16 catches in 14 games last season), but behind a premier offensive line in Detroit, Montgomery will again be a serviceable RB2 in 2024.

	G	CAR	YDS	TD	YPC	TGT	REC	YDS	TD	YPT	FPTS
2023	14	219	1015	13	4.6	25	16	117	0	4.7	207
PROJ	14	186	819	10	4.4	28	22	163	1	5.8	181

25 NAJEE HARRIS PIT · $5 · AGE 26 · BYE 9

A true volume grinder, Harris returns to Pittsburgh for his fourth season as the primary runner on early downs. He has totaled at least 255 carries and 1,000 rush yards for three straight seasons. However, he dipped to 11.5 fantasy points per game last season (RB26), and his receving totals continue to decline (career-low 29 receptions in 2023). A run-heavy approach from new offensive coordinator Arthur Smith is a bonus here, but with the expanding role for Jaylen Warren in the Steelers' backfield, Harris should be targeted as lower-tier flex only.

	G	CAR	YDS	TD	YPC	TGT	REC	YDS	TD	YPT	FPTS
2023	17	255	1035	8	4.1	38	29	170	0	4.5	196
PROJ	14	219	892	6	4.1	36	28	169	1	4.7	176

26 JAYLEN WARREN PIT · $5 · AGE 25 · BYE 9

Now entering his third pro season, Warren emerged as a playmaking talent with the Steelers in 2023, posting career highs across the board in rushing and receving. He posted a run of 10 or more yards on 15.5% of his carries while producing double-digit fantasy points in 10 of 17 games played. He's an explosive mover with perimeter juice and the open-field vision to produce as a screen target (18 receptions, 114 yards on screens last season). While he will share backfield touches with Najee Harris, he brings more fantasy upside as a dual-threat back under new offensive coordinator Arthur Smith. Target Warren as a high-end flex with RB2 upside.

	G	CAR	YDS	TD	YPC	TGT	REC	YDS	TD	YPT	FPTS
2023	17	149	784	4	5.3	75	61	370	0	4.9	196
PROJ	14	125	599	3	4.8	67	54	370	1	5.6	176

27 ZAMIR WHITE LV · $5 · AGE 24 · BYE 10

After spending 27 games as a scarcely used backup to Josh Jacobs, White finally got a chance to strut his stuff beginning in Week 15 last season after Jacobs was lost to a quadriceps injury. White rushed a league-high 84 times during his four-game audition, ranked fourth among RBs with 457 yards from scrimmage and 2.33 average yards after first contact, and was eighth among RBs in fantasy points per game in that span (15.2). It set the power back up nicely for a leading role in 2024, despite the Raiders' offseason addition of Alexander Mattison. White could have fantasy RB2 value on a matchups basis.

	G	CAR	YDS	TD	YPC	TGT	REC	YDS	TD	YPT	FPTS
2023	17	104	451	1	4.3	19	15	98	0	5.2	74
PROJ	14	200	860	5	4.3	46	35	248	1	5.4	180

28 JAVONTE WILLIAMS DEN · $2 · AGE 24 · BYE 14

Though Williams' numbers were lackluster, credit him for quickly returning to action. He proved ready to play in Week 1, 343 days after tearing the ACL, LCL and posterolateral corner in his right knee, and appeared in 16 games, including handling 15-plus touches nine times. That aggressive recovery, coupled with the hefty workload, might have contributed to the so-so numbers, and he wouldn't be the first player to take a bigger step forward the second year following such a significant operation. Williams has a fantasy RB2 ceiling, but he would be wisely selected as a flex while his team overhauls the quarterback position.

	G	CAR	YDS	TD	YPC	TGT	REC	YDS	TD	YPT	FPTS
2023	16	217	774	3	3.6	58	47	228	2	3.9	179
PROJ	14	180	712	4	4.0	58	44	269	1	4.7	174

29 TYJAE SPEARS TEN · $2 · AGE 23 · BYE 5

Spears enters his second NFL season with Derrick Henry out and Tony Pollard in as his competition for touches. This third-round pick capably handled the ninth-most targets among backs on the way to more than 800 scrimmage yards in an impressive rookie season. Spears' production as a receiving valve for Will Levis last season offers encouraging evidence he can again excel in a timeshare this season. Given the immense value of targets compared to carries and the natural expectation for Spears to take on more overall work in 2024, the arrow is pointing up for him as a mid-round RB2/flex option.

	G	CAR	YDS	TD	YPC	TGT	REC	YDS	TD	YPT	FPTS
2023	17	100	453	2	4.5	70	52	385	1	5.5	154
PROJ	14	123	536	3	4.4	66	50	400	2	6.0	172

30 TONY POLLARD TEN · $2 · AGE 27 · BYE 5

Pollard is entering his sixth season in the NFL, but it's still fair to ask, just who is this guy? Is he the ultra-efficient game-breaker from his Pro Bowl 2022 effort? Or is he the tailback who struggled to sustain steady production as the Cowboys' lead back last season? The reality could be somewhere between those extremes. The presence of Tyjae Spears is notable, as he consumed 150 TDs last season, including the majority of work on third downs. Given Spears' proficient receiving profile, it's likely that Pollard's ability to be efficient on early downs and in the red zone will dictate his fantasy stock this season. Targeting Pollard as a borderline RB2 or flex candidate could still prove rewarding on a team that aggressively went after him in free agency.

	G	CAR	YDS	TD	YPC	TGT	REC	YDS	TD	YPT	FPTS
2023	17	252	1005	6	4.0	67	55	311	0	4.6	223
PROJ	14	163	700	5	4.3	48	38	244	1	5.0	165

31 ZACK MOSS CIN · $2 · AGE 26 · BYE 12

Going into his fifth pro season, Moss joins his third team in Cincinnati, where he will replace Joe Mixon as the team's early-down runner. Moss saw eight starts for the Colts last season, producing three games of 20 or more fantasy points while logging at least 18 carries six times. A volume back with the skills to catch the ball on screens and unders, he will share touches with Chase Brown this season in Ohio. Playing in a high-scoring Bengals offense, Moss has flex upside, given his anticipated rushing volume and goal line role.

	G	CAR	YDS	TD	YPC	TGT	REC	YDS	TD	YPT	FPTS
2023	14	183	794	5	4.3	37	27	192	2	5.2	170
PROJ	14	184	792	7	4.3	37	28	190	1	5.2	173

32 AUSTIN EKELER WAS · $2 · AGE 29 · BYE 14

Ekeler signed with the Commanders after a thoroughly disappointing final season with the Chargers. He scored 38 touchdowns during the 2021 and 2022 seasons, which earned him much fantasy love and the top running back spot in many fantasy leagues, but his 2023 was a struggle. Ekeler suffered a high-ankle sprain in Week 1 (while scoring 26.4 PPR points!), missed three games and never really returned to prominence, seeing sketchy volume among his inefficiency. He recorded five top-10 weekly finishes at RB in 14 games. Ekeler will not cost a first-round pick this season—not in Washington's moribund offense—but if health and volume return, there is enticing bounce-back possibility as a TD-driven RB2 choice.

	G	CAR	YDS	TD	YPC	TGT	REC	YDS	TD	YPT	FPTS
2023	14	179	628	5	3.5	74	51	436	1	5.9	185
PROJ	14	110	442	3	4.0	68	50	446	2	6.5	170

33 DEVIN SINGLETARY NYG · $2 · AGE 27 · BYE 11

Singletary signed a three-year deal to join the Giants and essentially replace Saquon Barkley. Good luck. While Singletary delivered seven double-digit fantasy efforts for the Texans last season, he is not close to Barkley's level, averaging only 9.8 fantasy points per game. He is undersized and not a speed burner, but he has been a fairly consistent, durable contributor for five NFL seasons. The Giants may be poised to give him his best opportunity for touches, even though they drafted Tyrone Tracy Jr. late, but in a below-average offense with issues galore, it makes Singletary an RB3 at best.

	G	CAR	YDS	TD	YPC	TGT	REC	YDS	TD	YPT	FPTS
2023	17	216	898	4	4.2	38	30	193	0	5.1	167
PROJ	14	185	789	5	4.3	46	35	227	1	4.9	167

34 EZEKIEL ELLIOTT DAL · $2 · AGE 29 · BYE 7

After one underwhelming season with an even more underwhelming Patriots offense, the 29-year-old Elliott signed back with the Cowboys days after the franchise spent its draft picks on other positions. He will battle holdovers Rico Dowdle and Deuce Vaughn for touches. Elliott used to be one of the first picks in a fantasy draft, but his last RB1 season was 2019. He scored a solid 12 touchdowns during each of his final two inefficient seasons with Dallas, though, and he showed he can still catch passes last season in New England's terrible offense, so perhaps RB2 production remains attainable. Just don't draft him as an RB2.

	G	CAR	YDS	TD	YPC	TGT	REC	YDS	TD	YPT	FPTS
2023	17	184	642	3	3.5	65	51	313	2	4.8	175
PROJ	14	191	751	6	3.9	43	32	216	1	5.0	172

35 RAHEEM MOSTERT MIA · $2 · AGE 32 · BYE 6

Mostert, now in his third season with the Dolphins, is 32 and coming off a career year. He led the league in rushing touchdowns (18) and surpassed 200 rushing attempts and 1,000 rushing yards for the first time. Despite sharing the workload with exceptional rookie De'Von Achane, Mostert remains a key part of the explosive Dolphins offense, and our projections suggest Miami will continue with the committee approach. He is extremely unlikely to approach last season's touchdown count but should be viewed as a high-end flex option.

	G	CAR	YDS	TD	YPC	TGT	REC	YDS	TD	YPT	FPTS
2023	15	209	1012	18	4.8	33	25	175	3	5.3	268
PROJ	14	153	715	8	4.7	35	26	188	1	5.4	170

36 GUS EDWARDS LAC · $2 · AGE 29 · BYE 5

One of the game's more underrated rushers, Edwards found himself an advantageous arrangement by signing with the Chargers. Coach Jim Harbaugh, as well as offensive coordinator Greg Roman (who served in the same role for Edwards' 2019–22 Ravens teams), are committed to a run-heavy offense. In his six-year career, Edwards has averaged 4.9 yards and 2.07 yards after first contact per carry, as well as a 29.6% big-play rate, all of which rank among the position's top 20 (minimum 300 attempts) in that span. He also converted on a sparkling eight of nine goal-line tries in 2023. Because Edwards scarcely contributes in the receiving game, he's a better non-PPR pick than PPR, but he could serve as a weekly flex.

	G	CAR	YDS	TD	YPC	TGT	REC	YDS	TD	YPT	FPTS
2023	17	198	810	13	4.1	13	12	180	0	13.8	187
PROJ	14	180	762	6	4.2	22	17	134	1	6.2	143

37 NICK CHUBB CLE · $2 · AGE 28 · BYE 10

Chubb took a pay cut to return to the Browns for a seventh season, and the serious knee injury he suffered in Week 2 creates real concern about his future outlook. In previous seasons, he was a high-end fantasy option, finishing as RB6 in 2022 and RB13 in 2021. A powerful runner with open-field elusiveness and top-end speed, Chubb has been one of the more consistent fantasy running backs. However, with the emergence of Jerome Ford in Cleveland last season and the uncertainty around Chubb's eventual recovery from the knee injury, we would advise approaching this with caution. We see him in the lower-tier flex range.

	G	CAR	YDS	TD	YPC	TGT	REC	YDS	TD	YPT	FPTS
2023	2	28	170	0	6.1	4	4	21	0	5.3	23
PROJ	11	183	891	6	4.9	25	19	160	1	6.4	163

38 J.K. DOBBINS LAC · $2 · AGE 25 · BYE 5

Dobbins is another piece brought to Los Angeles as the Chargers assembled a sort of "Ravens West." He should compete with Gus Edwards, Isaiah Spiller and rookie Kimani Vidal in what's sure to be a heavily utilized running back corps. Dobbins is the ultimate risk/reward pickup. In 13 career games with double-digit carries, his 6.2 YPC and nine rushing touchdowns underscore his upside, but his 43 absences in 67 NFL contests serve as a reminder of his propensity for injury. Dobbins did his best work in Baltimore under Greg Roman, the offensive coordinator with whom he is now reunited, so monitor his preseason and be prepared to pounce on him as a late-round value pick if he's looking good.

	G	CAR	YDS	TD	YPC	TGT	REC	YDS	TD	YPT	FPTS
2023	1	8	22	1	2.8	3	2	15	0	5.0	12
PROJ	13	154	769	4	5.0	44	34	241	1	5.5	166

39 ZACH CHARBONNET SEA · $2 · AGE 23 · BYE 10

Charbonnet possesses an impressive blend of power and deft receiving skills, and he drew a lot of buzz after being selected by the Seahawks in the second round of last year's NFL draft. He was on the field for nearly the same number of snaps as Kenneth Walker III; however, he was not entrusted with an identical workload as a rookie. In fact, Charbonnet registered double-digit carries (an average of 16 per game) only when Walker was sidelined from Weeks 11 through 13 last season. He should have a slightly larger role moving forward but remains more insurance policy than legitimate starter for fantasy purposes.

	G	CAR	YDS	TD	YPC	TGT	REC	YDS	TD	YPT	FPTS
2023	16	108	462	1	4.3	41	33	209	0	5.1	106
PROJ	14	116	506	3	4.3	45	36	248	1	5.5	137

40 ANTONIO GIBSON NE · $2 · AGE 26 · BYE 14

Gibson enters his fifth season in the league but his first with the Patriots. With new head coach Jerod Mayo and offensive coordinator Alex Van Pelt, New England aims to revitalize a running game that ranked 26th in rushing yards per game last season. While Rhamondre Stevenson is expected to continue as the starter, Gibson will likely serve as a change-of-pace option and contribute on passing downs in the Patriots' committee approach. Gibson is worth considering in the double-digit rounds of your fantasy draft as an RB4.

	G	CAR	YDS	TD	YPC	TGT	REC	YDS	TD	YPT	FPTS
2023	16	65	265	1	4.1	60	48	389	2	6.5	127
PROJ	14	127	536	3	4.2	50	39	280	1	5.5	142

41 TYLER ALLGEIER ATL · $2 · AGE 24 · BYE 12

Allgeier was a red-zone vulture in Atlanta last season, taking opportunities away from Bijan Robinson without putting up huge numbers on his own. Allgeier had 35 rushing attempts inside the 20-yard line and just three touchdowns. Coach Arthur Smith has been replaced by Raheem Morris, so the running focus could fully shift to Robinson this season, which would make Allgeier more of an upper-tier insurance policy.

	G	CAR	YDS	TD	YPC	TGT	REC	YDS	TD	YPT	FPTS
2023	17	186	683	4	3.7	23	18	193	1	8.4	138
PROJ	14	141	576	5	4.1	34	28	214	1	6.2	144

42 JEROME FORD CLE · $2 · AGE 24 · BYE 10

Ford enters his third season with the Browns after posting career highs in rushing and receving yards in 2023. In relief of Nick Chubb (knee) during the Week 2 game versus the Steelers, Ford dropped 24.1 fantasy points on the Pittsburgh defense, though he averaged 12.9 points from Weeks 3 through 17. Ford has the lateral agility and power to shed tacklers plus the straight-line speed to create explosive plays in the run and pass game. With the uncertainty of Chubb's recovery from injury, Ford should be drafted in all formats with the potential upside of taking on a volume role this season.

	G	CAR	YDS	TD	YPC	TGT	REC	YDS	TD	YPT	FPTS
2023	17	204	813	4	4.0	64	44	319	5	5.0	211
PROJ	14	120	492	3	4.1	34	26	181	1	5.3	115

Zach Charbonnet

43 TY CHANDLER MIN · $1 · AGE 26 · BYE 6

Chandler returns to the Vikings for his third season, this time backing up new teammate Aaron Jones. Chandler took over as the starter in Week 15 last season and turned in a 26-touch, 157-yard performance, including a touchdown. Unfortunately, he failed to get enough volume in the subsequent weeks and couldn't crack the top 25 at RB. Chandler will continue his usual backup role in what may be one of the lowest-volume rush attacks in the league, so he's worth no more than a late pick.

	G	CAR	YDS	TD	YPC	TGT	REC	YDS	TD	YPT	FPTS
2023	17	102	461	3	4.5	25	21	159	0	6.4	101
PROJ	14	155	681	4	4.4	30	22	158	1	5.4	138

44 CHASE BROWN CIN · $1 · AGE 24 · BYE 12

Heading into his second pro season, Brown will occupy the No. 2 role behind Zack Moss in the Bengals' backfield. Brown has the ability to find interior daylight as a runner, plus he flashed as a receving target as a rookie. Last season, he averaged 14.4 yards per reception on screens, using his vision and contact balance to win in space. He is a smart insurance play behind Moss, and his receiving usage creates flex value in deeper leagues.

	G	CAR	YDS	TD	YPC	TGT	REC	YDS	TD	YPT	FPTS
2023	12	44	179	0	4.1	15	14	156	1	10.4	54
PROJ	14	91	386	3	4.3	49	39	289	1	5.9	133

45 TREY BENSON ARI · $1 · AGE 22 · BYE 11

Benson is big and fast and has a three-down skill set. His pro-ready frame (6 feet, 216 pounds) and impressive speed (4.39) make him a tough target to take down. He figures to cut his proverbial teeth behind James Conner before taking over the top RB spot in 2025, assuming Arizona doesn't re-sign the 29-year-old vet to a new deal. Given Conner's age and injury history, Benson should emerge as one of this season's most popular late-round insurance policies.

	G	CAR	YDS	TD	YPC	TGT	REC	YDS	TD	YPT	FPTS
2023	0	0	0	0	0.0	0	0	0	0	0.0	0
PROJ	14	115	507	3	4.4	28	22	153	1	5.5	109

46 BLAKE CORUM LAR · $1 · AGE 23 · BYE 6

Corum led the Wolverines' run-centric offense all the way to the national championship, regularly shimmying his way past defenders and through holes. While he proved he can handle a large volume of touches (he rushed for 1,245 yards and 27 touchdowns on 258 attempts in 2023), he likely won't emerge as the Rams' primary ball carrier, since Kyren Williams holds that honor. However, Corum could flirt with double-digit touches on a per-game basis and is likely to eat into Williams' snap count. Corum is worth a late-round pick in redraft leagues with deep benches, but his value would experience a sizable bump if Williams were to be sidelined.

	G	CAR	YDS	TD	YPC	TGT	REC	YDS	TD	YPT	FPTS
2023	0	0	0	0	0.0	0	0	0	0	0.0	0
PROJ	14	110	472	3	4.3	23	18	130	1	5.6	102

47 KENDRE MILLER NO · $- · AGE 22 · BYE 12

Injuries derailed Miller's rookie season, and he made it through only eight games, finishing with 41 carries, 156 yards and a touchdown. The TCU product should come into his sophomore season in a much healthier state, but he'll still have to deal with Alvin Kamara and Jamaal Williams in the backfield. He's only worth a late-round flier.

	G	CAR	YDS	TD	YPC	TGT	REC	YDS	TD	YPT	FPTS
2023	8	41	156	1	3.8	12	10	117	0	9.8	43
PROJ	14	71	310	2	4.3	39	30	241	1	6.2	104

48 JALEEL MCLAUGHLIN DEN · $- · AGE 23 · BYE 14

McLaughlin, the NCAA's all-time rushing leader, impressed the Broncos brass as an undrafted rookie with a sizzling four-touchdown preseason. That ultimately earned him a spot in the team's backfield rotation alongside Javonte Williams and Samaje Perine. McLaughlin certainly provided a spark, as 12 of his 76 rushing attempts went for 10-plus yards (sixth-best 15.8% rate, minimum 40 attempts), and he delivered a combined 37.3 fantasy points while filling in for an injured Williams in Weeks 4 and 5. McLaughlin should begin 2024 in a similar spot, making him a worthwhile late-round speculative pick who could be a home-run hitter with an expanded opportunity.

	G	CAR	YDS	TD	YPC	TGT	REC	YDS	TD	YPT	FPTS
2023	17	76	410	1	5.4	35	31	160	2	4.6	106
PROJ	14	96	431	2	4.5	39	30	208	1	5.3	114

49 MARSHAWN LLOYD GB · $- · AGE 23 · BYE 10

Lloyd joins the Packers after being drafted in the third round of this year's NFL draft. Lloyd is a big-play threat from USC, averaging 7.1 yards per carry for the Trojans last season. The Packers let Aaron Jones walk this offseason and AJ Dillon's only on a one-year deal, so Lloyd could be the backup of the future behind Josh Jacobs. As it stands, he is an explosive and talented rookie, but he likely won't get enough touches for fantasy relevance in 2024.

	G	CAR	YDS	TD	YPC	TGT	REC	YDS	TD	YPT	FPTS
2023	0	0	0	0	0.0	0	0	0	0	0.0	0
PROJ	14	74	324	2	4.4	33	25	182	1	5.5	94

50 ALEXANDER MATTISON LV · $- · AGE 26 · BYE 10

It's difficult to fathom how Mattison, who averaged 20.1 fantasy points per game in six fill-in starts for Dalvin Cook in 2020-21, could flop so significantly when finally granted a full-time starter's role in 2023. To illustrate, he failed to exceed 17.5 points in any of 13 starts before an ankle injury hobbled him in December, and he finished the season with beneath-league-average numbers in terms of yards per carry and explosive-play and first-down rates. It painted the picture of a depth piece, occasional fill-in and change-of-pace back rather than clear starter, and the Raiders inked Mattison in March for just that purpose. He could have his moments if asked again to pinch hit, but don't expect a full-timer's output.

	G	CAR	YDS	TD	YPC	TGT	REC	YDS	TD	YPT	FPTS
2023	16	180	700	0	3.9	45	30	192	3	4.3	133
PROJ	14	121	493	3	4.1	17	13	87	1	5.1	91

51 CHUBA HUBBARD CAR · $- · AGE 25 · BYE 11

Hubbard replaced Miles Sanders as the feature back for the worst offensive team in the league last season, finishing with 902 rush yards and five touchdowns. However, he wasn't exactly efficient in doing so, ranking in the 30s in explosive-run rate, forced missed tackles and yards after contact. Add in the fact that things are still a bit cloudy in Carolina with new head coach Dave Canales, along with the fact they drafted Jonathon Brooks with the 46th pick in the draft, and it's not hard to see Hubbard's fantasy value taking a hit. He'll be worth only a midround pick if Brooks (ACL recovery) misses time to open the season.

	G	CAR	YDS	TD	YPC	TGT	REC	YDS	TD	YPT	FPTS
2023	17	238	902	5	3.8	45	39	233	0	5.2	183
PROJ	14	100	409	3	4.1	28	22	147	0	5.4	100

52 MILES SANDERS CAR · $- · AGE 27 · BYE 11

Sanders had a disappointing season in several ways, including being beaten out by Chuba Hubbard for the role of lead back, as well as scoring just one touchdown for a shaky offense led by a rookie quarterback with little protection. A new coaching regime could help Sanders, as maybe he'll be looked upon more favorably, but the fact the Panthers also drafted Jonathon Brooks with the 46th pick could spell disaster for him. This smells like it could end in a crowded committee situation (at best), as Sanders will have to compete with not only Hubbard for the starting job and reps but with Brooks as well. Sanders will need a big training camp if he's going to be anything more than an injury insurance policy this season.

	G	CAR	YDS	TD	YPC	TGT	REC	YDS	TD	YPT	FPTS
2023	16	129	432	1	3.3	42	27	154	0	3.7	88
PROJ	14	83	357	2	4.3	19	13	96	0	5.0	73

53 RICO DOWDLE DAL · $- · AGE 26 · BYE 7

Dowdle saw limited offensive snaps during his first three NFL seasons after joining Dallas as an undrafted free agent, but Year 4 was his relative breakout with 505 yards from scrimmage. The main backup to now-departed Tony Pollard rushed for more than 50 yards in only one game, though he saw regular action on special teams. The Cowboys brought back franchise icon Ezekiel Elliott after a year away, and he figures to handle most of the touches, at least early on, diluting Dowdle's potential value. There is opportunity for a Dallas RB, but it is hard to see Dowdle as anything more than an RB5.

	G	CAR	YDS	TD	YPC	TGT	REC	YDS	TD	YPT	FPTS
2023	16	89	361	2	4.1	23	17	144	2	6.3	92
PROJ	14	113	480	3	4.3	30	23	177	1	5.8	114

54 KEATON MITCHELL BAL · $- · AGE 22 · BYE 14

As Mitchell enters his second pro season, all eyes will be on his recovery from an ACL injury suffered in Week 15 last season. When healthy, however, he should slot into a backup role behind Derrick Henry in Baltimore. Mitchell is an explosive runner with big-play chops, as 25.5% of his carries last season went for 10 or more yards. He can attack the perimeter and shift gears in space. While he saw only 10 targets last season, Mitchell has the traits to be schemed as a target for Lamar Jackson in the pass game, too. He fits as a potential deeper-league flex option once he returns to the field.

	G	CAR	YDS	TD	YPC	TGT	REC	YDS	TD	YPT	FPTS
2023	8	47	396	2	8.4	10	9	93	0	9.3	70
PROJ	8	41	183	1	4.4	13	10	78	1	5.8	48

55 KHALIL HERBERT CHI · $- · AGE 26 · BYE 7

Last season, Herbert was part of a three-headed committee in Chicago, sharing time with D'Onta Foreman and Roschon Johnson. This season, he will retain his committee role behind new teammate D'Andre Swift. Herbert missed five games in 2023 with a high-ankle sprain but flashed at times when getting volume. In three games with at least 20 touches, he finished as a top-12 running back in each one. Even with that production, the Bears didn't see him as a lead back, signing Swift to a three-year deal this offseason. Herbert is not worthy of draft consideration in leagues of 10-to-12 teams.

	G	CAR	YDS	TD	YPC	TGT	REC	YDS	TD	YPT	FPTS
2023	12	132	611	2	4.6	31	20	134	1	4.3	113
PROJ	14	105	476	2	4.6	17	12	87	1	5.2	85

56 CLYDE EDWARDS-HELAIRE KC · $- · AGE 25 · BYE 6

Edwards-Helaire was the first running back off the board in the 2020 NFL draft, but his stock has gone in the wrong direction in each of his four pro seasons. In 2023, his transformation into supporting cast member was complete: He averaged 4.7 fantasy points per game, 14.6 offensive snaps and 5.8 touches, and he scored in double figures only twice (Weeks 3 and 15). Re-signed as a free agent, Edwards-Helaire should serve as the Chiefs' insurance policy against an Isiah Pacheco injury, which is also his primary utility in fantasy leagues. It's possible that, in games the team dominates, both backs could deliver meaningful fantasy stats, but there's no reason otherwise to expect a significant career rebirth from Edwards-Helaire.

	G	CAR	YDS	TD	YPC	TGT	REC	YDS	TD	YPT	FPTS
2023	15	70	223	1	3.2	22	17	188	1	8.5	70
PROJ	14	87	375	2	4.3	32	24	206	2	6.4	109

57 RAY DAVIS BUF · $- · AGE 24 · BYE 12

Davis was selected 128th overall by the Bills in April's draft. He rushed for more than 1,100 yards last season at the University of Kentucky after rushing for more than 1,000 yards at Vanderbilt the previous year. Davis is also a solid pass-catcher. The Buffalo backfield belongs to James Cook, so Davis will be competing for touches with Ty Johnson. Davis isn't someone to target in redraft leagues.

	G	CAR	YDS	TD	YPC	TGT	REC	YDS	TD	YPT	FPTS
2023	0	0	0	0	0.0	0	0	0	0	0.0	0
PROJ	14	83	355	2	4.3	17	13	94	1	5.5	75

58 ROSCHON JOHNSON CHI · $- · AGE 23 · BYE 7

Johnson returns for his sophomore season, where he will share a backfield with D'Andre Swift and Khalil Herbert. The former fourth-rounder was efficient in his rookie season, finishing top 20 in fantasy points per touch and top 30 in yards per rush, targets, receptions and receiving yards. Unfortunately, he didn't touch the ball very much (49th among RBs), and his role doesn't look to change in 2024 with Swift, and perhaps Herbert, ahead of him. While talented, Johnson checks in outside the top 50 at the position and can be added off of waivers rather than drafted.

	G	CAR	YDS	TD	YPC	TGT	REC	YDS	TD	YPT	FPTS
2023	15	81	352	2	4.3	43	34	209	0	4.9	102
PROJ	14	75	324	2	4.3	20	15	101	1	5.2	74

59 JAYLEN WRIGHT MIA · $- · AGE 21 · BYE 6

Wright landed in one of the league's most productive running games in Miami. Fantasy managers saw how lethal De'Von Achane was last season when given opportunities for the Dolphins. Wright averaged 7.4 rushing yards per carry last season at the University of Tennessee and ran the 40-yard dash in 4.38 seconds. He's also a very capable receiver out of the backfield. Considering the age and injury history of Raheem Mostert, you should not hesitate to add Wright to your roster in the double-digit rounds. He has the potential to be a league winner if Mostert and/or Achane end up missing time.

	G	CAR	YDS	TD	YPC	TGT	REC	YDS	TD	YPT	FPTS
2023	0	0	0	0	0.0	0	0	0	0	0.0	0
PROJ	14	51	224	1	4.4	17	13	90	0	5.5	56

60 SAMAJE PERINE DEN · $- · AGE 28 · BYE 14

Last year, Perine was added as a pass-catching back and insurance policy in case Javonte Williams wasn't ready to return from ACL surgery. Perine proved more useful in the former department, placing 14th among running backs in receptions while only being called upon to start in an injured Williams' stead in Week 5, a game in which Perine scored a modest 11.5 fantasy points. He is probably destined for a mere pass-catching role for 2024 now that Williams is another year removed from surgery. In addition, sophomore Jaleel McLaughlin excelled in a pinch-hitting role last season, and the team drafted Audric Estimé for added depth. Consider Perine bench fodder in PPR leagues.

	G	CAR	YDS	TD	YPC	TGT	REC	YDS	TD	YPT	FPTS
2023	17	53	238	1	4.5	55	50	455	0	8.3	121
PROJ	14	58	251	1	4.3	45	37	270	1	5.9	102

61 TYRONE TRACY JR. NYG · $- · AGE 24 · BYE 11

The Giants chose Tracy in the fifth round of April's draft. He shined in his one year as a running back at Purdue after several seasons as a wide receiver in Iowa's troubling offense. Of course, the Giants signed former competent Texans/Bills veteran Devin Singletary in March, and he figures to handle the bulk of the work, but Singletary has never caught more than 40 passes or tallied 300 receiving yards in a season. Tracy may become the third-down back, but this still isn't a strong offense, so don't expect more than RB5 production.

	G	CAR	YDS	TD	YPC	TGT	REC	YDS	TD	YPT	FPTS
2023	0	0	0	0	0.0	0	0	0	0	0.0	0
PROJ	14	77	322	2	4.2	23	18	122	1	5.3	77

62 ELIJAH MITCHELL SF · $- · AGE 26 · BYE 9

Since Christian McCaffrey's arrival in San Francisco, Mitchell has recorded exactly 114 carries. Noting injuries (which have limited Mitchell to a total of 16 games over the past two seasons), that's an average of 7.6 attempts per contest. It's therefore difficult to consider the Louisiana product a true backup. He did, however, handle the ball 16 times for 67 scrimmage yards and a rushing score when CMC was resting during Week 18 last season. Heading into the final year of his rookie deal, it's unlikely Mitchell will provide much value to fantasy managers moving forward. His stock took an additional hit with the addition of metrics marvel Isaac Guerendo, whom the 49ers traded up to select in the fourth round of April's draft.

	G	CAR	YDS	TD	YPC	TGT	REC	YDS	TD	YPT	FPTS
2023	11	75	281	2	3.7	8	6	14	0	1.8	48
PROJ	13	80	327	3	4.1	15	12	79	0	5.4	73

63 JAMAAL WILLIAMS NO · $- · AGE 29 · BYE 12

Williams backed up Alvin Kamara while rookie Kendre Miller spent most of last season on the injury report. Coming off a career year in 2022 when he scored 17 TDs with Detroit, Williams did very little with his 106 carries in 2023, averaging 2.9 yards per tote and scoring just one meaningless (and controversial) touchdown in Week 18. That makes him tough to roster in fantasy, outside of being an insurance policy for Kamara's fantasy managers. Miller should come into this season healthy, which will further hinder Williams.

	G	CAR	YDS	TD	YPC	TGT	REC	YDS	TD	YPT	FPTS
2023	13	106	306	1	2.9	20	18	62	0	3.1	61
PROJ	14	85	341	2	4.0	23	19	110	0	4.9	77

64 TANK BIGSBY JAX · $- · AGE 23 · BYE 12

A third-round selection in the spring of 2023, Bigsby's first run in the league didn't include much, well, running. He toted the ball just 50 times, finishing with the fewest yards per touch of all backs with as many attempts.Given the team's draft investment, Bigsby still has a chance to surface as a contributor to the Jaguars' offense in 2024, albeit with tempered expectations, given his perch behind a proven three-down option in Travis Etienne Jr. Given Bigsby's blend of collegiate production and NFL draft stock, he should be considered as a worthy late-round insurance option in most formats.

	G	CAR	YDS	TD	YPC	TGT	REC	YDS	TD	YPT	FPTS
2023	17	50	132	2	2.6	4	1	6	0	1.5	23
PROJ	14	83	346	3	4.2	17	13	91	1	5.3	74

65 KENNETH GAINWELL PHI · $- · AGE 25 · BYE 5

Gainwell has averaged nearly 300 rushing yards and 30 receptions over his first three seasons, but it hasn't added up to much fantasy relevance. The Eagles simply haven't thrown much to their running backs in the Jalen Hurts era, though that may change with the Saquon Barkley acquisition. A healthy Barkley did not share much volume as a Giant, so Gainwell—more of a change-of-pace option due to his smaller stature—may find it difficult to hit his season averages unless Barkley is hurt again. The drafting of Will Shipley is another sign that, even if Barkley goes down, Gainwell may not be next, so consider him in the later rounds, if at all.

	G	CAR	YDS	TD	YPC	TGT	REC	YDS	TD	YPT	FPTS
2023	16	84	364	2	4.3	37	30	183	0	4.9	97
PROJ	14	61	266	2	4.3	26	20	139	0	5.4	74

66 ISRAEL ABANIKANDA NYJ · $- · AGE 21 · BYE 12

Abanikanda is entering his second NFL season with an opportunity to earn primary backup duties behind Breece Hall. A 2023 fifth-round pick, he showed plenty of promise in 2023, leading the Jets to part ways with Dalvin Cook and Michael Carter. Abanikanda will now compete with Day 3 rookies Braelon Allen and Isaiah Davis for the No. 2 gig. This should be an improved Jets offense with a healthy Aaron Rodgers under center, so Abanikanda can be considered late in your draft as a viable insurance RB should he beat out Allen and Davis.

	G	CAR	YDS	TD	YPC	TGT	REC	YDS	TD	YPT	FPTS
2023	6	22	70	0	3.2	11	7	43	0	3.9	16
PROJ	14	78	334	2	4.3	17	13	94	1	5.5	74

67 BRAELON ALLEN NYJ · $- · AGE 20 · BYE 12

Allen finds himself in a crowded running back room in New York alongside Breece Hall, Israel Abanikanda and fellow rookie Isaiah Davis, who was selected in Round 5. Allen, a solid all-around back from the University of Wisconsin, profiles more as a two-down backup at the NFL level and isn't expected to contribute much as a receiver out of the backfield. He should be targeted late in fantasy drafts as an insurance option, only if he wins the No. 2 job behind Hall.

	G	CAR	YDS	TD	YPC	TGT	REC	YDS	TD	YPT	FPTS
2023	0	0	0	0	0.0	0	0	0	0	0.0	0
PROJ	14	74	318	2	4.3	17	13	93	1	5.6	72

68 BUCKY IRVING TB · $- · AGE 22 · BYE 11

Irving was taken with with the 125th pick in the draft by the Buccaneers and will look to complement Rachaad White in the Tampa backfield. He is quick and gets up to speed in a hurry, but he doesn't possess breakaway speed. He also doesn't appear to be anything more than a check-down option in the passing game. White is still the starter for the Buccaneers, and Irving will simply be hoping to battle with Chase Edmonds in order to become the team's RB2. Irving is no more than a late-round insurance flier.

	G	CAR	YDS	TD	YPC	TGT	REC	YDS	TD	YPT	FPTS
2023	0	0	0	0	0.0	0	0	0	0	0.0	0
PROJ	14	69	299	2	4.3	12	9	64	0	5.4	57

69 WILL SHIPLEY PHI · $- · AGE 22 · BYE 5

The Eagles selected Shipley in the fourth round of the draft, which may have surprised some, since the franchise spent big money to secure Saquon Barkley earlier in the offseason. Then again, Barkley has been known to miss games, and Shipley caught 69 passes over his final two seasons at Clemson, so the Eagles could use him to lessen Barkley's load on third downs. Either way, Shipley has little value when Barkley is healthy, but he should leapfrog Kenneth Gainwell on the depth chart, making him a reasonable late-round fantasy choice.

	G	CAR	YDS	TD	YPC	TGT	REC	YDS	TD	YPT	FPTS
2023	0	0	0	0	0.0	0	0	0	0	0.0	0
PROJ	14	37	158	1	4.3	10	8	56	0	5.5	38

70 DAMEON PIERCE HOU · $- · AGE 24 · BYE 14

Another offseason spells increased competition for meaningful work in Houston's backfield. Pierce might have a stake in this trend when we consider that he ranked 66th out of the 68 backs with at least 50 carries last season in yards per touch. Given Joe Mixon's established profile and the potential presence of rookie Jawhar Jordan on the depth chart, Pierce is positioned as merely a late-round insurance policy in drafts.

	G	CAR	YDS	TD	YPC	TGT	REC	YDS	TD	YPT	FPTS
2023	14	145	416	2	2.9	16	13	101	0	6.3	83
PROJ	14	78	299	2	3.8	9	7	43	0	5.0	55

71 D'ONTA FOREMAN CLE · $- · AGE 28 · BYE 10

After a one-year run with the Bears, Foreman joins the Browns for his seventh pro season, adding depth to the Cleveland backfield. Playing in a rotational role for the Bears as an early-down runner, he had two games with 15 or more fantasy points last season, including a 30-point game against the Raiders in Week 7. There could be an early-season opening for Foreman if Nick Chubb (knee) isn't back to full strength, but he lacks any real fantasy upside, given the current depth chart in Cleveland and the fact that he is not much of a factor in the pass game.

	G	CAR	YDS	TD	YPC	TGT	REC	YDS	TD	YPT	FPTS
2023	9	109	425	4	3.9	15	11	77	1	5.1	91
PROJ	13	63	262	2	4.2	7	6	41	0	5.6	49

72 AJ DILLON GB · $- · AGE 26 · BYE 10

Dillon returns for his fifth season with the Packers on a one-year deal. The 26-year-old known as "Quadzilla" has never finished higher than RB23 in fantasy. His game is predicated on being a demolishing between-the-tackles back, yet despite that bruising reputation, he's never been an elite touchdown maker, with only 16 rushing touchdowns in his four-year career. Dillon is now splitting his backup role with rookie MarShawn Lloyd out of USC and will likely be third in line for touches. With Josh Jacobs handling the majority of the work and an exciting rookie in the mix, Dillon should go undrafted in standard ESPN fantasy leagues.

	G	CAR	YDS	TD	YPC	TGT	REC	YDS	TD	YPT	FPTS
2023	15	178	613	2	3.4	27	22	223	0	8.3	118
PROJ	14	49	194	1	3.9	11	8	64	0	6.0	44

73 DEUCE VAUGHN DAL · $- · AGE 22 · BYE 7

Vaughn's rookie season amounted to little production, as the sixth-round draft pick from Kansas State saw precious few touches during the first month of the season and then was a healthy inactive most of the rest of the way. The diminutive Vaughn (5-foot-6, 175 pounds) was expected to handle change-of-pace duties and catch passes, but he ended up with only 30 touches in seven games, including seven receptions. Tony Pollard is gone, but Ezekiel Elliott has returned after a year away, and Rico Dowdle is also in the way for meaningful touches. Vaughn has little value.

	G	CAR	YDS	TD	YPC	TGT	REC	YDS	TD	YPT	FPTS
2023	7	23	40	0	1.7	7	7	40	0	5.7	15
PROJ	14	29	124	1	4.3	18	14	101	1	5.5	45

74 JUSTICE HILL BAL · $- · AGE 26 · BYE 14

The fifth-year pro saw a bump in volume last season with J.K. Dobbins and Keaton Mitchell suffering injuries, finishing with career highs in rushing yards and receiving totals. If Mitchell has to start the season on the PUP list, Hill could potentially have some deeper-league fantasy value if he can hold off rookie fifth-round pick Rasheen Ali. However, if Mitchell is healthy as the No. 2 behind Derrick Henry, then Hill lacks the fantasy value to warrant a draft pick.

	G	CAR	YDS	TD	YPC	TGT	REC	YDS	TD	YPT	FPTS
2023	16	84	387	3	4.6	39	28	206	1	5.3	109
PROJ	14	53	234	2	4.4	24	18	136	1	5.6	69

WIDE RECEIVERS

The NFL continues to be a passing game, making top WRs essential to your roster

BY MATT BOWEN
PLAYER PROJECTIONS BY MIKE CLAY

IN TODAY'S NFL, offenses are built on the pass game, including a focus on creating big plays through the air. And wide receivers are cashing in.

Last season, CeeDee Lamb led all PPR scorers with 403.2 total points, and four of the top 10 were wide receivers (Lamb, Tyreek Hill, Amon-Ra St. Brown, Puka Nacua). In fact, there were 33 wide receivers who scored at least 200 fantasy points in 2023, with 18 averaging at least 15 points per game (among those with at least 10 games played).

Want more evidence that passing games are exploding right now? Think about this: 35 wide receivers saw at least 100 targets last season, while 27 eclipsed 1,000 yards receiving. You want to see the ball in the end zone? A total of 26 wide receivers caught at least seven touchdowns, including six who had 10 or more, led by Hill and Mike Evans with 13.

The overall passing volume is up and will remain at a high level. Last season, 24 of the 32 NFL teams attempted 550 or more passes, and 11 had 600-plus. It's the dropback pass game, play-action and RPOs, with built-in concepts to attack defensive coverage trends.

NFL defenses played zone coverage at a 57.5% rate in 2023, with split-safety alignments on 44.3% of opponent dropbacks, both of which were the highest marks of the past five seasons.

TIERED RANKINGS

Tiers allow you to identify players you should value similarly at various points of your draft.

RANK	PLAYER, TEAM	ROUND
1	CEEDEE LAMB, DAL	1
2	TYREEK HILL, MIA	1
3	JA'MARR CHASE, CIN	1
4	AMON-RA ST. BROWN, DET	1
5	JUSTIN JEFFERSON, MIN	1
6	A.J. BROWN, PHI	1/2
7	PUKA NACUA, LAR	2
8	GARRETT WILSON, NYJ	2
9	DAVANTE ADAMS, LV	2
10	CHRIS OLAVE, NO	2
11	MICHAEL PITTMAN JR., IND	2/3
12	MIKE EVANS, TB	2/3
13	MARVIN HARRISON JR., ARI	4
14	DRAKE LONDON, ATL	4
15	NICO COLLINS, HOU	4
16	DK METCALF, SEA	4
17	BRANDON AIYUK, SF	4
18	DEEBO SAMUEL, SF	4/5
19	STEFON DIGGS, HOU	4/5
20	DJ MOORE, CHI	4/5
21	DEVONTA SMITH, PHI	4/5

And offensive playcallers have answers to carve out open voids, create catch-and-run opportunities or dial up the vertical shot plays.

There is obviously impressive depth at wide receiver in fantasy football, with multiple tiers of players who can contribute viable production for your lineup. However, when setting your draft board, it's still best to jump early and target a wideout—in Round 1 or 2—who can provide consistent scoring and volume opportunities, with breakout-game potential.

Regardless of your scoring format or whether your starting lineup features two or three wide receivers (or more, if you include flex slots), the value of landing a top-tier pass-catcher has never been greater. Grab one early and then build out the rest of your roster with receivers who play in high-volume/high-scoring passing offenses. The pro game has changed, and it's not going back.

We got next: Rookie wide receivers are more developed than ever, with pro-ready skill sets and playmaking traits. Seven receivers were selected in Round 1 of April's draft, led by Marvin Harrison Jr. (Cardinals), Malik Nabers (Giants) and Rome Odunze (Bears). It's OK to target the upside of first-year wide receivers who landed in positive team/scheme situations, or when looking for that late-round flier.

ABOUT OUR PROJECTIONS: All are for a 17-game season, with some degree of player maintenance and injury risk factored in and then rounded up or down as appropriate. Player ages are as of Sept. 5, 2024.

CeeDee Lamb

1 CEEDEE LAMB DAL · $55 · AGE 25 · BYE 7

Lamb led the entire fantasy football world in fantasy points in 2023, surpassing 25 points in eight games and truly dominating the second half of the season. He started slow—it's a career theme—but from Week 8 on, he averaged 28.5 fantasy points per game. His 313.6 fantasy points in the final 11 weeks alone topped the full-season performance of all but eight other NFL players. Lamb is not only a clear top-five fantasy pick, but with his durability and the Cowboys' high-octane offense, the case can be made for him as a solid choice to go No. 1 overall.

	G	CAR	YDS	TD	TGT	REC	YDS	TD	YPT	C%	FPTS
2023	17	14	113	2	181	135	1749	12	9.7	75%	403
PROJ	15	13	86	1	166	117	1463	9	8.8	71%	328

2 TYREEK HILL MIA · $54 · AGE 30 · BYE 6

Hill enters his third season with the Dolphins after another exquisite season in which he averaged 10.7 targets and 23.5 fantasy points per game. He was one of only eight players in the league who had at least 90 receptions and 1,200 receiving yards in 2023. Targets are among the most predictable year-to-year counting stats for wide receivers, and Hill remains the top option in a Dolphins offense that ranked first in passing yards last season, a trend that's expected to continue. Despite the fact that he's entering his age-30 season, Hill should still be one of the first receivers selected in fantasy drafts.

	G	CAR	YDS	TD	TGT	REC	YDS	TD	YPT	C%	FPTS
2023	16	6	15	0	171	119	1799	13	10.5	70%	376
PROJ	15	4	25	0	156	106	1438	8	9.2	68%	298

Mike Evans

3 JA'MARR CHASE CIN · $53 · AGE 24 · BYE 12

Chase starts his fourth pro season with the Bengals looking to boost his numbers with a healthy Joe Burrow back running the offense. Chase averaged 16.4 fantasy PPG in 2023, down from the 20.0 PPG he registered in 2022 (WR4). However, he still posted five games with 20 or more points, including a 52.2-point performance in Week 5 versus the Cardinals. Chase has totaled 29 touchdowns in his career and is one of the league's premier players at the position due to his big-play ability and upper-tier play strength. You'd be smart to lock him in as a top 10 player overall in fantasy this season.

	G	CAR	YDS	TD	TGT	REC	YDS	TD	YPT	C%	FPTS
2023	16	3	-6	0	144	100	1216	7	8.4	69%	263
PROJ	15	4	18	0	152	106	1343	8	8.8	69%	292

4 AMON-RA ST. BROWN DET · $53 · AGE 24 · BYE 5

After inking a new four-year contract this offseason, St. Brown returns as the leader of the Lions' receiving corps. One of most consistent wide receivers in fantasy, ARSB had an outstanding 11 games with at least 18 fantasy points in 2023. No wide receiver had more top-20 weekly finishes, and only Tyreek Hill had more weeks finishing seventh or better. Possessing both a high floor and ceiling, St. Brown was top five in every major receiving category last season and returns to an offense that looks to be just as potent. He is showing no signs of slowing down and is poised to be a top-five fantasy wide receiver in 2024.

	G	CAR	YDS	TD	TGT	REC	YDS	TD	YPT	C%	FPTS
2023	16	4	24	0	165	119	1515	10	9.2	72%	331
PROJ	15	4	29	0	153	110	1264	7	8.3	72%	284

5 JUSTIN JEFFERSON MIN · $52 · AGE 25 · BYE 6

Jefferson enters his fifth season with the Vikings after missing significant time due to injury last year for the first time in his career. In his eight healthy weeks of 2023, he averaged 24 fantasy points per game and was one of only four wide receivers to have at least six games with 23 fantasy points. In a season where the Vikings started Kirk Cousins, Nick Mullens, Joshua Dobbs and Jaren Hall, Jefferson proved himself QB-proof. This season, he'll have Sam Darnold and rookie J.J. McCarthy under center. While there could be some growing pains in this offense, Jefferson is one of the few WRs who can make magic happen with subpar QB play. He is once again a top-five fantasy wide receiver.

	G	CAR	YDS	TD	TGT	REC	YDS	TD	YPT	C%	FPTS
2023	10	1	-12	0	100	68	1074	5	10.7	68%	202
PROJ	15	2	10	0	165	107	1364	7	8.3	65%	286

6 A.J. BROWN PHI · $46 · AGE 27 · BYE 5

Brown's second season in Philadelphia statistically mirrored his excellent debut, as he was fifth in receiving yards and provided a cool 17 fantasy points per game, eighth among wide receivers. The way he statistically achieved his numbers was a bit disturbing for fantasy managers (and the stumbling Eagles), as he dominated over a six-game stretch early on, *averaging* 138 receiving yards and tallying five touchdowns from Weeks 3 through 8, but then reaching 100 yards in just one of the final nine contests. Still, QB Jalen Hurts leads an elite offense, and even with WR DeVonta Smith and new RB Saquon Barkley in the mix, Brown will see ample targets and end zone opportunities. Expect another season as a WR1 option and potential first-round choice.

	G	CAR	YDS	TD	TGT	REC	YDS	TD	YPT	C%	FPTS
2023	17	0	0	0	159	106	1456	7	9.2	67%	290
PROJ	15	0	0	0	144	93	1304	8	9.1	65%	271

23 COOPER KUPP LAR · $15 · AGE 31 · BYE 6

It was an up-and-down effort in 2023 from Kupp, who missed the first four weeks with a hamstring issue and has now missed 13 games the past two seasons. On the plus side, he posted four 100-yard efforts and five outings of 15 or more fantasy points. Unfortunately, he was also held below 40 yards in six of 12 contests. Kupp's nose for the end zone saved fantasy managers, as the 31-year-old scored four times from Weeks 13 through 17. Obviously, Puka Nacua's emergence negatively affected Kupp's volume, though the vet remained Matthew Stafford's favorite high-value target. He led the team in red zone opportunities (19, WR9). While he appears past peak value, Kupp's savvy and chemistry with Stafford are solid enough for him to deliver low-end WR2 numbers in PPR formats.

	G	CAR	YDS	TD	TGT	REC	YDS	TD	YPT	C%	FPTS
2023	12	1	-3	0	97	59	737	5	7.6	61%	164
PROJ	15	2	12	0	118	78	1000	7	8.4	66%	219

24 ZAY FLOWERS BAL · $15 · AGE 23 · BYE 14

Flowers kicks off his second pro season after averaging 12.9 fantasy PPG in his rookie year, with four games of 19 or more points. He's an explosive mover with electric ability in space, as 45.1% of his receving yards came after the catch. In Baltimore's system, he can be schemed on screens and manufactured touches in addition to his multilevel route-running ability. With Flowers expected to see No. 1 volume this season, he should be drafted as a flex/WR2.

	G	CAR	YDS	TD	TGT	REC	YDS	TD	YPT	C%	FPTS
2023	16	8	56	1	108	77	858	5	7.9	71%	206
PROJ	15	9	55	1	117	78	970	6	8.3	67%	217

25 CALVIN RIDLEY TEN · $14 · AGE 29 · BYE 5

Joining the Titans in free agency via a rich new pact was a bit surprising, and also very interesting. Ridley's return to NFL action in 2023 resulted in a somewhat volatile season in Jacksonville. He had seven games with at least 83 receiving yards and nine with 40 yards or fewer. A sluggish catch rate of 55% (among the lowest among the top 40 in targets) was a key culprit. The Titans paid Ridley handsomely to help open the downfield offense next to DeAndre Hopkins while aiding Will Levis' progression as a professional passer. Much like last season, a blend of volume and variance is likely the story with Ridley. There will be valleys but also impressive peaks. Taking him in the middle rounds on the fringes of WR2 and WR3 pricing could prove very rewarding.

	G	CAR	YDS	TD	TGT	REC	YDS	TD	YPT	C%	FPTS
2023	17	9	23	0	137	76	1016	8	7.4	55%	230
PROJ	15	4	19	0	127	73	994	7	7.8	57%	214

26 MALIK NABERS NYG · $13 · AGE 21 · BYE 11

The Giants desperately needed an offensive game-breaker with big-play ability at wide receiver, someone they can line up anywhere, and they got him by securing Nabers with the sixth overall pick in the April draft. He dominated at LSU, averaging better than 12 yards per target in his final season and with a huge target share, but things are quite different in the New York offense. The Giants struggle to throw the football downfield with Daniel Jones at QB. Nabers has the skills to change the offense and become a fantasy star, but it's tough to recommend him as more than WR3 initially.

	G	CAR	YDS	TD	TGT	REC	YDS	TD	YPT	C%	FPTS
2023	0	0	0	0	0	0	0	0	0.0	0%	0
PROJ	15	0	0	0	127	78	1033	5	8.1	62%	214

27 TEE HIGGINS CIN · $13 · AGE 25 · BYE 12

Higgins is back—on the franchise tag—for his fifth pro season with the Bengals. In 12 games played last season, he averaged 11.5 fantasy PPG but was inconsistent, scoring 22 or more points three times but below 10 points on seven occasions. Higgins will remain unpredictable at times as the secondary target behind Ja'Marr Chase, but he has ability to win on the boundary or as a seam-stretcher from the slot. Having a healthy Joe Burrow back on the field for this high-powered offense puts Higgins in the mid-tier flex range, with WR2 upside.

	G	CAR	YDS	TD	TGT	REC	YDS	TD	YPT	C%	FPTS
2023	12	0	0	0	77	42	656	5	8.5	55%	138
PROJ	15	0	0	0	116	70	1031	7	8.9	60%	216

28 TANK DELL HOU · $11 · AGE 24 · BYE 14

If Dell's first season saw him set a franchise rookie record for receiving scores in just 11 games, a second season bears real excitement. He is expected to be fully back from a broken fibula that shortened his prolific first year in the league, and fortunately, he shouldn't be limited by a shooting wound incurred in the offseason. As he forges a dynamic duo with C.J. Stroud to create one of the most exciting big-play tandems in the NFL, Year 2 could be even more compelling. Target competition is a real factor on a depth chart that includes Nico Collins and Stefon Diggs, but as last season suggests, Dell can do a lot of damage without immense volume. The history of second-year receiving ascension also bodes well for him, making him a worthy WR3 target as a key part of a rising offense.

	G	CAR	YDS	TD	TGT	REC	YDS	TD	YPT	C%	FPTS
2023	11	11	51	0	75	47	709	7	9.5	63%	165
PROJ	15	16	93	1	112	70	933	6	8.3	62%	210

29 KEENAN ALLEN CHI · $11 · AGE 32 · BYE 7

Allen joins the Bears after spending the past 11 seasons with the Chargers. A dominant possession receiver, he is coming off the second-best fantasy season and the highest points per game mark of his storied career. Now that he's 32 and starting over with rookie quarterback Caleb Williams, Allen's best fantasy days may be behind him. And while he's still a legitimate threat, he is now in a crowded WR room with an inexperienced signal-caller, so he should be viewed as a WR3 heading into the season.

	G	CAR	YDS	TD	TGT	REC	YDS	TD	YPT	C%	FPTS
2023	13	2	6	0	151	108	1243	7	8.2	72%	279
PROJ	14	2	12	0	123	84	882	5	7.2	68%	202

30 CHRIS GODWIN TB · $10 · AGE 28 · BYE 11

Godwin finished last season as fantasy's WR28 and eclipsed 1,000 yards for the third straight year. Baker Mayfield had a solid season, and Godwin excelled as a result, but he was once again lacking in the touchdown department, and his fantasy upside is impacted by playing in the shadow of Mike Evans. The 28-year-old Godwin still has some life left in his legs but will have to improve on his 12.3 fantasy points per game if he's going to be more than a WR3 again this season.

	G	CAR	YDS	TD	TGT	REC	YDS	TD	YPT	C%	FPTS
2023	17	4	38	1	134	83	1024	2	7.6	62%	209
PROJ	15	4	25	0	124	81	973	5	7.9	66%	214

31 AMARI COOPER CLE · $10 · AGE 30 · BYE 10

Cooper is entering his 10th pro season, his third with the Browns. One of the top route technicians in the league, he averaged 14.5 PPG last season (WR17), highlighted by his 51.5-point performance in Week 16 versus the Texans. Cooper has now seen 100 or more targets in six straight seasons, with at least 68 receptions each year during that stretch. The Browns traded for wide receiver Jerry Jeudy, but Cooper will remain the top target in Cleveland's schemed pass game. You can feel comfortable drafting him as a reliable flex option.

	G	CAR	YDS	TD	TGT	REC	YDS	TD	YPT	C%	FPTS
2023	15	0	0	0	129	72	1250	5	9.7	56%	227
PROJ	15	0	0	0	118	72	1028	5	8.7	61%	207

32 GEORGE PICKENS PIT · $10 · AGE 23 · BYE 9

Heading into his third pro season, Pickens is the unquestioned top target in Pittsburgh after the club traded Diontae Johnson to Carolina. Last season, Pickens averaged 12.3 PPG despite having inconsistent quarterback play. He flashed his big-play ability, as he logged four games of 20 or more points, including a season-high 35.5 against the Bengals in Week 16. Given his vertical ability (14 receptions on throws of 20 or more air yards), he has real fantasy potential if the Steelers can get a higher level of play at quarterback from either Russell Wilson or Justin Fields. You can draft Pickens as a flex, but he certainly has the ability to produce breakout games that can win you a week.

	G	CAR	YDS	TD	TGT	REC	YDS	TD	YPT	C%	FPTS
2023	17	3	18	0	105	63	1140	5	10.9	60%	209
PROJ	15	4	29	0	113	68	1040	4	9.2	60%	201

33 DEANDRE HOPKINS TEN · $10 · AGE 32 · BYE 5

Hopkins is entering his 12th NFL season, but he hasn't shown serious signs of aging just yet. Last season, he posted his highest yards per catch since his first All-Pro effort in 2017. The days of triple-digit reception totals are likely in the past, but a concentrated Titans offense could still afford him well over 100 targets working with a big-armed second-year QB in Will Levis. There is always a degree of risk investing in a receiver in his age-32 season, though it's reasonable to note that Hopkins wins at the catch point with a mixture of guile and hands that remains rare at the position. Given his track record, don't be surprised by another solid WR2 showing found at WR3 pricing.

	G	CAR	YDS	TD	TGT	REC	YDS	TD	YPT	C%	FPTS
2023	17	2	9	0	138	75	1057	7	7.7	54%	224
PROJ	15	0	0	0	127	76	1012	5	8.0	60%	204

34 RASHEE RICE KC · $9 · AGE 24 · BYE 6

Rice was arguably the one thing that went right in a 2023 Chiefs wide receiver room that seemed to get everything else wrong. He delivered 212.5 fantasy points (eighth best among all rookies) and had seven top-25 positional weekly scores. Though he did most of his damage in the short game—his 4.9 aDOT was lowest among wide receivers—he quickly developed into a go-to target for Patrick Mahomes. Rice was WR8 in the season's final seven weeks, despite sitting out Week 18. He is tricky to rank, as he could be facing a multi-game suspension due to an off-the-field incident, but he has WR2 value when active. His usage should be similar to 2023, even after the team's offseason addition of deep threats Marquise Brown and Xavier Worthy.

	G	CAR	YDS	TD	TGT	REC	YDS	TD	YPT	C%	FPTS
2023	16	1	-3	0	103	79	938	7	9.1	77%	213
PROJ	13	2	10	0	94	68	792	7	8.4	73%	189

Terry McLaurin

35 DIONTAE JOHNSON CAR · $4 · AGE 28 · BYE 11

Johnson was traded to Carolina during the offseason after spending his first five seasons in Pittsburgh. He has seen his production dip over the past two seasons (41st in fantasy PPG both years) but showed he could deliver high-end numbers with good quarterback play (22nd and ninth with Ben Roethlisberger in 2020 and 2021, respectively). Johnson is an elite route-runner who has managed a target share of at least 23% in four consecutive seasons. He's a good bet to lead an improved Carolina offense in targets, and especially if Bryce Young makes a Year 2 leap, Johnson is likely to return to fantasy relevance. Target Johnson as a WR3/flex with WR2 upside.

	G	CAR	YDS	TD	TGT	REC	YDS	TD	YPT	C%	FPTS
2023	13	0	0	0	86	51	717	5	8.3	59%	153
PROJ	15	2	13	0	111	68	936	6	8.4	61%	198

36 TERRY MCLAURIN WAS · $4 · AGE 28 · BYE 14

McLaurin's fifth NFL season looked quite a bit like his prior ones, as he crossed 1,000 receiving yards in the fourth consecutive campaign, quite the feat considering Washington's quarterback play during his career. This is a new era, with Jayden Daniels at quarterback, and that helps everyone. The consistent McLaurin has caught between 77 and 87 passes in each of the past four seasons, and he has scored four or more touchdowns each year. What looked different in 2023 was how he got those numbers, with a career-worst 7.6 yards per target and 12.7 yards per reception. Fantasy managers can no longer comfortably choose the durable McLaurin as a WR2, as 27 wide receivers scored more fantasy points last season, but he isn't far from that range, either.

	G	CAR	YDS	TD	TGT	REC	YDS	TD	YPT	C%	FPTS
2023	17	0	0	0	131	79	1002	4	7.6	60%	209
PROJ	15	0	0	0	119	72	988	3	8.3	61%	191

37 CHRISTIAN KIRK JAX · $4 · AGE 27 · BYE 12

A return to the top of the Jaguars' depth chart could define Kirk's 2024. Calvin Ridley's arrival in Jacksonville last season saw Kirk assume a smaller share of the passing market, resulting in per-game production in the WR3 and flex tier among receivers. A core injury that required surgery and an IR stint also slowed his production. This marked a decline from Kirk's surprisingly strong finish in his 2022 debut season with the team. But with Ridley off to the rival Titans and the arrival of lower-volume field-stretcher Gabe Davis and rookie Brian Thomas Jr., Kirk has a realistic path to pace the depth chart in opportunities as a top option for Trevor Lawrence. Consider Kirk as a flex.

	G	CAR	YDS	TD	TGT	REC	YDS	TD	YPT	C%	FPTS
2023	12	1	6	0	83	57	787	3	9.5	69%	150
PROJ	15	2	12	0	118	79	899	4	7.6	67%	195

38 JORDAN ADDISON MIN · $4 · AGE 22 · BYE 6

Addison had some ups and downs in his rookie season. Playing with four different QBs and taking over WR1 responsibilities while Justin Jefferson was out, he turned in seven performances with at least 15 fantasy points, third most among rookie wide receivers. Most impressive, his 10 touchdowns were tied for fourth-most among all wideouts. Expect those touchdowns to come down with Jefferson fully healthy and Kirk Cousins in Atlanta. While he's super-talented, Addison is the No. 2 pass-catcher for a rookie QB at arguably the deepest position in fantasy football, so it's best to view him as a WR4 or WR5 entering draft season.

	G	CAR	YDS	TD	TGT	REC	YDS	TD	YPT	C%	FPTS
2023	17	1	2	0	108	70	911	10	8.4	65%	221
PROJ	15	0	0	0	116	71	880	5	7.6	61%	191

39 COURTLAND SUTTON DEN · $4 · AGE 28 · BYE 14

Following along with what was a team-wide theme, Sutton fell short of expectations again in 2023, marking three consecutive seasons in which he has failed to crack the positional top 30 in fantasy points despite pacing the Broncos in both routes run and targets. Though his career-best 10 touchdowns were a bright spot, advanced measures deemed it a fortunate total. And since he entered the season with just 14 TDs in 65 career games, it was quite a surprise. He enters his age-28 season working with his ninth quarterback, and one probably a step down talent-wise from Russell Wilson. Still, the offseason trade of Jerry Jeudy opens up some targets and paves the way for Sutton to be the Broncos' receiving alpha dog. He's best drafted as a WR3 with potential receptions upside.

	G	CAR	YDS	TD	TGT	REC	YDS	TD	YPT	C%	FPTS
2023	16	0	0	0	92	59	772	10	8.4	64%	190
PROJ	15	0	0	0	120	70	895	5	7.5	58%	188

40 CHRISTIAN WATSON GB · $3 · AGE 25 · BYE 10

Watson is back in Green Bay as one of the most difficult players to figure out in fantasy. A big-play WR with multiple boom games to his name, he was second in points per reception and finished eighth in end zone targets despite playing only nine games last season. The biggest knock against him is his faulty hamstrings, which have kept him from staying on the field thus far in his young career. Watson has missed 11 games over his first two seasons, and he's now in a very full wide receiver room. Watson carries risk, but his ceiling remains off the charts. He's best viewed as a high-upside WR4.

	G	CAR	YDS	TD	TGT	REC	YDS	TD	YPT	C%	FPTS
2023	9	4	11	0	53	28	422	5	8.0	53%	101
PROJ	15	6	39	0	95	55	837	8	8.8	57%	189

41 JAYDEN REED GB · $3 · AGE 24 · BYE 10

Reed impressed as a rookie and is back to do it again in his second season with the Packers. The former second-round pick showcased his talent down the stretch with at least 15 fantasy points in seven of his final eight games. In fact, over that stretch, Reed was WR10! The upside is obvious—the only problem is the number of options Jordan Love has at his disposal. Christian Watson is a potential star when healthy, Romeo Doubs has shown his knack for the end zone and Dontayvion Wicks even flashed last season. It's just a deep WR room, and it's the deepest position in fantasy. Because of that, Reed checks in as a flex with WR3 upside.

	G	CAR	YDS	TD	TGT	REC	YDS	TD	YPT	C%	FPTS
2023	16	11	119	2	94	64	793	8	8.4	68%	217
PROJ	15	13	88	1	95	62	760	5	8.0	66%	181

42 JAXON SMITH-NJIGBA SEA · $3 · AGE 22 · BYE 10

Eventually finding his footing as the Seahawks' No. 3 WR, Smith-Njigba was largely deployed via the slot as a rookie (64.3% rate) working as a complement to DK Metcalf and Tyler Lockett. Smith-Njigba is a smooth and reliable receiver who uses agility and crisp routes to gain separation, and at just 22 years old, he figures to eventually grow into a starring role. With Lockett and Noah Fant returning, however, targets may be hard to come by in 2024. Seattle's new coaching regime figures to shake things up from a scheme perspective, but how many opportunities they'll immediately grant Smith-Njigba remains to be seen. An injury to the 31-year-old Lockett would pave the way for a potential breakout for JSN, who presents with plenty of theoretical upside.

	G	CAR	YDS	TD	TGT	REC	YDS	TD	YPT	C%	FPTS
2023	17	0	0	0	93	63	628	4	6.8	68%	150
PROJ	15	0	0	0	107	72	841	5	7.9	67%	183

43 MIKE WILLIAMS NYJ · $3 · AGE 29 · BYE 12

This is Williams' first season with the Jets after spending his first seven NFL seasons with the Chargers. He offers a much-needed boost to a team that struggled with Allen Lazard and Xavier Gipson as their next-best WRs behind Garrett Wilson. Despite suffering a torn ACL last September, Williams is expected to be fully recovered by the start of the 2024 season. The 29-year-old has maintained an average of 7.7 targets and 14.8 fantasy points per game over the past three seasons. With Aaron Rodgers at quarterback, Williams should see enough targets to warrant consideration as a boom/bust flex option in 2024.

	G	CAR	YDS	TD	TGT	REC	YDS	TD	YPT	C%	FPTS
2023	3	1	3	0	26	19	249	1	9.6	73%	50
PROJ	14	0	0	0	91	60	821	6	9.0	65%	179

44 TYLER LOCKETT SEA · $3 · AGE 31 · BYE 10

It was assumed that after nine seasons in Seattle and on the heels of Pete Carroll's departure, Lockett would land with a different squad in 2024. But the organization was motivated to keep the team together, re-signing Lockett to a two-year deal worth $34 million. Failing to clear 1,000 receiving yards for the first time in four years and recording 11.3 YPR (WR71), he is unlikely to deliver better than WR3 numbers for fantasy purposes. Jaxon Smith-Njigba's presence further lowers his ceiling. Still, he's a valued vet with a solid floor, and he should remain a stabilizing presence in Seattle and for fans of the virtual game this season.

	G	CAR	YDS	TD	TGT	REC	YDS	TD	YPT	C%	FPTS
2023	17	0	0	0	123	79	894	5	7.3	64%	202
PROJ	15	0	0	0	107	74	821	4	7.7	69%	182

45 MARQUISE BROWN KC · $2 · AGE 27 · BYE 6

The most accomplished deep-threat receiver the Chiefs have signed since Tyreek Hill departed, Brown brings the worry of having been a near-total flop in his two years in Arizona but also the tantalizing upside of a weekly fantasy WR2. He never clicked with Kliff Kingsbury's offensive system in 2022 and was held back by injury (foot) and poor quarterback play in 2023, but he also had seven touchdowns of 40 yards or greater during his three seasons in Baltimore (2019-21), third best in the league. Having one of the game's best quarterbacks, Patrick Mahomes, should help fuel a rebound for Brown, but be forewarned that due to his probable role, and with the speedy Xavier Worthy also now on the roster, Brown will likely be a boom-or-bust type.

	G	CAR	YDS	TD	TGT	REC	YDS	TD	YPT	C%	FPTS
2023	14	2	23	0	101	51	574	4	5.7	50%	135
PROJ	15	2	13	0	98	55	804	6	8.2	56%	176

46 ROME ODUNZE CHI · $2 · AGE 22 · BYE 7

Odunze joins the Bears as the ninth overall pick in the 2024 NFL draft. He's a big (6-foot-3, 212 pounds), physical receiver who knows how to use his size and body when making contested catches. He's the real deal, and his numbers during his final season at the University of Washington show that (92-1,640-13). Odunze has the makeup of a star in this league, but in 2024 he'll be third in line for targets behind DJ Moore and Keenan Allen. Add a rookie QB to the mix and a run-heavy scheme, and we're looking at a WR4/5 with upside.

	G	CAR	YDS	TD	TGT	REC	YDS	TD	YPT	C%	FPTS
2023	0	0	0	0	0	0	0	0	0.0	0%	0
PROJ	15	2	13	0	100	60	804	6	8.0	60%	175

47 XAVIER WORTHY KC · $2 · AGE 21 · BYE 6

That the Chiefs paid handsomely to move up to 28th overall in the NFL draft to select Worthy speaks volumes about their regard for his big-play ability. In his final season at Texas, he averaged 7.7 yards after the catch per target and broke 15 tackles, and he ultimately set the 40-yard dash record at the NFL combine (4.21 seconds). Though the Chiefs' receiving depth should afford them patience with Worthy's development, his ability to stretch the field will prove handy for them from Day 1. If he clicks, he could deliver fantasy WR3 numbers right from the start. Bear in mind, however, that players of his ilk often have their single-game statistical peaks and valleys.

	G	CAR	YDS	TD	TGT	REC	YDS	TD	YPT	C%	FPTS
2023	0	0	0	0	0	0	0	0	0.0	0%	0
PROJ	15	6	35	0	90	56	754	6	8.3	62%	175

48 LADD MCCONKEY LAC · $2 · AGE 22 · BYE 5

Though Puka Nacua did it just last season, it's not common historically that an unheralded draft pick emerges as his team's go-to receiver. McConkey has a very real chance to do just that, considering the Chargers' aggressive move to trade up for him at No. 34 overall, addressing what was an especially weak spot on the team. He's a polished route-runner who, despite a disappointing and injury-limited senior season at Georgia, excelled at the combine (4.39 40 time), a reminder of his elite speed and quickness. Expect McConkey to get an extended look during the preseason, with a high probability of emerging as Justin Herbert's preferred target before the 2024 season concludes. There's WR3 upside here.

	G	CAR	YDS	TD	TGT	REC	YDS	TD	YPT	C%	FPTS
2023	0	0	0	0	0	0	0	0	0.0	0%	0
PROJ	15	2	14	0	98	63	797	5	8.1	65%	174

49 KEON COLEMAN BUF · $2 · AGE 21 · BYE 12

Coleman was selected by Buffalo in the second round of April's draft and was immediately tethered to one of the league's best quarterbacks in Josh Allen. He easily could pace the Bills in targets out of the gate after Stefon Diggs and Gabe Davis left this offseason. The rookie out of Florida State led the Seminoles in receptions, yards and touchdowns in his final collegiate season. With his downfield prowess and red zone potential, Coleman should be on your radar in the middle rounds.

	G	CAR	YDS	TD	TGT	REC	YDS	TD	YPT	C%	FPTS
2023	0	0	0	0	0	0	0	0	0.0	0%	0
PROJ	15	0	0	0	96	58	810	5	8.4	60%	170

50 BRIAN THOMAS JR. JAX · $2 · AGE 21 · BYE 12

Selecting Thomas in the first round highlights the Jaguars' clear agenda to provide Trevor Lawrence with an upgraded collection of downfield playmakers. Overshadowed to a degree by LSU teammate Malik Nabers, Thomas established quite the collegiate career of his own. After all, his 12 touchdown hauls on passes of at least 20 yards downfield last season marked the most by any FBS player in a season since ESPN Stats & Information began tracking air yards in 2011. Lawrence, meanwhile, is third in the NFL in passes of least 10 air yards since the start of the 2022 campaign. Taking Thomas, the rare rookie from this class with a projection for a triple-digit target workload, in the late-middle rounds of your draft could prove profitable.

	G	CAR	YDS	TD	TGT	REC	YDS	TD	YPT	C%	FPTS
2023	0	0	0	0	0	0	0	0	0.0	0%	0
PROJ	15	0	0	0	100	61	814	5	8.1	61%	171

51 DARNELL MOONEY ATL · $1 · AGE 26 · BYE 12

Mooney had a highly disappointing campaign for the Bears, thanks to injuries and playing in Chicago's offense, but he'll get a fresh start in Atlanta, where he's expected to be a deep threat alongside Drake London and Kyle Pitts for new quarterback Kirk Cousins. Mooney had just 31 catches for 414 yards and one touchdown in a lost season, but he should be unchallenged as the WR2 in Atlanta. If he can stay healthy, he could be primed for a breakout season in Atlanta's high-powered air attack, making him a strong sleeper option for his new team.

	G	CAR	YDS	TD	TGT	REC	YDS	TD	YPT	C%	FPTS
2023	15	2	5	0	58	31	414	1	7.1	53%	79
PROJ	15	4	25	0	93	56	819	6	8.8	60%	175

52 JAKOBI MEYERS LV · $1 · AGE 27 · BYE 10

Meyers' familiarity with Josh McDaniels' system afforded him a hot start to 2023. He was 20th among WRs through eight weeks with 108.4 fantasy points. After the Raiders dispatched McDaniels, Meyers' production dipped, as he averaged 3.3 fewer points and 2.6 fewer targets per game from that point forward. Ultimately, he finished 24th in fantasy production among wide receivers, a good enough stat line to earn him No. 2 target status again in the Raiders' 2024 offense and a fantasy flex valuation. The team's iffy quarterback situation, however, might mean the second-half version is the more likely Meyers we'll see this year.

	G	CAR	YDS	TD	TGT	REC	YDS	TD	YPT	C%	FPTS
2023	16	4	24	2	107	71	807	8	7.5	66%	219
PROJ	15	4	25	0	108	73	783	3	7.2	68%	175

53 JERRY JEUDY CLE · $1 · AGE 25 · BYE 10

Jeudy enters his fifth pro season in a new home after being traded from Denver to Cleveland. The former first-round pick logged his best numbers in 2022 with the Broncos, posting 13.6 PPG with six touchdowns. His totals dropped last season, as he struggled to find the end zone (two touchdowns) and finished at 8.9 PPG. The Browns gave Jeudy a three-year contract extension, so they believe in his upside. He's a explosive mover with three-level separation ability. However, he will compete for targets with Amari Cooper, David Njoku and Elijah Moore in an offense hoping for Deshaun Watson to elevate his game. That keeps Jeudy down in the lower-tier flex range.

	G	CAR	YDS	TD	TGT	REC	YDS	TD	YPT	C%	FPTS
2023	16	0	0	0	86	54	758	2	8.8	63%	142
PROJ	15	0	0	0	96	61	907	4	9.4	63%	174

54 ADAM THIELEN CAR · $1 · AGE 34 · BYE 11

Thielen is entering his 11th NFL season (his second in Carolina) after a surprising rebound campaign in 2023, in which he cleared both 100 receptions and 1,000 yards. He benefited from heavy usage as Bryce Young's only reliable target, ranking third among WRs in routes (605), 17th in target share (25%) and ninth in receptions (103). Thielen played well (his 76% catch rate ranked third) and ended up 17th at the position in fantasy points despite Carolina's overall offensive struggles. He is likely headed for a step back in 2024, however, as he's now 34 and has substantially more competition for targets (Diontae Johnson, Xavier Legette). Thielen should be valued as a low-ceiling flex option.

	G	CAR	YDS	TD	TGT	REC	YDS	TD	YPT	C%	FPTS
2023	17	1	6	0	136	103	1014	4	7.5	76%	231
PROJ	15	0	0	0	100	74	708	5	7.1	74%	171

55 CURTIS SAMUEL BUF · $1 · AGE 28 · BYE 12

Samuel signed with the Bills this offseason after showcasing versatility over the past two seasons with the Commanders. In 33 regular-season games, he hauled in 126 of 183 targets for 1,269 receiving yards and eight touchdowns, proving effective as both a receiver and a rusher. Now part of a Bills offense that ranked fourth in total yards per game and sixth in points scored per game with Josh Allen at QB, he has a clear path to targets, especially with Stefon Diggs and Gabe Davis departing this offseason. However, rookie Keon Coleman will also be actively involved. Samuel can be considered a flex option in deeper formats.

	G	CAR	YDS	TD	TGT	REC	YDS	TD	YPT	C%	FPTS
2023	16	7	39	1	92	62	613	4	6.7	67%	157
PROJ	15	13	65	1	90	63	643	4	7.1	69%	165

56 JAMESON WILLIAMS DET · $1 · AGE 23 · BYE 5

Williams returns as the WR2 behind Amon-Ra St. Brown in a critical third year with the Lions. Jamo has played only 18 of a possible 34 games in his young career with the Lions, with only 50 targets in that span. The former 12th overall pick is a dangerous playmaker who finished fourth in fantasy points per reception last season, but he'll need more volume if he's going to be attractive to fantasy managers. He carries breakout upside but also substantial risk if he doesn't see the necessary increase in opportunities. Williams is best viewed as a WR5/6 with big, but risky, upside.

	G	CAR	YDS	TD	TGT	REC	YDS	TD	YPT	C%	FPTS
2023	12	3	29	1	41	24	354	2	8.6	59%	80
PROJ	15	4	34	0	90	54	777	4	8.6	60%	162

57 XAVIER LEGETTE CAR · $1 · AGE 23 · BYE 11

The Panthers selected Legette with the 32nd pick in the draft, giving young QB Bryce Young another receiver to target in a retooled Carolina offense under coach Dave Canales. Veterans Adam Thielen and Diontae Johnson should still dominate targets for the Panthers, which will make it tough for the rookie to emerge this season, particularly in the early games. But Legette does have incredibly strong hands and a nice combination of both speed and power, which is why Carolina spent such a valuable pick on him. Given Young's inconsistency and the state of the team's offense last season, it's hard to see Legette breaking out as long as Thielen and Johnson are the preferred targets in front of him on the depth chart. He's a clear dynasty target and a player to keep an eye on during training camp for redraft leagues.

	G	CAR	YDS	TD	TGT	REC	YDS	TD	YPT	C%	FPTS
2023	0	0	0	0	0	0	0	0	0.0	0%	0
PROJ	15	6	39	0	88	55	724	4	8.3	62%	156

58 GABE DAVIS JAX · $1 · AGE 25 · BYE 12

Davis and Bills fans will always have that legendary four-score playoff performance to remember, but the future for this vertical threat has him donning teal and gold. The Jaguars boldly committed to Davis to add verticality to their playbook. Of the 111 NFL receivers with at least 100 total targets since the start of the 2021 season, he ranks second, with a robust 16.6 yards per reception. Speaking to the team's intentions with Davis, Trevor Lawrence ranks third in the NFL behind only Josh Allen and Tua Tagovailoa with 375 attempts of at least 10 air yards over the past two seasons. With the team investing heavily in fellow big-play threat Brian Thomas Jr. in the draft, it's worth wondering if Davis will see enough targets to deliver sustainable fantasy success.

	G	CAR	YDS	TD	TGT	REC	YDS	TD	YPT	C%	FPTS
2023	17	1	-2	0	80	45	746	7	9.3	56%	161
PROJ	15	0	0	0	94	52	797	6	8.5	56%	170

59 RASHID SHAHEED NO · $1 · AGE 26 · BYE 12

Shaheed is an intriguing breakout candidate in his third NFL season after primarily operating in a situational role during his first two campaigns. The 2022 UDFA posted the sixth-highest aDOT (14.4) among WRs last year, which led to a lot of big plays (five TDs, 15.6 YPR) but inconsistent production (five top-25 fantasy weeks, but no other finishes better than 45th). With Michael Thomas gone, Shaheed's top competition for New Orleans' No. 2 WR role behind Chris Olave is A.T. Perry, Cedrick Wilson and fifth-round rookie Bub Means. It's possible he never emerges as anything more than a boom/bust situational player, but his path to heavy usage makes him well worth a late-round flier.

	G	CAR	YDS	TD	TGT	REC	YDS	TD	YPT	C%	FPTS
2023	15	7	37	0	75	46	719	5	9.6	61%	156
PROJ	15	4	27	0	86	54	740	4	8.6	63%	159

60 DEMARIO DOUGLAS NE · $- · AGE 23 · BYE 14

Douglas is entering his second season with the Patriots. The passing game for New England struggled last season, which helps explain his failure to score a touchdown, but No. 3 overall pick Drake Maye could help change that in 2024. Douglas operated primarily from the slot, with 68% of his targets coming from there last season. From Week 7 on, he had a 21% target share and 25% air yards share, which was encouraging. He has a shot to lead the Patriots in targets, with Kendrick Bourne and rookie Ja'Lynn Polk the top competition. Douglas is worth a late-round flier.

	G	CAR	YDS	TD	TGT	REC	YDS	TD	YPT	C%	FPTS
2023	14	8	41	0	77	49	561	0	7.3	64%	107
PROJ	15	12	72	0	90	55	722	3	8.0	61%	155

61 ROMEO DOUBS GB · $- · AGE 24 · BYE 10

Doubs is back for his third season with the Packers. There were low expectations entering the 2023 season, but he continually showed a connection with Jordan Love and a knack for getting into the painted area. He had five games with at least 16 fantasy points and the fourth-most end zone targets among WRs. The biggest roadblock is the oft-injured Christian Watson, who relegates Doubs to the No. 3 WR when healthy. As only the fourth-best option in this Packers offense, Doubs checks in as bench material in fantasy.

	G	CAR	YDS	TD	TGT	REC	YDS	TD	YPT	C%	FPTS
2023	17	0	0	0	97	59	674	8	6.9	61%	174
PROJ	15	0	0	0	89	55	682	5	7.7	62%	155

62 JA'LYNN POLK NE · $- · AGE 22 · BYE 14

The Patriots did not select a traditional X receiver in the draft to address their biggest open spot within their receiver group, but Polk's consistency and ability to attack all three levels of the defense were attractive to New England. While the Patriots will look to revitalize their passing game with rookie quarterback Drake Maye, it would not be wise to expect Polk to receive steady targets. However, he doesn't have much competition for snaps, so the rookie is a fine late-round lottery ticket.

	G	CAR	YDS	TD	TGT	REC	YDS	TD	YPT	C%	FPTS
2023	0	0	0	0	0	0	0	0	0.0	0%	0
PROJ	15	0	0	0	84	51	636	3	7.6	61%	131

63 ADONAI MITCHELL IND · $- · AGE 21 · BYE 14

The Colts selected this big and rangy receiver in the second round of April's draft. The intent to deploy Mitchell on the outside as a field-stretcher appears clear, given a collegiate career average of 15.1 yards per catch across three seasons split between Georgia and Texas. Capable versus both man and press coverage, it further helps his case for starting snaps at the X that he placed in the 94th percentile among positional prospects in the 40-yard dash over the past 25 years, all while measuring at just above 6-foot-2. Target volume could hold him back from being a part of starting fantasy lineups early on, but the upside is clear for a player ideally matched for Anthony Richardson's rocket right arm.

	G	CAR	YDS	TD	TGT	REC	YDS	TD	YPT	C%	FPTS
2023	0	0	0	0	0	0	0	0	0.0	0%	0
PROJ	15	0	0	0	80	46	643	3	8.1	58%	130

64 QUENTIN JOHNSTON LAC · $- · AGE 22 · BYE 5

Few rookies disappointed to the degree that Johnston did in 2023, especially in light of the opportunity that injuries to Mike Williams and Keenan Allen provided. Among receivers with at least 50 targets, his 6.5 yards per target were ninth fewest, and his 57.6% catch and 13.2% big-play rates were significantly beneath the league's averages. Allen and Williams are now gone, expanding Johnston's opportunity, but bear in mind that he totaled 25.5 fantasy points in the four games Allen and Williams missed. Ladd McConkey's arrival presents another obstacle to a Johnston breakout, limiting him to late-round fantasy consideration.

	G	CAR	YDS	TD	TGT	REC	YDS	TD	YPT	C%	FPTS
2023	17	3	9	0	66	38	431	2	6.5	58%	94
PROJ	15	2	13	0	76	47	601	4	7.9	62%	131

65 JOSH PALMER LAC · $- · AGE 24 · BYE 5

Tasked with serving as the Chargers' No. 1 receiver more often than expected due to injuries for Mike Williams and Keenan Allen, Palmer delivered a pair of 100-yard performances and finished second on the team in receiving yards in 2023. Unfortunately, he was a top-30 positional scorer only three times, and he was limited to 10 games because of knee and concussion issues. Palmer could factor as a perimeter starter again, but that's more a of statement about the Chargers' lack of positional depth than his own talent. He's a depth piece for PPR formats who shouldn't be expected to provide any miracles.

	G	CAR	YDS	TD	TGT	REC	YDS	TD	YPT	C%	FPTS
2023	10	1	6	0	61	38	581	2	9.5	62%	107
PROJ	15	0	0	0	82	53	630	4	7.7	65%	139

66 BRANDIN COOKS DAL · $- · AGE 30 · BYE 7

Cooks averaged 10.8 fantasy points during his first season with the Cowboys, making him barely a top-50 fantasy WR, with the highlight being a surprising eight touchdown receptions. His overall production, however, was below expectations. The 30-year-old Cooks boasts six seasons with more than 1,000 receiving yards for four other franchises, but he has been held to less than 700 yards in consecutive seasons, a troubling trend. The Cowboys throw a lot—no team had more completions in 2023—but Cooks is no longer more than a reliable WR4 fantasy option, especially when his touchdown rate from last season regresses.

	G	CAR	YDS	TD	TGT	REC	YDS	TD	YPT	C%	FPTS
2023	16	5	35	0	81	54	657	8	8.1	67%	173
PROJ	15	4	26	0	86	57	667	5	7.8	67%	155

67 KENDRICK BOURNE NE · $- · AGE 29 · BYE 14

Bourne, entering his eighth season (his fourth with the Patriots), is returning from an ACL tear that sidelined him for the final nine games of last season. Despite New England's dreadful passing game in 2023, he managed to average 7.1 targets and 12.5 fantasy points per game. No. 3 overall pick Drake Maye is projected to be the Patriots' starting quarterback, and Bourne is a candidate to pace the team in targets. Bourne is a fine late-round selection.

	G	CAR	YDS	TD	TGT	REC	YDS	TD	YPT	C%	FPTS
2023	8	1	4	0	57	37	406	4	7.1	65%	100
PROJ	15	2	13	0	84	56	666	4	7.9	66%	145

68 MARVIN MIMS JR. DEN · $- · AGE 22 · BYE 14

A popular sleeper as a rookie, Mims caught 60- and 53-yard passes while returning a punt 45 yards in what appeared to be a breakthrough Week 2, only to be minimally used by Sean Payton over his next 14 games. Come year's end, he had run a route on only 37% of the Broncos' dropbacks despite placing 10th among wide receivers (minimum 30 targets) in aDOT (15.0) and 18th in big-play reception rate (27.3%). Following Jerry Jeudy's offseason trade to Cleveland, the path was seemingly clear for Mims to take over as the team's No. 2 target, though the selection of Troy Franklin, the signing of Josh Reynolds and the return of Tim Patrick tosses some cold water on the early excitement. Mims still has a path to a fantasy breakout, but he'll need to be sharp during the preseason to remain an attractive late-round pick.

	G	CAR	YDS	TD	TGT	REC	YDS	TD	YPT	C%	FPTS
2023	16	9	30	0	33	22	377	1	11.4	67%	71
PROJ	15	8	44	0	80	48	644	3	8.1	61%	142

69 KHALIL SHAKIR BUF · $- · AGE 24 · BYE 12

Now in his third year with the Bills, Shakir primarily operated from the slot last season, accumulating 91.5% of his receiving yards from that position. With Stefon Diggs traded and Gabe Davis moving to the Jaguars, Shakir has a clearer path to more targets in 2024. Though he's tied to a Josh Allen-led offense, he's projected to see the fourth-most targets behind Dalton Kincaid, Keon Coleman and Curtis Samuel. Shakir is not a priority pick in most leagues.

	G	CAR	YDS	TD	TGT	REC	YDS	TD	YPT	C%	FPTS
2023	17	1	10	0	46	39	611	2	13.3	85%	113
PROJ	15	0	0	0	73	52	614	3	8.4	71%	133

70 JOSH DOWNS IND · $- · AGE 23 · BYE 14

In a modern NFL rife with three-receiver sets, being deemed a slot maven isn't nearly as limiting as it once was. Downs, for instance, enters his second season building on a strong rookie showing that included finishing seventh in total fantasy points among first-year receivers in what was a strong class for the position. Designation as a slot option doesn't disqualify his potential to help fantasy managers at times in 2024, but it could signal a less exciting upper end of outcomes. Three-quarters of Downs' routes came from a slot alignment as a rookie, and it's likely we'll see similar deployment for the smaller receiver in his second campaign. With a limited ceiling in mind, Downs can be targeted in the later rounds of drafts.

	G	CAR	YDS	TD	TGT	REC	YDS	TD	YPT	C%	FPTS
2023	17	0	0	0	98	68	771	2	7.9	69%	157
PROJ	15	0	0	0	80	53	596	2	7.4	66%	126

Marvin Mims Jr.

71 JAHAN DOTSON WAS · $- · AGE 24 · BYE 14

The good news is that Dotson played more than 80% of Washington's snaps in his second season, but he scored more fantasy points as a rookie. Dotson surpassed 70 receiving yards in only one game—Week 8 against the struggling Eagles secondary—and that was the lone game in which he caught more than five passes. Sure, the Commanders lacked top quarterback play, but things are different now with Jayden Daniels leading the way. Dotson, a first-round pick from 2022, needs to prove himself again, especially with the Commanders investing in WR Luke McCaffrey too. Fantasy managers should not expect better than WR4 production.

	G	CAR	YDS	TD	TGT	REC	YDS	TD	YPT	C%	FPTS
2023	17	0	0	0	81	49	518	4	6.4	60%	125
PROJ	15	0	0	0	85	50	594	3	7.0	59%	125

72 RICKY PEARSALL SF · $- · AGE 23 · BYE 9

Pearsall is a favorite among metrics mavens, presenting with elite testing numbers that include burst and agility scores above the 95th percentile. He gives off Christian Kirk vibes, as he's likely best deployed via the slot, but he has the route savvy, strength and catch radius to successfully work all levels of the field. Pearsall is buried on the depth chart to begin his career but is one injury away from fantasy relevance. He's a wonderful fit for Kyle Shanahan's offense and is worth a late-round fantasy pick.

	G	CAR	YDS	TD	TGT	REC	YDS	TD	YPT	C%	FPTS
2023	0	0	0	0	0	0	0	0	0.0	0%	0
PROJ	15	5	29	0	46	29	385	3	8.4	63%	87

73 DEMARCUS ROBINSON LAR · $- · AGE 29 · BYE 6

After a one-year stint in Baltimore, Robinson arrived in Los Angeles, eventually working his way up the depth chart and emerging as the Rams' No. 3 WR. After drawing just a single target prior to the team's Week 10 bye, Robinson finished strong. Demonstrating his vertical ability, the 29-year-old posted double-digit fantasy points, finding the end zone or clearing 80 receiving yards from Weeks 13 through 17. Signed to a one-year deal worth $5 million, Robinson could find himself back on the fantasy radar if Puka Nacua or Cooper Kupp were to miss time in 2024. His big-play prowess could additionally provide late-round value to best-ball enthusiasts.

	G	CAR	YDS	TD	TGT	REC	YDS	TD	YPT	C%	FPTS
2023	16	1	23	0	38	26	371	4	9.8	68%	87
PROJ	15	0	0	0	88	58	700	4	8.0	66%	153

74 TYLER BOYD TEN · $- · AGE 29 · BYE 5

Boyd signed with the Titans during the offseason after spending his first eight NFL campaigns with the Bengals. He has been one of the league's best slot receivers over the past decade, but that hasn't translated to much fantasy upside. He was a top-20 scorer way back in in 2018-19 but has finished 36th or lower in fantasy PPG each of the past four seasons. That includes a 60th-place finish in 2023, in which he posted a career-low 6.8 average depth of target (eighth lowest among WRs). Still just 29, Boyd has something left in the tank, but same as in Cincinnati, he won't be a priority target in Tennessee with DeAndre Hopkins and Calvin Ridley leading the WR room. He is a low-ceiling bench option in PPR formats.

	G	CAR	YDS	TD	TGT	REC	YDS	TD	YPT	C%	FPTS
2023	17	2	11	0	98	67	667	2	6.8	68%	145
PROJ	15	2	11	0	83	58	573	2	6.9	69%	128

75 WAN'DALE ROBINSON NYG · $- · AGE 23 · BYE 11

Robinson's second NFL season went twice as well statistically as his first, as the Kentucky product led the team in receptions. The problem is he was not a threat down the field, averaging 8.8 yards per catch. He mainly handles slot duties, and if the Giants care to give him more rushing opportunities like the 49ers' Deebo Samuel [Robinson scored a rushing touchdown in Week 17], then we are interested. He earned nine rushes last season. Underwhelming quarterback play doesn't help, and the franchise investing in Malik Nabers early in Round 1 is a clear sign as well. Robinson is a former second-round pick the Giants would love to develop alongside Nabers, but the upside is muted, making him no more than a WR6.

	G	CAR	YDS	TD	TGT	REC	YDS	TD	YPT	C%	FPTS
2023	15	9	87	1	76	60	525	1	6.9	79%	133
PROJ	15	8	51	0	81	58	534	1	6.6	72%	125

76 JERMAINE BURTON CIN · $- · AGE 23 · BYE 12

Burton was selected in the third round of April's draft. He has the play strength to work through contact at multiple levels of the field, with the ability to separate at the third level due to his 4.45 speed. He is also a strong hands-catcher who can work on the boundary. He joins a highly talented [and crowded] wide receiver room in Cincinnati, where he'll be in a position to compete for the No. 3 role in the Bengals' offense. Burton has plenty of upside in dynasty formats with Tee Higgins slated to play this season on the franchise tag.

	G	CAR	YDS	TD	TGT	REC	YDS	TD	YPT	C%	FPTS
2023	0	0	0	0	0	0	0	0	0.0	0%	0
PROJ	15	0	0	0	72	47	562	4	7.8	65%	124

77 DJ CHARK JR. LAC · $- · AGE 27 · BYE 5

Chark signed with the Chargers after one-year stops in Detroit and Carolina the past two seasons. The 2018 second-round pick looked like a budding fantasy star when he posted a 73-1,008-8 receiving line in 2019, but he's struggled with injuries [zero career full seasons] and hasn't cleared 35 receptions or 525 yards in a season since 2020. The 27-year-old has a path to a major role in a wide-open Los Angeles WR room that also includes Quentin Johnston, Josh Palmer and rookie Ladd McConkey, but the most likely outcome is that the targets will be too few and far between to allow consistent fantasy production. The shaky depth chart and presence of Justin Herbert are just enough to make Chark worth late-round consideration.

	G	CAR	YDS	TD	TGT	REC	YDS	TD	YPT	C%	FPTS
2023	15	0	0	0	67	35	525	5	7.8	52%	116
PROJ	15	0	0	0	70	38	567	5	8.1	55%	123

78 ZAY JONES ARI · $- · AGE 29 · BYE 11

An injury-marred 2023 season makes it easy to forget Jones finishing 17th in receptions and 26th in total fantasy points among receivers in 2022 with the Jaguars. That big season reads like an outlier when you assess his seven-year run in the league, but it also offers evidence that relevant production can emerge if he gets the opportunity. After landing in Arizona, he will be behind Marvin Harrison Jr. and Trey McBride for targets, and he'll have to battle with Michael Wilson and maybe even Greg Dortch for looks as well. Keep an eye on training camp to see whether Jones is making his mark in his new surroundings, but even if he does, he's nothing more than a late-round pick in deeper formats.

	G	CAR	YDS	TD	TGT	REC	YDS	TD	YPT	C%	FPTS
2023	9	0	0	0	64	34	321	2	5.0	53%	78
PROJ	15	0	0	0	78	47	555	3	7.1	60%	122

79 RASHOD BATEMAN BAL · $- · AGE 24 · BYE 14

Bateman heads into his fourth pro season after playing in a career-high 16 games in 2023, yet he averaged just 4.8 PPG and produced only one game of 50 or more yards receiving. Drops have also been an issue [five last season], and he simply hasn't found the end zone enough [four career touchdowns]. As the third option in the Baltimore route tree behind tight end Mark Andrews and wide receiver Zay Flowers, you can bet on the talent, play strength and frame of Bateman, but only as a late-round flier.

	G	CAR	YDS	TD	TGT	REC	YDS	TD	YPT	C%	FPTS
2023	16	1	18	0	54	32	367	1	6.8	59%	77
PROJ	15	0	0	0	76	46	602	3	7.9	60%	121

80 MICHAEL WILSON ARI · $- · AGE 24 · BYE 11

Selected by the Cardinals in the third round of the 2023 NFL draft, Wilson flashed during his rookie campaign despite missing four weeks with a shoulder injury and while dealing with chaotic QB play. An excellent route-runner with impressive timing and awareness, the Stanford product demonstrated ace concentration and efficiency, recording a top-15 true catch rate [95%] and a +15.3 production premium [WR5]. His rapport with Kyler Murray also appeared to improve over the final weeks of the season, as Wilson closed things out by catching all six targets for a season-high 95 yards in Week 18. Marvin Harrison Jr. and Trey McBride are Murray's top targets, but Wilson figures to battle Zay Jones to be third in line and could serve as a fine late-round flier.

	G	CAR	YDS	TD	TGT	REC	YDS	TD	YPT	C%	FPTS
2023	13	0	0	0	56	38	565	3	10.1	68%	115
PROJ	15	0	0	0	72	48	556	3	7.7	66%	120

81 MALACHI CORLEY NYJ · $- · AGE 22 · BYE 12

Garrett Wilson and Mike Williams are locked into the top two spots in the Jets' WR room, but Corley, who was selected 65th overall in the draft, could emerge as the team's No. 3 receiver. He accumulated 2,277 yards and 22 touchdowns in his two final collegiate seasons at Western Kentucky. Corley figures to be third or fourth on the team in targets, with Wilson, Williams, Tyler Conklin and Breece Hall also in the mix. The "RAC King" should not be drafted in standard leagues but belongs on your watch list.

	G	CAR	YDS	TD	TGT	REC	YDS	TD	YPT	C%	FPTS
2023	0	0	0	0	0	0	0	0	0.0	0%	0
PROJ	15	9	54	0	56	39	439	3	7.9	70%	107

82 DONTAYVION WICKS GB · $- · AGE 23 · BYE 10

Wicks is back for his second season as the WR4 in Green Bay. Playing behind Christian Watson, Jayden Reed and Romeo Doubs last year, the former fifth-round pick showed flashes late, finishing top 20 at the position in Week 15 and top five in Week 18. Other than those two weeks, however, he was largely outside the top 40. He's talented, but he's clearly the fifth option [at best] in this offense. Wicks is a dynasty stash who doesn't need to be drafted in standard ESPN leagues.

	G	CAR	YDS	TD	TGT	REC	YDS	TD	YPT	C%	FPTS
2023	15	1	1	0	58	39	581	4	10.0	67%	120
PROJ	15	0	0	0	55	36	427	3	7.7	65%	95

83 ODELL BECKHAM JR. MIA · $- · AGE 31 · BYE 6

Beckham signed with the Dolphins after appearing in 14 regular-season games with Baltimore in 2023. He showed he still had something left in the tank by hitting for the occasional big play, but he also wasn't utilized much (his 49% snap share and 16% target share when active were both career lows). Beckham also missed three games and has been sidelined for at least three outings in four consecutive seasons. He is now 31 years old and hasn't scored more than six TDs in a season since 2016. He'll work as a situational player behind Tyreek Hill and Jaylen Waddle and would only be on the flex radar if one of those two were to miss time. Beckham is barely worth late-round consideration in deep leagues.

	G	CAR	YDS	TD	TGT	REC	YDS	TD	YPT	C%	FPTS
2023	14	0	0	0	64	35	565	3	8.8	55%	108
PROJ	14	0	0	0	57	32	468	3	8.2	56%	99

84 ELIJAH MOORE CLE · $- · AGE 24 · BYE 10

Heading into his fourth pro season, his second with the Browns, Moore posted career highs in receptions, targets and receiving yards last season. However, he averaged just 7.8 fantasy PPG and logged only five games with double-digit fantasy production. He has the ability to play in the slot or outside the numbers, and he can be schemed on manufactured touches. But with the Browns trading for Jerry Jeudy and both Amari Cooper and David Njoku commanding targets, Moore won't see enough volume to have consistent, week-to-week fantasy relevance. He's worth a late-round flier only.

	G	CAR	YDS	TD	TGT	REC	YDS	TD	YPT	C%	FPTS
2023	17	9	11	0	103	59	640	2	6.2	57%	132
PROJ	15	4	22	0	64	37	494	3	7.7	59%	105

85 DARIUS SLAYTON NYG · $- · AGE 27 · BYE 11

Slayton led the Giants in receiving yards last season, but 770 yards is hardly eye-popping. That said, it was the most the former Auburn speedster had amassed over five NFL campaigns. His best weeks were the final three games, as he averaged 86 receiving yards in that span (picking on the sputtering Eagles twice) and scored three of his four touchdowns. Slayton still offers the ability to stretch the field, but with top draft pick Malik Nabers joining the team and quarterback Daniel Jones unlikely to stretch the field, Slayton becomes forgettable. He hasn't caught more than 50 passes in any season, and 2024 figures to be more of the same, making him likely waiver-wire fodder.

	G	CAR	YDS	TD	TGT	REC	YDS	TD	YPT	C%	FPTS
2023	17	0	0	0	79	50	770	4	9.7	63%	151
PROJ	15	0	0	0	63	37	512	2	8.1	59%	100

86 JALIN HYATT NYG · $- · AGE 22 · BYE 11

Hyatt played in all 17 games as a rookie, but the third-round pick from Tennessee did little damage on his 41 targets, scoring nary a touchdown. He did, however, average 16.2 yards when he managed to catch the football, which would have been a top-10 mark in the league with more volume, and three catches went for more than 40 yards. The Giants covet explosive playmakers and utilized their top draft pick on Malik Nabers, a future star. Hyatt has the skills to shine, but fantasy managers should not expect top-50 fantasy wide receiver numbers.

	G	CAR	YDS	TD	TGT	REC	YDS	TD	YPT	C%	FPTS
2023	17	0	0	0	41	23	373	0	9.1	56%	60
PROJ	15	0	0	0	63	38	484	2	7.7	60%	99

87 RONDALE MOORE ATL · $- · AGE 24 · BYE 12

Moore had a disappointing campaign for the Cardinals last year, catching just 40 passes for 352 yards and one touchdown despite playing in every game. He'll get a fresh start in Atlanta playing for new coach Raheem Morris and with quarterback Kirk Cousins. He should be locked in as the WR3 for the Falcons, and if he can develop chemistry and a connection with Cousins, he should have a solid bounce-back season in Atlanta. The only question is, will there be enough footballs to feed to all the capable mouths the Falcons have now assembled offensively? Moore isn't worth drafting in most formats.

	G	CAR	YDS	TD	TGT	REC	YDS	TD	YPT	C%	FPTS
2023	17	28	178	1	63	40	352	1	5.6	63%	105
PROJ	15	8	51	0	58	42	429	3	7.4	72%	107

88 TREY PALMER TB · $- · AGE 23 · BYE 11

Palmer was a solid find by the Buccaneers in the sixth round of the 2023 NFL draft. The Nebraska product quickly earned slot duties between Mike Evans and Chris Godwin and proceeded to run 433 routes (45th among WRs) during his rookie campaign. Though he was on the field a fair share, Palmer wasn't a fantasy option, having cleared 51 yards and 8.8 fantasy points in only one game (Week 17). The 23-year-old has added competition for No. 3 duties this season in third-round rookie Jalen McMillan, which means he likely wouldn't be fantasy-viable even if Evans or Godwin were to miss time. Palmer is not worth considering on draft day.

	G	CAR	YDS	TD	TGT	REC	YDS	TD	YPT	C%	FPTS
2023	17	3	22	0	68	39	385	3	5.7	57%	96
PROJ	15	4	24	0	58	35	440	3	7.6	59%	98

89 JALEN MCMILLAN TB · $- · AGE 22 · BYE 11

The Buccaneers took McMillan with the 92nd pick of this year's draft. The University of Washington product had a nice showing at the NFL combine and should emerge as a No. 3 or No. 4 receiver option for Tampa Bay this season. But with veterans like Mike Evans, Chris Godwin and Trey Palmer in front of him on the depth chart, it's hard to imagine him having any kind of breakout campaign as a rookie. It would likely take multiple injuries to the aforementioned trio of teammates for McMillan to be worth using in fantasy this season.

	G	CAR	YDS	TD	TGT	REC	YDS	TD	YPT	C%	FPTS
2023	0	0	0	0	0	0	0	0	0.0	0%	0
PROJ	15	0	0	0	52	33	395	2	7.5	62%	87

90 ROMAN WILSON PIT · $- · AGE 23 · BYE 9

Wilson was selected in the third round of April's draft. The Michigan product is an inside target with the 4.39 speed to stress defenses on deep over routes and vertical concepts. He should man the slot for the Steelers in their three-wide receiver sets. He'll work the underneath levels, too, but look for offensive coordinator Arthur Smith to scheme up play-action shots for him to create big-play opportunities. With the expected volume for Steelers No. 1 wide receiver George Pickens and Smith's run-heavy approach, Wilson can be targeted as a late-round flier in deeper re-draft leagues, but he has more upside in dynasty formats.

	G	CAR	YDS	TD	TGT	REC	YDS	TD	YPT	C%	FPTS
2023	0	0	0	0	0	0	0	0	0.0	0%	0
PROJ	15	0	0	0	46	28	366	2	8.0	62%	76

TIGHT ENDS

The value of the TE continues to grow thanks to a crop of prolific newbies along with dependable veterans

BY LIZ LOZA
PLAYER PROJECTIONS
BY MIKE CLAY

TIGHT ENDS HAVE seemingly become the Renaissance men of the NFL. Tasked with mastering a wide variety of skills and techniques, the tight end position has evolved tremendously over the past decade. In 2023, TEs accounted for their largest share of total targets (21.4%), total receptions (22.5%) and total receiving yards (21.1%) in any of the past five seasons. A position that often felt full of busts appears to be booming now.

While that makes for creative offensive scheming and exciting on-field play, it can also be frustrating for fantasy managers. For a long time, phrases like "the tight end wasteland" and "rookie TEs don't produce in their first year" were widely accepted tropes. Those notions haven't been obliterated, as there's still some truth to both. However, more players are challenging the nature of these previously long-held beliefs.

Last season, a pair of rookies had tremendous seasons. Sam LaPorta burst onto the scene, managing an 86-889-10 stat line and finishing his freshman campaign as fantasy's TE1 in terms of total points. (Travis Kelce led in PPG.) Dalton Kincaid also put together a historic greenhorn effort, recording the fourth-most regular-season receptions (73) by a rookie tight end. And while Trey McBride wasn't a first-year player, he had remained a largely unknown commodity before emerging down the stretch to average nearly 11 fantasy points per game for the season (TE7).

Meanwhile, battle-tested vets are still posting big numbers. Kelce finished below 1,000 receiving yards for the first time in seven years but continued his dominant run at the position by averaging 14.6 fantasy points per game. Mark Andrews was limited to 10 games but was a force when he was on the field, registering the fifth-most fantasy points per game (13.5) while also leading the Ravens in receiving yards per contest (54.4). And George Kittle logged a career-best 11.3 yards per target and 15.7 yards per reception (both tops among TEs) while thriving as the 49ers' second-most-targeted option in the passing game. The "big three" may be beyond their fantasy peaks, but they're all prominent members of high-scoring offenses and, as a result, will likely come off draft boards by the end of Round 6.

Nabbing an elite fantasy producer at the position certainly offers managers an edge. Yet it's worth noting that 33 non-quarterbacks registered more fantasy points per game than Kelce in 2023. Given the aforementioned depth at the position, fantasy enthusiasts aren't faced with the same "all-or-nothing" dilemma of passing on a promising WR or RB in the hopes of securing the unequivocally most productive tight end. Plus, players like Kyle Pitts and Brock Bowers offer later-round upside, while someone like David Njoku presents a decent floor, allowing potential investors more wiggle room in the first half of their drafts.

Ultimately, the growth of the position has provided dependable second- and third-tier options. It is this collection of players that figures to deliver the healthiest return on investment relative to draft capital—and where savvy managers should focus their attention.

TIERED RANKINGS

Tiers allow you to identify players you should value similarly at various points of your draft.

RANK	PLAYER, TEAM	ROUND
1	SAM LAPORTA, DET	3
2	TRAVIS KELCE, KC	3
3	MARK ANDREWS, BAL	5/6
4	EVAN ENGRAM, JAX	6/7
5	TREY MCBRIDE, ARI	6/7
6	GEORGE KITTLE, SF	7
7	DAVID NJOKU, CLE	7/8
8	DALTON KINCAID, BUF	7/8
9	JAKE FERGUSON, DAL	9
10	KYLE PITTS, ATL	9
11	DALLAS GOEDERT, PHI	9/10
12	T.J. HOCKENSON, MIN	9/10
13	BROCK BOWERS, LV	13/14
14	DALTON SCHULTZ, NYG	13/14
15	PAT FREIERMUTH, HOU	14
16	COLE KMET, PIT	14
17	TYLER CONKLIN, CHI	14/15

ABOUT OUR PROJECTIONS: All are for a 17-game season, with some degree of player maintenance and injury risk factored in and then rounded up or down as appropriate. Player ages are as of Sept. 5, 2024.

Sam LaPorta

1 SAM LAPORTA DET · $30 · AGE 23 · BYE 5

LaPorta is back as the Lions' starting tight end after putting together a historic rookie season that saw him finish the season as TE1. LaPorta and Jared Goff immediately hit it off, with the former Iowa star becoming a trusted target and ranking top five in routes, targets, receptions, receiving yards, touchdowns and end zone targets, as well as finishing second in team target share. Fantasy managers can expect more of the same in 2024 with the Lions returning the majority of their starting offense. LaPorta should be the top tight end off the board on draft day.

	G	CAR	YDS	TD	TGT	REC	YDS	TD	YPT	C%	FPTS
2023	17	1	4	0	121	86	889	10	7.3	71%	239
PROJ	15	0	0	0	119	84	861	7	7.3	71%	210

2 TRAVIS KELCE KC · $29 · AGE 34 · BYE 6

The stats back Kelce as best tight end in fantasy football history. He has 2,116.7 points since 2016, by far the most any tight end has scored over an eight-year period, and he has six positional first-place finishes in that span, never finishing worse than third. Still, Kelce's detractors cite his 10.6 yards per reception and 12.9% big-play rates from 2023, both the worst of his NFL career. We counter that the Chiefs' problems at wide receiver put oodles of pressure on him to perform and made it easier for opponents to defend him. Kelce's days of being a mid-first-round pick and virtual TE1 lock might be behind him, but he's still Patrick Mahomes' go-to guy and plenty capable of a 2023 repeat.

	G	CAR	YDS	TD	TGT	REC	YDS	TD	YPT	C%	FPTS
2023	15	0	0	0	121	93	984	5	8.1	77%	219
PROJ	15	2	1	0	108	83	836	7	7.8	77%	209

Travis Kelce

3 MARK ANDREWS BAL · $12 · AGE 28 · BYE 14

Still in his prime playing years, Andrews heads into his seventh season with the Ravens. He played in only 10 games last season (ankle), but he averaged 13.5 PPG while seeing 14 red zone targets. Andrews is a natural seam stretcher with the frame to win contested catches, and he will continue to be a prime option for quarterback Lamar Jackson as a middle-of-the-field option with third-level ability on schemed concepts. Andrews is a top-three player at the position.

	G	CAR	YDS	TD	TGT	REC	YDS	TD	YPT	C%	FPTS
2023	10	1	0	0	62	45	544	6	8.8	73%	135
PROJ	15	0	0	0	107	74	819	7	7.7	69%	198

4 EVAN ENGRAM JAX · $9 · AGE 30 · BYE 12

Can Engram match an awesome 2023 that saw him finish just two catches shy of Jimmy Smith's single-season franchise record for receptions? Adding to the historic nature of last season, Engram also produced the fewest yards ever for a player with at least 114 catches. His constant command of Trevor Lawrence's attention led to a career year in which he finished as TE2. Gone are Calvin Ridley's 137 targets from last season, so Engram is again set for a sizable stake in this passing game in 2024. Even with some regression possible in the target and reception departments, he is the rare early-round tight end in fantasy with an entirely reasonable projection for at least 120 looks in this offense.

	G	CAR	YDS	TD	TGT	REC	YDS	TD	YPT	C%	FPTS
2023	17	0	0	0	143	114	963	4	6.7	80%	230
PROJ	15	0	0	0	118	87	787	3	6.7	73%	183

5 TREY MCBRIDE ARI · $9 · AGE 24 · BYE 11

McBride put together a breakout sophomore effort, leading all Arizona pass-catchers in targets (108), receptions (81) and yards (825). The Colorado State product averaged more than eight targets per contest from Weeks 8 through 18 after Zach Ertz was placed on injured reserve and eventually waived. McBride quickly earned Kyler Murray's trust, drawing a team-high five end zone looks and recording a catch rate of 80% over the final eight games of the season. He figures to remain an integral part of the Cardinals' aerial attack heading into 2024.

	G	CAR	YDS	TD	TGT	REC	YDS	TD	YPT	C%	FPTS
2023	17	0	0	0	108	81	825	3	7.6	75%	182
PROJ	15	0	0	0	112	83	796	3	7.1	74%	183

6 GEORGE KITTLE SF · $6 · AGE 30 · BYE 9

Despite experiencing a dip in overall efficiency, Kittle buoyed his fantasy stock by scoring 11 TDs in 2022. A regression was therefore anticipated heading into 2023. His TDs did, in fact, decline (with three of his six scores occurring in Week 5), but the 30-year-old still posted a top-five positional fantasy finish, recording a career high in yards per target (11.3) and yards per reception (15.7), both best among TEs. While Kittle was second on the team in targets (behind Brandon Aiyuk), his week-to-week volume fluctuated, presenting a frustrating conundrum for fantasy managers. His do-it-all skill set combined with the depth of pass-catchers in the 49ers' offense figures to lead to boom-or-bust play again in 2024.

	G	CAR	YDS	TD	TGT	REC	YDS	TD	YPT	C%	FPTS
2023	16	1	2	0	90	65	1020	6	11.3	72%	203
PROJ	15	0	0	0	88	63	846	5	9.6	71%	175

23 LUKE MUSGRAVE GB · $- · AGE 24 · BYE 10

Musgrave is back with the Packers for his sophomore campaign after finishing as TE31 last season. He began 2023 as the starter but put up only two top-13 weeks in his first 10 games before missing six weeks with a lacerated kidney. Despite being a talented tight end, the former second-rounder is buried in the pecking order behind a plethora of young WRs and his fellow TE Tucker Kraft. Musgrave should not be drafted in 2024.

	G	CAR	YDS	TD	TGT	REC	YDS	TD	YPT	C%	FPTS
2023	11	0	0	0	46	34	352	1	7.7	74%	75
PROJ	15	0	0	0	47	34	338	2	7.1	72%	80

24 NOAH FANT SEA · $- · AGE 26 · BYE 10

Fant was a red zone stalwart at Iowa but has failed to fully break out since joining the NFL, never once cracking the top-10 fantasy TEs in his five years as a pro. Coming off of a career-low campaign, it seemed the 26-year-old was destined to land on a new team in free agency. Interestingly, however, the Seahawks opted to sign him to a two-year contract while parting ways with Will Dissly and Colby Parkinson. That figures to keep the intrigue surrounding Fant alive for at least one more season. Likely the fourth option in Ryan Grubb's scheme, he won't draw enough looks for weekly consideration, but his ever-present potential provides TE2 upside for streaming purposes.

	G	CAR	YDS	TD	TGT	REC	YDS	TD	YPT	C%	FPTS
2023	17	0	0	0	43	32	414	0	9.6	74%	73
PROJ	15	0	0	0	62	46	458	2	7.4	74%	103

25 CADE OTTON TB · $- · AGE 25 · BYE 11

Otton is entering his third season with the Buccaneers. The 2022 fourth-round pick has settled in as a solid player, but without much fantasy upside. He posted a 42-391-2 receiving line on 66 targets as a rookie and saw the slightest of upticks in all four categories in 2023. Otton runs a lot of routes (he's fourth in the category since he was drafted), but he won't see enough of Baker Mayfield's targets to vault him into the TE1 discussion. He's a low-ceiling TE2.

	G	CAR	YDS	TD	TGT	REC	YDS	TD	YPT	C%	FPTS
2023	17	0	0	0	69	47	455	4	6.6	68%	117
PROJ	15	0	0	0	65	43	456	3	7.0	66%	110

26 HAYDEN HURST LAC · $- · AGE 31 · BYE 5

A 2018 first-rounder who has one positional top-20 fantasy season in his career (2020, 10th) and has finished outside the top 30 in four of six years, Hurst struggled through a miserable 2023 with the Panthers. He committed as many drops (two) as he had in his previous five seasons combined, caught 56.3% of his passes and continued to battle injuries, missing the final eight games with a concussion. Hurst reunited with offensive coordinator Greg Roman during the offseason, where he could serve as the Chargers' pass-catching tight end. But between Will Dissly providing competition and Hurst's injury history, he's a dicey pick in standard ESPN leagues.

	G	CAR	YDS	TD	TGT	REC	YDS	TD	YPT	C%	FPTS
2023	9	0	0	0	32	18	184	1	5.8	56%	42
PROJ	15	0	0	0	60	41	393	3	6.6	69%	99

27 JONNU SMITH MIA · $- · AGE 29 · BYE 6

Now in his eighth season and first with the Dolphins, Smith joins an offense that ranked No. 1 in total yards last year. While Tua Tagovailoa led the league in passing, the majority of the yards came from Tyreek Hill and Jaylen Waddle. With Hill and Waddle projected to continue as the primary targets, Smith's fantasy prospects are limited, especially considering the Dolphins' strong running game with De'Von Achane and Raheem Mostert, who will score a fair share of touchdowns. Given the returning key playmakers for 2024, fantasy managers should consider Smith as no more than a TE3.

	G	CAR	YDS	TD	TGT	REC	YDS	TD	YPT	C%	FPTS
2023	17	1	0	0	70	50	582	3	8.3	71%	124
PROJ	15	2	2	0	46	32	370	2	8.0	68%	83

28 DAWSON KNOX BUF · $- · AGE 27 · BYE 12

Knox enters his sixth year with the Bills. This offseason, he reworked his contract to free up additional cap space for Buffalo. After Dalton Kincaid became a major factor in the offense in 2023, Knox's role in the offense declined. He also missed five games with a wrist injury. Last season's 186 receiving yards represented a big dip after consecutive seasons with 500-plus yards and a total of 15 touchdowns. It's hard to see him having a major offensive role unless Kincaid misses time, so Knox shouldn't be drafted in most fantasy leagues.

	G	CAR	YDS	TD	TGT	REC	YDS	TD	YPT	C%	FPTS
2023	12	0	0	0	37	22	186	2	5.0	59%	55
PROJ	15	0	0	0	45	29	323	3	7.2	64%	82

29 JELANI WOODS IND · $- · AGE 25 · BYE 14

A recurrent hamstring injury cost Woods his 2023 campaign, yet reports suggest he's on track to contribute to the offense as he embarks on his third season with the Colts. Not only did this 6-foot-7 tight end reach the end zone on his first two career catches as a rookie, he converted 16 first downs on his 25 catches in 2022. The Colts have leaned on a frustrating committee approach at the position for several seasons, including Shane Steichen's first year at the helm. If the team pivots to instead consolidate work in Woods' favor, the ingredients for a sleeper season are present. It further helps that the team didn't pick a tight end in the draft. Speculating on Woods will only require a very late investment in most drafts.

	G	CAR	YDS	TD	TGT	REC	YDS	TD	YPT	C%	FPTS
2023	0	0	0	0	0	0	0	0	0.0	0%	0
PROJ	15	0	0	0	48	32	350	2	7.3	67%	81

30 DANIEL BELLINGER NYG · $- · AGE 23 · BYE 11

Bellinger is back for his third season with the Giants. The 2022 fourth-round pick hasn't been utilized much in the passing game, though he's a candidate for slightly more work this season, following Darren Waller's retirement. With Waller sidelined for five games last season, Bellinger played 87% of the snaps and posted an 11-138-0 receiving line on 12 targets. Rookie Theo Johnson could quickly overtake Bellinger on the depth chart, so there's simply not much fantasy appeal here, especially in an offense that is expected to struggle.

	G	CAR	YDS	TD	TGT	REC	YDS	TD	YPT	C%	FPTS
2023	17	0	0	0	28	25	255	0	9.1	89%	51
PROJ	15	0	0	0	46	35	292	1	6.3	76%	72

31 TYLER HIGBEE LAR · $- · AGE 31 · BYE 6

With Cooper Kupp and Puka Nacua vying for looks, Higbee recorded his fewest number of targets per game (4.7) as a member of the Matthew Stafford era. In fact, two of his four double-digit fantasy outings came while Kupp was sidelined at the top of the season. Higbee also struggled near the end zone, posting two TDs, both of which came in the same game at Arizona. A rebound appears unlikely for the 31-year-old, especially given that he's likely to miss time after tearing his ACL and MCL this past January.

	G	CAR	YDS	TD	TGT	REC	YDS	TD	YPT	C%	FPTS
2023	15	0	0	0	70	47	495	2	7.1	67%	109
PROJ	11	0	0	0	49	33	348	2	7.0	68%	77

32 BEN SINNOTT WAS · $- · AGE 22 · BYE 14

The Commanders invested a second-round pick on Sinnott in this year's draft, and there is instant opportunity for him to shine with only veteran Zach Ertz, entering his age-33 season, in his way on the depth chart. Sinnott led Kansas State in receiving yards and touchdown receptions, and he shined at the combine, showing speed and fluid movement. Rookie tight ends can be risky in fantasy, especially when paired with a rookie quarterback (Jayden Daniels), but Sinnott has the skills to be an instant TE2 if given the opportunity.

	G	CAR	YDS	TD	TGT	REC	YDS	TD	YPT	C%	FPTS
2023	0	0	0	0	0	0	0	0	0.0	0%	0
PROJ	15	0	0	0	45	30	312	2	7.0	68%	72

33 COLBY PARKINSON LAR · $- · AGE 25 · BYE 6

With Tyler Higbee's availability in question (knee), the Rams added Parkinson, inking the Stanford product to a three-year deal worth $22.5 million. He split TE snaps with Will Dissly and Noah Fant in Seattle last season, running a paltry 13.6 routes per game (TE38) and drawing fewer than two looks per contest (TE41). A better blocker than he is a receiver (particularly in the passing game), Parkinson is unlikely to deliver anything better than streaming value, even if he does emerge as the Rams' TE1.

	G	CAR	YDS	TD	TGT	REC	YDS	TD	YPT	C%	FPTS
2023	17	0	0	0	33	25	247	2	7.5	76%	62
PROJ	15	0	0	0	44	31	305	2	7.0	71%	76

34 GREG DULCICH DEN · $- · AGE 24 · BYE 14

Head coach Sean Payton's arrival, coupled with the reemergence of the hamstring issues that cost Dulcich seven games as a rookie, presented him with insurmountable obstacles as a sophomore. Payton brought in Adam Trautman, one of his tight ends from New Orleans, to provide competition, while Dulcich got hurt in the season opener, only to suffer a season-ending setback 11 snaps into his Week 6 return. When healthy, he offers greater field-stretching potential than a typical tight end—his 10.6 aDOT from 2022-23 was second best among tight ends (minimum 50 targets)—but he'd need a huge preseason to emerge as more than an in-season pickup.

	G	CAR	YDS	TD	TGT	REC	YDS	TD	YPT	C%	FPTS
2023	2	0	0	0	4	3	25	0	6.3	75%	6
PROJ	15	0	0	0	46	29	329	1	7.2	63%	70

35 ZACH ERTZ WAS · $- · AGE 33 · BYE 14

Ertz signed a one-year contract with the Commanders, reuniting with former Cardinals coach Kliff Kingsbury, now Washington's offensive coordinator. Ertz, 33, is no longer the player he used to be with the Eagles, succumbing to age and a serious knee injury in recent seasons. However, he was on pace to exceed 50 catches for last season's Cardinals before his November release, and he was in line to replace the departed Logan Thomas before the Commanders drafted Ben Sinnott in the second round. There is mild target opportunity for Washington's tight ends, but Sinnott is the future for the franchise at TE.

	G	CAR	YDS	TD	TGT	REC	YDS	TD	YPT	C%	FPTS
2023	7	0	0	0	40	27	187	1	4.7	68%	52
PROJ	15	0	0	0	48	30	289	2	6.0	63%	72

36 ISAIAH LIKELY BAL · $- · AGE 24 · BYE 14

As Likely enters his third pro season, his fantasy ceiling is tied to the health of teammate Mark Andrews. In the six late-season games Likely started with Andrews out (ankle), he averaged 13.9 PPG from Weeks 12 through 18, including three games of 18 or more points. However, in the games with Andrews on the field (Weeks 2 through 11), he averaged only 1.7 PPG. He's able to uncover, and he's slippery after the catch, but as long as Andrews is in the mix, Likely simply doesn't carry enough fantasy value to be drafted.

	G	CAR	YDS	TD	TGT	REC	YDS	TD	YPT	C%	FPTS
2023	17	0	0	0	41	30	411	5	10.0	73%	101
PROJ	15	0	0	0	35	24	264	2	7.5	67%	63

37 MICHAEL MAYER LV · $- · AGE 23 · BYE 10

The learning curve for tight ends at the NFL level can be lengthy, and Mayer's 2023 season was representative of that. He began playing sparingly behind Austin Hooper, but over his final nine games, he played 82% of the Raiders' offensive snaps, averaging 21.8 routes, 3.9 targets and 6.9 fantasy points per game, before a toe issue cost him the season's final three weeks. That might have been a stepping stone to bigger things for Mayer, but the team added free agent Harrison Bryant, then drafted Brock Bowers 13th overall in April, greatly clouding the sophomore's 2024 outlook. On a skills basis, Mayer possesses plenty of upside, but he might need a change of scenery to claim the playing time needed to be fantasy-relevant.

	G	CAR	YDS	TD	TGT	REC	YDS	TD	YPT	C%	FPTS
2023	14	0	0	0	40	27	304	2	7.6	68%	71
PROJ	15	0	0	0	39	27	283	1	7.2	69%	63

38 MIKE GESICKI CIN · $- · AGE 28 · BYE 12

The seventh-year pro posted uninspiring numbers in New England last season, averaging 3.8 fantasy points per game and scoring only two touchdowns. In Cincinnati, Gesicki will get an upgrade with quarterback Joe Burrow, as he plays the role of the primary pass-catching tight end in 11 personnel sets. Given the receving volume that wide receivers Ja'Marr Chase and Tee Higgins will demand this season, however, Gesicki has a limited fantasy ceiling and shouldn't be drafted.

	G	CAR	YDS	TD	TGT	REC	YDS	TD	YPT	C%	FPTS
2023	17	0	0	0	43	29	244	2	5.7	67%	65
PROJ	15	0	0	0	36	24	244	2	6.7	66%	62

Michael Mayer

39 JOHNNY MUNDT MIN · $- · AGE 29 · BYE 6

With T.J. Hockenson recovering from a torn ACL suffered in Week 16 last season, Mundt is poised to work as Minnesota's starting tight end to begin 2024. We saw this usage during the final two games of 2023, and Mundt delivered receiving lines of 4-39-1 and 5-58-0 on 13 total targets. Both showings were enough for top-12 fantasy production. The 29-year-old is a sneaky bet for fringe TE1 production early in the season, though he'll return to clear backup duties once Hockenson is back on the field. Only consider drafting him in leagues that start two tight ends.

	G	CAR	YDS	TD	TGT	REC	YDS	TD	YPT	C%	FPTS
2023	17	0	0	0	23	17	172	1	7.5	74%	40
PROJ	15	0	0	0	30	21	197	1	6.6	70%	48

40 NOAH GRAY KC · $- · AGE 25 · BYE 6

Gray is back for his fourth season with the Chiefs. Travis Kelce's primary backup, he has recorded almost identical stats each of the past two seasons, posting a 28-299-1 receiving line in 2022 and 28-305-2 line in 2023. Gray is obviously without stand-alone fantasy value, but he's a name to know should Kelce miss time. Kelce was out in Week 1 last season, and while Gray had a fairly quiet game, he played 87% of the snaps and was targeted five times. Gray should not be drafted, but scoop him up if Kelce is ever sidelined.

	G	CAR	YDS	TD	TGT	REC	YDS	TD	YPT	C%	FPTS
2023	17	1	1	0	44	28	305	2	6.9	64%	71
PROJ	15	0	0	0	41	29	288	2	7.0	69%	71

41 WILL DISSLY LAC · $- · AGE 28 · BYE 5

A quality blocker who has had his moments in the receiving game, Dissly was swiftly scooped up by Jim Harbaugh's Chargers only days after his release by the Seahawks. In L.A., Dissly will certainly be more role player than fantasy standout, although he could contribute a useful game or two, especially in weeks where Hayden Hurst or Donald Parham Jr. (or both) is sidelined. Something to tuck away as you plan your weekly matchups: Dissly is a noted hot starter, having caught eight of his 13 career touchdowns in the month of September.

	G	CAR	YDS	TD	TGT	REC	YDS	TD	YPT	C%	FPTS
2023	16	0	0	0	22	17	172	1	7.8	77%	40
PROJ	15	0	0	0	38	30	266	1	7.0	79%	65

42 GERALD EVERETT CHI · $- · AGE 30 · BYE 7

Entering his eighth season, Everett joins the Bears after spending the past two with the Chargers. His highest fantasy finish was TE12 in 2022, when he was the lone tight end in a Justin Herbert-led offense. In Chicago, he'll play second fiddle to Cole Kmet and will instead catch passes from Caleb Williams, a clear downgrade in situations. While Everett is still talented, he is not worth drafting in fantasy.

	G	CAR	YDS	TD	TGT	REC	YDS	TD	YPT	C%	FPTS
2023	15	3	10	0	70	51	411	3	5.9	73%	111
PROJ	15	2	2	0	28	20	181	1	6.5	70%	46

43 THEO JOHNSON NYG · $- · AGE 23 · BYE 11

The Giants selected Johnson in the fourth round of April's draft. The Penn State product stands 6-foot-6, 259 pounds and showed his ability with a dominant combine, which included a class-best 119 speed score (4.57 40-yard dash). Following the retirement of Darren Waller, Johnson joins a depth chart that includes the likes of Daniel Bellinger and Chris Manhertz. Bellinger figures to get the early-season starts, but Johnson has a real opportunity to pace the unit in targets. Expectations should always be kept in check for rookie tight ends (especially those drafted on Day 3 in shaky offenses), so Johnson should be targeted in dynasty leagues only.

	G	CAR	YDS	TD	TGT	REC	YDS	TD	YPT	C%	FPTS
2023	0	0	0	0	0	0	0	0	0.0	0%	0
PROJ	15	0	0	0	35	24	233	1	6.7	69%	55

KICKERS

Accuracy (obviously) matters here, but there are a range of other variables to consider at your draft

BY ERIC MOODY
PLAYER PROJECTIONS
BY MIKE CLAY

KICKERS ARE OFTEN an afterthought in fantasy football. That's mostly because their fantasy output is very difficult to predict from week to week, and that variance is why it's not worth your time to select one until the final two rounds of your draft.

Last season, just 37 fantasy points separated the No. 1 kicker (Brandon Aubrey) from No. 10 (Blake Grupe). As an example of the weekly variance, consider Cameron Dicker, who tied for seventh-most points among kickers last season. He scored five or fewer points five times, but he scored 12 or more fantasy points five times. Since you can't predict how many field goals a kicker will make in a given week—which obviously drives up the point total—it's best to choose kickers with a high floor.

Streaming is a popular strategy for finding a quality option on the waiver wire each week during the season. When drafting kickers or considering streaming options, here are a few things to think about:

▶ **Target a kicker from a team with a high-powered offense.** While field goal attempts may be difficult to forecast, pinpointing teams with the highest expected point totals in a given week can provide a safe floor for the kicker's fantasy output, with the potential for a big day if/when the offense bogs down in an opponent's territory. Your kicker can't score fantasy points if his team can't cross the 50-yard line. Last year, seven of the top 11 NFL teams in points per game also had a kicker finish in the top 11 in fantasy points.

▶ **Identify teams that struggle in the red zone.** While real-life NFL teams

Justin Tucker

crave a touchdown and six points, fantasy managers prefer their kickers to have a field goal attempt worth three or more points instead of a point after a touchdown. Identifying teams that consistently struggle inside the red zone can make a difference. Cairo Santos (tied for second), Harrison Butker (fifth), Jason Myers (sixth) and Cameron Dicker (tied for seventh) all finished seventh or better among fantasy kickers last season, but their respective teams ranked 15th or worse in scoring. No team scored fewer touchdowns than the Jets last season, yet their kicker (Greg Zuerlein) was the No. 12 kicker in fantasy—despite missing a game—because he was one off the NFL lead with 35 field goals made.

▶ **Prioritize accuracy, leg strength.** While demanding accuracy from your kicker would seem to be obvious—there's nothing quite like rostering a kicker, like Justin Tucker, who is nearly automatic inside 50 yards—it's important to know which kickers have historically been successful from 50 or more yards out, since most leagues award more points for longer kicks. Last season, Aubrey was a remarkable 10-for-10 on attempts of 50+ yards. If you're seeking a larger sample size, Chris Boswell is the only kicker to make at least six from that distance in each of the past three seasons.

▶ **Dome kickers serve as good tiebreakers.** The three factors above are much more reliable indicators of potential fantasy success, but taking a kicker who plays at least half his games in a climate-controlled environment can be a useful tiebreaker when you're having a hard time choosing between kickers.

Not into streaming? If you don't want to spend time managing the position, you can simply pick a kicker whose bye week comes in the latter half of the season. This will help you avoid hitting the waiver wire for at least a couple of months, and when the bye week arrives, you can pick up another kicker whose bye has already passed.

▶ **Don't draft a kicker, if your league rules allow.** Some sites don't make you fill out your entire starting lineup during the draft. If that's the case in your league, you can draft another flex-eligible player. This affords you the opportunity to evaluate another player's potential role before you must decide which player to drop once you're forced to grab a kicker for Week 1.

ABOUT OUR PROJECTIONS: All are for a 17-game season, with some degree of player maintenance and injury risk factored in and then rounded up or down as appropriate. Player ages are as of Sept. 5, 2024.

1 HARRISON BUTKER KC · $1 · AGE 29 · BYE 6

After missing four games due to an ankle injury in 2022 and posting the worst field goal accuracy numbers of his NFL career, Butker rebounded in a big way for the eventual Super Bowl champions. He set a personal best with his 94.3% field goal success rate and was a perfect 12-for-12 on his attempts of 40 yards or greater. Butker returns as the placekicker for one of the game's most potent offenses, a prerequisite for the position, which makes him one of the top options in the draft.

	G	XP	XP%	FG	FG%	0-39	40-49	50+	FPTS
2023	17	38/38	100%	33/35	94%	21/23	7/7	5/5	153
PROJ	17	49/50	97%	28/32	88%	16/17	7/9	5/7	146

2 BRANDON AUBREY DAL · $1 · AGE 29 · BYE 7

He was the NFL's leading scorer last season with 157 points and 180 fantasy points and an unprecedented story. Aubrey played soccer at Notre Dame and two seasons of pro soccer before becoming a traditional kicker in the USFL. The Cowboys took a chance and enjoyed a league-leading 36 field goals, including an NFL-record 35 straight, to begin his career, and an historic 10-of-10 from 50 yards and beyond. He should see ample opportunities for extra points and field goals thanks to a high-volume offense.

	G	XP	XP%	FG	FG%	0-39	40-49	50+	FPTS
2023	17	49/52	94%	36/38	95%	22/24	4/4	10/10	180
PROJ	17	42/43	98%	29/33	89%	17/17	8/9	5/7	142

3 JUSTIN TUCKER BAL · $1 · AGE 34 · BYE 14

One of the league's most consistent placekickers, with the leg strength to drive the ball on deeper attempts, Tucker logged 155 fantasy points last season (second most in the league) while converting on 86.5% of field goals and hitting 98.1% of his extra point attempts. Surprisingly, he struggled from 50-plus yards in 2023, converting just one of five attempts. Given his track record, however, plus the opportunities he will get from Baltimore's prolific offense, Tucker remains a top-five fantasy kicker.

	G	XP	XP%	FG	FG%	0-39	40-49	50+	FPTS
2023	17	51/52	98%	32/37	86%	20/20	11/12	1/5	155
PROJ	17	44/45	97%	29/32	88%	16/17	7/9	5/7	142

4 JAKE ELLIOTT PHI · $1 · AGE 29 · BYE 5

Elliott's seventh NFL season was his most accurate, and it included a career-best seven field goals of 50 yards or more. He also reached 44 extra points made for the third consecutive season. He doesn't always get the volume of his peers, thanks to Philadelphia's red zone efficiency and desire to go for it (and succeed) on fourth downs. He signed a four-year contract extension and figures to be one of the most reliable, safe kickers yet again. Elliott won't be the first kicker off the board, but he definitely belongs in the top 10.

	G	XP	XP%	FG	FG%	0-39	40-49	50+	FPTS
2023	17	45/46	98%	30/32	94%	16/17	7/7	7/8	155
PROJ	17	43/44	98%	29/32	89%	17/17	8/9	5/7	144

5 GREG ZUERLEIN NYJ · $1 · AGE 36 · BYE 12

Zuerlein is entering his third season with the Jets. He made 35 of 38 field goals last season, his most accurate campaign (92.1%) since 2017. The Jets struggled without Aaron Rodgers under center, finishing the 2023 season ranked 31st in total yards and 29th in points scored per game. With Rodgers back under center in 2024, the Jets should be much better on offense, which will give Zuerlein a considerably higher scoring floor. He should be viewed as a top-10 fantasy kicker.

	G	XP	XP%	FG	FG%	0-39	40-49	50+	FPTS
2023	16	15/16	94%	35/38	92%	17/18	13/14	5/6	140
PROJ	17	43/45	97%	28/32	87%	16/17	7/9	5/7	141

6 KA'IMI FAIRBAIRN HOU · $1 · AGE 30 · BYE 14

A gifted kicker entering his eighth season with the Texans, Fairbairn was limited to a dozen regular-season games last season due to a quad injury. While active, he averaged 2.3 field goal attempts per game, a pace that would have seen him finish third in the NFL had he sustained it over a full schedule. Tied to an ascendant Houston offense and with a leg that merits trust from all over the field from his coaching staff, it makes sense to consider Fairbairn among the better fantasy options at this often fickle position.

	G	XP	XP%	FG	FG%	0-39	40-49	50+	FPTS
2023	12	21/22	95%	27/28	96%	20/20	2/2	5/6	113
PROJ	17	41/42	98%	29/33	88%	17/17	8/9	5/7	140

7 EVAN MCPHERSON CIN · $1 · AGE 25 · BYE 12

McPherson converted 83.9% of field goal attempts last season while hitting seven of 12 from 50-plus yards. He was perfect on extra points, and he finished the season with 135 fantasy points. With a healthy Joe Burrow back to lead an explosive Bengals offense, McPherson should produce top-10 numbers this season.

	G	XP	XP%	FG	FG%	0-39	40-49	50+	FPTS
2023	17	40/40	100%	26/31	84%	11/11	8/8	7/12	135
PROJ	17	42/43	96%	28/33	87%	16/17	7/9	5/7	139

8 JAKE MOODY SF · $1 · AGE 24 · BYE 9

Moody gained notoriety after converting all 148 extra points at Michigan, eventually becoming the first kicker selected in the 2023 NFL draft. The heir to Robbie Gould's uprights, he made good on 21 of 25 field goal attempts (84%) while nailing all but one extra point (60 of 61 attempts) during his rookie campaign. Tied to an elite scoring offense, Moody is capable of posting top-five fantasy numbers at the position.

	G	XP	XP%	FG	FG%	0-39	40-49	50+	FPTS
2023	17	60/61	98%	21/25	84%	15/16	4/6	2/3	127
PROJ	17	47/50	93%	27/32	84%	16/17	7/9	4/7	139

9 CAMERON DICKER LAC · $1 · AGE 24 · BYE 5

Dicker has been quite a find for the Chargers, who scooped him up off waivers in mid-2022. In 28 games, he has converted all but three field goal attempts, including a perfect 45-for-45 on kicks shorter than 50 yards, and he hasn't missed any of his 59 extra-point attempts. Dicker was seventh in total fantasy points and ninth in top-10 weekly performances in 2023. He'll serve in the same capacity in 2024 for a run-heavy Chargers offense that might find itself in an advantageous number of field goal situations.

	G	XP	XP%	FG	FG%	0-39	40-49	50+	FPTS
2023	17	35/35	100%	31/33	94%	15/15	9/9	7/9	149
PROJ	17	38/39	98%	29/33	89%	17/17	8/9	5/7	138

10 CAIRO SANTOS CHI · $1 · AGE 32 · BYE 7

Santos finished tied for second-best kicker in fantasy in 2023, and he has made better than 90% of his FGs in three of his past four seasons. The Bears used the No. 1 overall pick on Caleb Williams and have put a plethora of talent around him, hoping to ignite their offense. But growing pains should be expected, so Santos may have some additional opportunities. It's not a foregone conclusion, but the Bears are set up to be a more potent offense in 2024, which makes Santos a fringe starting kicker in fantasy.

	G	XP	XP%	FG	FG%	0-39	40-49	50+	FPTS
2023	17	31/33	94%	35/38	92%	20/20	8/10	7/8	155
PROJ	17	38/38	98%	29/33	88%	17/17	8/9	5/7	137

DEFENSE & SPECIAL TEAMS

Your best bet when drafting a D/ST unit is to wait as long as possible—and keep an eye on the offenses they face each week

BY TRISTAN H. COCKCROFT
PROJECTIONS BY MIKE CLAY

DEFENSE DOES *NOT* WIN fantasy football championships.

In fantasy, few positions are a bigger waste of precious draft resources than defense. You should wait until the final two or three rounds of your draft, and arguably the final round, to select your defense. This is due to the position's week-to-week statistical volatility, the influence weekly matchups have upon scoring and, perhaps most important, our collective difficulty, at least during the preseason, in predicting just *what* makes a great defense.

This strategy might come as a surprise to those who remember 2023 as a higher-scoring year for fantasy D/STs. Yes, last season saw the Cowboys and Ravens defenses score 172 fantasy points to tie for the positional lead, the first time since 2017 that two D/STs managed at least that many points in a season. The collective point total by the top-10 fantasy D/STs was also the highest since that same 2017 campaign.

Value in fantasy football, however, revolves around performance relative to replacement level, meaning what is available on your league's waiver wire. As position-wide scoring increases, so does the productivity of said replacement level. Last season, the Cowboys and Ravens scored 45 fantasy points more than the No. 11 D/ST. With 10 D/STs in a standard league's lineup each week, that would be the first one on the sidelines and presumably available in free agency.

To compare that to the lowest scoring of the skill positions last season (tight end), those 45 points paled in comparison to the 57.8 points that separated the No. 1 and No. 7 tight ends.

As for the difficulty determining what makes a "great" defense, our collective track record picking the No. 1 unit is spotty at best. In the past five seasons, the D/ST selected first averaged 7.66 fantasy points per game and delivered a top-10 weekly positional score 47% of the time. Top-three D/STs in ADP, meanwhile, averaged 6.43 points per game and had a top-10 point total 42% of the time.

To compare, the D/STs that finished in the top three over the past five seasons averaged 9.21 fantasy points and had a top-10 weekly score 59% of the time. And most important, this group had a positional ADP of 11.9.

The upshot? Stream D/STs weekly. Had you decided to pick the defense that faced only the Jets last season, you'd have totaled 30 more fantasy points than either the Cowboys or Ravens. In fact, had you picked on the Panthers, Giants, Patriots or Commanders instead of the Jets, you'd *still* have outscored the Cowboys and Ravens for the season.

Determining this year's terrible offense is obviously the challenge. But for 2024, the Patriots, Giants, Broncos, Titans and Commanders appear likely to be offenses against which to stream. Target them as opponents for your early-season D/STs, and rest assured, we'll have much more advice on the topic in our "D/ST Roadmap" at espn.com/fantasy during the season.

D/ST RANKINGS

The top 10 teams for 2024.

RANK	TEAM
1	CLEVELAND BROWNS
2	DALLAS COWBOYS
3	NEW YORK JETS
4	BALTIMORE RAVENS
5	SAN FRANCISCO 49ERS
6	PITTSBURGH STEELERS
7	MIAMI DOLPHINS
8	JACKSONVILLE JAGUARS
9	NEW ORLEANS SAINTS
10	CINCINNATI BENGALS

Cleveland's defense rocks

ABOUT OUR PROJECTIONS: All are for a 17-game season, with some degree of player maintenance and injury risk factored in and then rounded up or down as appropriate. Player ages are as of Sept. 5, 2024.

1 CLEVELAND BROWNS $1 · BYE 10

The Browns finished as the No. 3 D/ST last season (9.8 PPG) while ranking top 10 in sacks and interceptions. This is an aggressive scheme under defensive coordinator Jim Schwartz, one that held opposing offenses to only 4.5 yards per play, the lowest in the league. Led by elite pass rusher Myles Garrett with playmakers Jeremiah Owusu-Koramoah and Denzel Ward on the back end, the Browns should again be an elite fantasy defense during the 2024 season.

	TD	INT	FR	SK	PPG	YPG	FPTS
2023	3	18	10	49	19.3	270.2	166
PROJ	3	14	9	46	18.5	318.7	141

2 DALLAS COWBOYS $1 · BYE 7

The Cowboys D/ST finished tied for first in fantasy points in 2023 (with the Ravens), extending a strong three-year run coinciding with the drafting of dominant edge Micah Parsons, now a three-time Pro Bowler. Dallas led the league in fantasy points in 2021 and was fourth in 2022. The Cowboys forced 26 turnovers last season and scored seven touchdowns. That rate figures to regress, but the Cowboys should deliver another strong fantasy campaign, perhaps the best in the league once again.

	TD	INT	FR	SK	PPG	YPG	FPTS
2023	7	17	9	46	18.2	299.7	172
PROJ	2	13	9	46	19.4	328.6	131

3 NEW YORK JETS $1 · BYE 12

The Jets finished as the No. 4 D/ST last season, averaging 9.4 points per game. New York's defense was great despite its offensive woes. The team allowed 292.3 total yards per game, the third fewest in the league, and also gave up only 20.1 points per game, which ranked 12th. Most of their key defensive players return, and the Jets' offense should be better with Aaron Rodgers back under center, which will keep the defense a bit fresher. This Jets defense should be targeted as one of the top fantasy units.

	TD	INT	FR	SK	PPG	YPG	FPTS
2023	4	17	10	48	20.1	292.3	159
PROJ	3	15	9	41	19.1	331.4	131

4 BALTIMORE RAVENS $1 · BYE 14

The Ravens are going through a transition after the departure of coordinator Mike Macdonald, but new defensive playcaller Zach Orr takes over a unit that averaged 10.1 fantasy PPG last season (tied for the most with Dallas) while leading the league in sacks and points allowed per game (15.8). Using a mix of coverage and disguised pressure, the Ravens have talent at all three levels of the field, with defensive tackle Justin Madubuike, linebacker Roquan Smith and safety Kyle Hamilton leading the way.

	TD	INT	FR	SK	PPG	YPG	FPTS
2023	2	18	13	60	15.8	301.4	172
PROJ	3	15	9	46	19.8	331.4	130

5 SAN FRANCISCO 49ERS $1 · BYE 9

While not as staunch as in previous years, the 49ers D/ST remained a formidable unit in 2023, tallying 48 sacks and 22 INTs and allowing the fourth-fewest completions of 40+ yards (five). San Francisco's defensive line experienced a good amount of turnover this offseason, losing Arik Armstead, Chase Young and Javon Kinlaw while adding Leonard Floyd, Yetur Gross-Matos and Maliek Collins. The team also addressed the secondary via the draft, adding DBs in the second and fourth rounds.

	TD	INT	FR	SK	PPG	YPG	FPTS
2023	1	22	6	48	17.2	303.9	136
PROJ	3	15	9	43	19.3	333.7	126

6 PITTSBURGH STEELERS $1 · BYE 9

Pittsburgh checked in as the No. 11 D/ST last season and finished just outside of the top 10 in sacks and interceptions. The Steelers feature one of the best edge rushing combos in the NFL with T.J. Watt (league-best 19 sacks) and Alex Highsmith, and the addition of linebacker Patrick Queen elevates the second level of the defense. With Minkah Fitzpatrick anchoring the secondary and a pressure-oriented scheme that can heat up the pocket, the Steelers project as a top-10 fantasy defense in 2024.

	TD	INT	FR	SK	PPG	YPG	FPTS
2023	2	16	11	47	19.1	342.1	127
PROJ	3	13	9	44	20.1	328.3	128

7 MIAMI DOLPHINS $1 · BYE 6

The Dolphins D/ST finished 2023 as the No. 7 unit, averaging 8.2 PPG. Miami ranked third in sacks and 10th in total yards allowed, but new defensive coordinator Anthony Weaver has some holes to fill since Christian Wilkins, Raekwon Davis, Jerome Baker and others are gone. To fill the void, the Dolphins added Jordan Poyer, Shaq Barrett and others in the offseason. Following the purge of so many players, Miami gave Weaver a blank canvas. Even so, the Dolphins can still be considered a top-10 fantasy defense.

	TD	INT	FR	SK	PPG	YPG	FPTS
2023	4	15	12	56	21.6	318.3	139
PROJ	3	13	9	41	20.0	334.6	117

8 JACKSONVILLE JAGUARS $1 · BYE 12

Save for the emergence of the recently extended linebacker Josh Allen, a series of high-end draft investments along the front seven the past few seasons has failed to pay significant dividends for Jacksonville. New defensive coordinator Ryan Nielsen tended to favor man coverage looks while running the Falcons' defense, an ask that could put pressure on a Jaguars secondary that struggled last season. Allen, along with a gifted tandem of linebackers, will be tasked with carrying out Nielsen's attacking scheme.

	TD	INT	FR	SK	PPG	YPG	FPTS
2023	2	16	11	40	21.5	342.8	105
PROJ	3	13	9	42	20.7	332.1	118

9 NEW ORLEANS SAINTS $1 · BYE 12

The Saints D/ST finished as the 10th best in fantasy last season on the strength of 29 takeaways (fourth most in the NFL) and three touchdowns. The mountains were high (six weeks with at least 12 fantasy points) and the valleys were low (seven weeks with four or fewer points), and many of their top players are getting long in the tooth, which is cause for concern. But if they can stay healthy and improve the pass rush (34 sacks ranked tied for 28th), this unit may have another top-10 run in the tank.

	TD	INT	FR	SK	PPG	YPG	FPTS
2023	3	18	11	34	18.5	327.2	129
PROJ	3	14	9	40	20.2	335.3	114

10 CINCINNATI BENGALS $1 · BYE 12

The Bengals produced just 5.4 fantasy points per game last season (24th at D/ST) while surrendering a league high in both yards per play (6.1) and yards per pass attempt (8.2). The club added defensive tackle Sheldon Rankins in free agency, as well as safety Geno Stone after he logged seven interceptions in Baltimore last season. That's a boost for proven defensive coordinator Lou Anarumo. However, the Bengals will need to limit opposing offenses at a much higher rate to be considered a borderline top-10 fantasy defense.

	TD	INT	FR	SK	PPG	YPG	FPTS
2023	2	17	9	44	22.2	374.6	91
PROJ	3	14	9	45	20.6	338.7	116

INDIVIDUAL DEFENSIVE PLAYERS

When making your IDP selections, target players who get the most opportunities for snaps and tackles

BY JIM McCORMICK
PROJECTIONS BY MIKE CLAY

CHANGE HAS BEEN a constant in fantasy football. Many leagues have adapted along with the sport, and incorporating individual defensive players (IDP) is a dynamic way to gamify the gridiron. IDP leagues present a shift from the sometimes vague volatility of outcomes for team defenses and instead focus on quantifying specific defensive contributions. Imagine not accurately accounting for a 14-catch Justin Jefferson opus. This is akin to allowing a dominant 15-tackle Fred Warner outing to go unrecognized.

Organizing players as defensive linemen, linebackers and defensive backs is the conventional positional approach. ESPN's IDP rankings rely on a scoring key that seeks to value volume-driven stats, such as tackles and assists, as well as scarcer splash plays, such as sacks and takeaways. Here are some tips to identify and roster the most consistently productive defenders on the field.

▶ **Tackles and snaps fuel fantasy fun.** When it comes to skill players, we covet opportunities. These materialize in the form of snaps, routes, targets and carries. On defense, opportunity rates similarly surface in snap counts, as being on the field is a prerequisite for statistics. Of the seven defensive backs who accrued at least 190 fantasy points last season, five ranked in the top 12 in total snaps at the position, and all were in the top 35. All of these DBs were safeties, as only a few cornerbacks crack the top tier in fantasy points each season. At linebacker, topping 130 total tackles is a demand to be considered in the LB1 tier. On the defensive line, 60 tackles and double-digit sacks have become essential thresholds. Big plays still matter, just as touchdowns do on offense, but it all starts with having surpassed a high threshold of tackle production.

In each of the three position groups, we naturally focus on players who rarely take their helmets off. There can be exceptions with certain edge players who are elite at getting to the pocket, but the best path to prolific fantasy production remains every-down, high-volume tackle talents.

▶ **Target elite linebackers.** Linebackers accounted for 18 of the top 20 (and 38 of the top 50) tackle leaders in 2023. This also matches the eye test, as Warner, Roquan Smith and the ageless Bobby Wagner embody the archetype of a position that places them around the ball on nearly every run down or short-yardage passing play. Star-level linebackers can be viewed as comparable to every-down running backs or 100-catch receivers.

▶ **Patience pays.** On draft day, it's savviest to wait on defensive selections until you've developed a strong offensive core. While it's certainly important to build your roster via the draft, it will need some tweaking throughout the season. It's also vital to not invest too early or at too high a price. Netting at least one elite defensive lineman and top-tier linebacker as mid-to-late-round priorities can prove prudent. This also rings true for the handful of special defensive backs, such as Antoine Winfield Jr. and Jessie Bates III.

TOP 30 DEFENSIVE PLAYERS

Overall fantasy ranking for all three positions.

RANK	PLAYER
1	ERNEST JONES IV, LAR (LB)
2	FOYESADE OLUOKUN, JAX (LB)
3	MAXX CROSBY, LV (DL)
4	BOBBY OKEREKE, NYG (LB)
5	T.J. WATT, PIT (DL)
6	ZAIRE FRANKLIN, IND (LB)
7	ROQUAN SMITH, BAL (LB)
8	FRED WARNER, SF (LB)
9	LAVONTE DAVID, TB (LB)
10	MICAH PARSONS, DAL (DL)
11	KHALIL MACK, LAC (DL)
12	ANTOINE WINFIELD JR., TB (DB)
13	JOSH ALLEN, JAX (DL)
14	DANIELLE HUNTER, HOU (DL)
15	T.J. EDWARDS, CHI (LB)
16	E.J. SPEED, IND (LB)
17	AIDAN HUTCHINSON, DET (DL)
18	MYLES GARRETT, CLE (DL)
19	NICK BOLTON, KC (LB)
20	TERREL BERNARD, BUF (LB)
21	BOBBY WAGNER, WAS (LB)
22	CAMRYN BYNUM, MIN (DB)
23	JESSIE BATES III, ATL (DB)
24	AZEEZ AL-SHAAIR, HOU (LB)
25	QUINCY WILLIAMS, NYJ (LB)
26	DERRICK BROWN, CAR (DL)
27	BRIAN BURNS, NYG (DL)
28	BRIAN BRANCH, DET (DB)
29	DERWIN JAMES JR., LAC (DB)
30	QUAY WALKER, GB (LB)

ABOUT OUR PROJECTIONS: All are for a 17-game season, with some degree of player maintenance and injury risk factored in and then rounded up or down as appropriate. Player ages are as of Sept. 5, 2024.

How do IDP leagues work?

You start various individual defenders based on your league's setup and adhere to a specific scoring key. An easy way to format IDP rosters could be starting two players at each positional group while also establishing two flex spots, thus asking teams to start eight defenders each week.

ESPN's default scoring key is as follows:

- **Solo tackle:** 1.5 points
- **Assisted tackle:** 0.75 points
- **Tackle for loss:** 2 points
- **Sack:** 4 points
- **Interception:** 5 points
- **Forced fumble:** 4 points
- **Fumble recovery:** 4 points
- **Defensive TD:** 6 points
- **Safety:** 2 points
- **Pass defensed:** 1.5 points

Rams linebacker Ernest Jones IV

DEFENSIVE LINEMEN

1 MAXX CROSBY LV · AGE 27 · BYE 10

Only James Harrison's 2008 DPOY campaign matches Crosby's blend of tackles, sacks and forced fumbles from last season. He's a true peer of T.J. Watt in fantasy terms.

	G	SNAP	TKL	SOLO	AST	SK	INT	FF	FPTS
2023	17	1037	90	55	35	14.5	0	2	228
PROJ	17	989	82	50	32	11.5	0	2	200

2 T.J. WATT PIT · AGE 29 · BYE 9

Not only has he paced the league in sacks in three of the past four years, Watt also just tied a career high in tackles. No. 90 should be one of the first defenders off the board in nearly any format.

	G	SNAP	TKL	SOLO	AST	SK	INT	FF	FPTS
2023	17	883	68	48	20	19	1	4	252
PROJ	17	835	63	39	25	13	0	3	193

3 MICAH PARSONS DAL · AGE 25 · BYE 7

No one registered more pressures on passers than Parsons last season. If those doubles convert into homers at a higher clip, we could see a 20-sack season emerge from this relentless rusher.

	G	SNAP	TKL	SOLO	AST	SK	INT	FF	FPTS
2023	17	818	64	36	28	14	0	1	178
PROJ	17	880	67	41	26	14.5	0	1	184

4 KHALIL MACK LAC · AGE 33 · BYE 5

Mack just netted his best statistical effort in his 10th NFL season. New defensive coordinator Jesse Minter loves to create chaos with shifting fronts, upping the excitement for Year 11.

	G	SNAP	TKL	SOLO	AST	SK	INT	FF	FPTS
2023	17	902	74	57	17	17	0	5	243
PROJ	17	776	60	36	23	9	0	3	169

5 JOSH ALLEN JAX · AGE 27 · BYE 12

Allen erupted last season, leading to a massive new contract and momentum for another special season. Like Nick Bosa, Allen was near the top in nearly every meaningful pressure metric.

	G	SNAP	TKL	SOLO	AST	SK	INT	FF	FPTS
2023	17	852	66	43	23	17.5	1	2	200
PROJ	17	859	65	40	26	10.5	0	2	173

6 DANIELLE HUNTER HOU · AGE 29 · BYE 14

While durability was once a real concern, Hunter has played every game the past two seasons and was one of only six linemen to log 1,000 snaps last season.

	G	SNAP	TKL	SOLO	AST	SK	INT	FF	FPTS
2023	17	1,006	83	54	29	16.5	0	4	234
PROJ	17	820	67	41	26	9	0	3	172

7 AIDAN HUTCHINSON DET · AGE 24 · BYE 5

Hutch was third among linemen in total snaps and joined Parsons as the only players with at least 100 pressures last season. He has validated lofty draft status in both real and fantasy terms.

	G	SNAP	TKL	SOLO	AST	SK	INT	FF	FPTS
2023	17	935	51	36	15	11.5	1	3	175
PROJ	17	969	56	34	22	10.5	0	2	162

8 MYLES GARRETT CLE · AGE 28 · BYE 10

The reigning DPOY was second only to Parsons in ESPN's pass rush win rate metric among edge players last season, and second only to Watt in total sacks the past three seasons.

	G	SNAP	TKL	SOLO	AST	SK	INT	FF	FPTS
2023	16	766	42	33	9	14	0	4	171
PROJ	17	852	52	32	20	12	0	3	170

9 DERRICK BROWN CAR · AGE 26 · BYE 11

On the field for 89% of the Panthers' defensive snaps, the highest of any interior lineman last season, Brown also led the position in run stop win rate. Another 100-tackle effort is viable.

	G	SNAP	TKL	SOLO	AST	SK	INT	FF	FPTS
2023	17	905	103	57	46	2	1	0	156
PROJ	17	963	99	51	47	5	0	0	151

10 BRIAN BURNS NYG · AGE 26 · BYE 11

The requisite ingredients are present for Burns to deliver his best statistical season yet as he joins a deep and talented Giants front seven after five seasons in Carolina.

	G	SNAP	TKL	SOLO	AST	SK	INT	FF	FPTS
2023	16	782	50	32	18	8	0	1	137
PROJ	17	918	60	36	23	9	0	1	159

11 JADEVEON CLOWNEY CAR · AGE 31 · BYE 11

A quietly stellar season in Baltimore included tying his career high in sacks while ranking fifth among edge defenders in pass rush win rate. With potential to get back to the 800-snap range in Carolina, Clowney could flirt with DL1 results.

	G	SNAP	TKL	SOLO	AST	SK	INT	FF	FPTS
2023	17	621	43	24	19	9.5	0	2	126
PROJ	17	779	50	31	20	13	0	2	151

12 NICK BOSA SF · AGE 26 · BYE 9

Even though his sack tally dipped last season, advanced metrics reveal continued dominance from the baby Bosa. After all, he was third in pressures, second in QB hits and fourth in hurries. Buy the dip.

	G	SNAP	TKL	SOLO	AST	SK	INT	FF	FPTS
2023	17	779	53	34	19	10.5	0	2	157
PROJ	17	833	56	34	22	10	0	2	154

13 JONATHAN GREENARD MIN · AGE 27 · BYE 6

Swapping teams and roles with Houston's Hunter, Greenard could build on last season's sack binge as the main edge menace in Brian Flores' pressure-driven defensive scheme.

	G	SNAP	TKL	SOLO	AST	SK	INT	FF	FPTS
2023	15	594	52	36	16	12.5	0	1	153
PROJ	17	724	57	34	22	10	0	1	151

14 BYRON YOUNG LAR · AGE 26 · BYE 6

An older rookie with an atypical path to the pros, Young thrived in his first season with the Rams due to rare success collapsing opposing pockets. If he can sustain such production sans Aaron Donald, Young makes for a savvy sleeper.

	G	SNAP	TKL	SOLO	AST	SK	INT	FF	FPTS
2023	17	917	61	42	19	8	0	2	137
PROJ	17	922	61	37	24	7	0	2	141

15 MICHAEL HOECHT LAR · AGE 26 · BYE 6

The rare Brown University product in the NFL, Hoecht thrived off the edge for the Rams last season, finishing among the positional leaders in tackles.

	G	SNAP	TKL	SOLO	AST	SK	INT	FF	FPTS
2023	17	908	77	43	34	6	0	1	135
PROJ	17	759	62	38	24	5	0	1	126

16 ALEX HIGHSMITH PIT · AGE 27 · BYE 9

Would you believe Highsmith actually tallied 14 more pressures last season than in his 14.5-sack breakout in 2022? This signals he's due for a positive correction in getting to QBs this season.

	G	SNAP	TKL	SOLO	AST	SK	INT	FF	FPTS
2023	17	867	57	34	23	7	2	2	141
PROJ	17	857	57	35	22	9	0	2	142

17 HAROLD LANDRY III TEN · AGE 28 · BYE 5

Consecutive seasons with at least 70 tackles and double-digit sack production merits acclaim and attention from fantasy investors. Creative alignments via first-time coordinator Dennard Wilson could be a boon.

	G	SNAP	TKL	SOLO	AST	SK	INT	FF	FPTS
2023	17	804	70	45	25	10.5	0	0	156
PROJ	17	793	65	39	25	8	0	1	144

18 TREY HENDRICKSON CIN · AGE 29 · BYE 12

Hendrickson is fifth in sacks since joining the Bengals three seasons ago and 10th among ends in pass rush win rate following last year's career-best output.

	G	SNAP	TKL	SOLO	AST	SK	INT	FF	FPTS
2023	17	714	43	28	15	17.5	0	3	172
PROJ	17	731	43	26	17	12	0	3	149

19 MONTEZ SWEAT CHI · AGE 28 · BYE 7

It's not often that a midseason deal reveals such success as Sweat's arrival in Chicago did. Regarded as a quality run-stopper off the edge, Sweat's emergence as a double-digit sack artist opens a new level of fantasy fun.

	G	SNAP	TKL	SOLO	AST	SK	INT	FF	FPTS
2023	17	738	57	38	19	12.5	0	3	167
PROJ	17	752	54	33	21	9	0	2	144

20 DEFOREST BUCKNER IND · AGE 30 · BYE 14

This versatile inside lineman joined Crosby and Hunter as the only players with at least 80 tackles, eight sacks and two forced fumbles last season.

	G	SNAP	TKL	SOLO	AST	SK	INT	FF	FPTS
2023	17	817	81	45	36	8	0	2	177
PROJ	17	776	71	37	34	7	0	1	139

21 JONATHON COOPER DEN · AGE 26 · BYE 14

One of just eight players with at least 70 tackles and eight sacks last season, Cooper enters his fourth pro season with a viable path to 900 snaps as one of Denver's top edge rushers.

	G	SNAP	TKL	SOLO	AST	SK	INT	FF	FPTS
2023	17	794	70	43	27	8.5	1	1	161
PROJ	17	759	64	39	25	7	0	1	133

22 KAYVON THIBODEAUX NYG · AGE 23 · BYE 11

One of seven players to produce at least 50 tackles, 11 sacks and three forced fumbles in 2023, Thibodeaux should see a rewarding increase in one-on-one matchups, given the arrival of Brian Burns.

	G	SNAP	TKL	SOLO	AST	SK	INT	FF	FPTS
2023	17	947	50	26	24	11.5	0	3	149
PROJ	17	874	50	30	20	8	0	2	139

23 MATTHEW JUDON NE · AGE 32 · BYE 14

In just four appearances before a season-ending injury, Judon averaged a sack per game and had multiple QB hits in each outing. Risks are likely baked in, creating the potential for surplus value.

	G	SNAP	TKL	SOLO	AST	SK	INT	FF	FPTS
2023	4	177	13	10	3	4	0	0	45
PROJ	17	753	54	33	21	9	0	1	139

24 SAM HUBBARD CIN · AGE 29 · BYE 12

He's logged a snap rate of at least 75% in each of the past five years, averaging 64 tackles and six sacks during this span. Expect another high-floor outcome.

	G	SNAP	TKL	SOLO	AST	SK	INT	FF	FPTS
2023	15	686	58	38	20	6	0	0	118
PROJ	17	785	62	38	24	7	0	1	134

LINEBACKERS

1 ERNEST JONES IV LAR · AGE 24 · BYE 6

One of just two players to compile at least 140 tackles and four sacks last season, Jones will rock the green dot for Chris Shula's aggressive defensive scheme in 2024.

	G	SNAP	TKL	SOLO	AST	SK	INT	FF	FPTS
2023	15	887	145	74	71	4.5	0	0	219
PROJ	17	998	157	95	62	4.5	1	1	256

2 FOYESADE OLUOKUN JAX · AGE 29 · BYE 12

A rich extension means the player with the most tackles over the past two seasons will continue to chase down ball carriers at an absurd clip for Jacksonville. And he's also a potent pass rusher.

	G	SNAP	TKL	SOLO	AST	SK	INT	FF	FPTS
2023	17	1075	173	111	62	2.5	1	1	275
PROJ	17	1020	159	96	63	2	1	1	238

3 BOBBY OKEREKE NYG · AGE 28 · BYE 11

Fears of Okereke's production dipping after shifting teams were answered in his first season with the Giants, which included career highs in sacks, passes defended and forced fumbles.

	G	SNAP	TKL	SOLO	AST	SK	INT	FF	FPTS
2023	17	1091	149	92	57	2.5	2	4	254
PROJ	17	1038	141	86	56	3	2	3	243

4 ZAIRE FRANKLIN IND · AGE 28 · BYE 14

Last season, Franklin became just the eighth player since 1987 to produce at least 179 tackles and more than one sack. Expect another big season as a fixture of the Colts' front seven.

	G	SNAP	TKL	SOLO	AST	SK	INT	FF	FPTS
2023	16	1055	179	107	72	1.5	0	2	244
PROJ	17	1013	165	100	65	1	1	2	238

5 ROQUAN SMITH BAL · AGE 27 · BYE 14

With more than one sack in each NFL season and nearly 500 tackles across the past three years, Smith embodies sideline-to-sideline playmaking at the position.

	G	SNAP	TKL	SOLO	AST	SK	INT	FF	FPTS
2023	16	1019	158	84	74	1.5	1	1	219
PROJ	17	1018	157	95	62	2.5	1	1	237

6 FRED WARNER SF · AGE 27 · BYE 9

A high weekly floor fueled by one of the most stable tackle rates meets elite ball-hawking in coverage. Warner's All-Pro status in three of the past four seasons includes a bevy of big plays.

	G	SNAP	TKL	SOLO	AST	SK	INT	FF	FPTS
2023	17	932	132	82	50	2.5	4	4	235
PROJ	17	1015	144	87	57	2	2	3	238

7 LAVONTE DAVID TB · AGE 34 · BYE 11

Taken 11 picks after Bobby Wagner in 2012, David joins his peer with a Canton-bound résumé and continuously prolific production deep into his career, remaining a special fantasy option.

	G	SNAP	TKL	SOLO	AST	SK	INT	FF	FPTS
2023	15	920	134	86	48	4.5	0	1	229
PROJ	17	975	140	85	55	3	1	2	237

8 T.J. EDWARDS CHI · AGE 28 · BYE 7

After joining the Bears in free agency last offseason, Edwards continued to shine. He is one of five players with at least 300 tackles and four sacks across the past two seasons.

	G	SNAP	TKL	SOLO	AST	SK	INT	FF	FPTS
2023	17	1008	153	90	63	2.5	3	1	246
PROJ	17	1020	152	92	60	2.0	1	1	233

9 E.J. SPEED IND · AGE 29 · BYE 14

Seventy-six percent of Speed's tackles last season were of the more valuable solo variety. With an anticipated uptick in snap rate, he might just be one of the better sleepers in 2024.

	G	SNAP	TKL	SOLO	AST	SK	INT	FF	FPTS
2023	16	702	100	76	24	1	0	3	178
PROJ	17	969	138	83	54	2	1	3	234

10 NICK BOLTON KC · AGE 24 · BYE 6

Injuries limited Bolton in 2023, but an awesome playoff run reminded us that in 2022, Bolton became one of just three players since 2000 to have 180 tackles and two sacks. Bet on a big year.

	G	SNAP	TKL	SOLO	AST	SK	INT	FF	FPTS
2023	8	423	60	38	22	0	1	0	85
PROJ	17	1018	153	93	60	2	1	0	225

11 TERREL BERNARD BUF · AGE 25 · BYE 12

The list of seasons with at least 140 tackles, 6.5 sacks and three interceptions includes Lavonte David's 2013 opus and Bernard's last year. He has entered the LB1 club.

	G	SNAP	TKL	SOLO	AST	SK	INT	FF	FPTS
2023	17	943	143	84	59	6.5	3	0	251
PROJ	17	989	145	88	57	3	1	0	224

12 BOBBY WAGNER WAS · AGE 34 · BYE 14

The ageless wonder led the league while setting a career high in tackles last season. He's set to be the maestro in the middle for Dan Quinn in Washington, so it's unwise to fade Wagner.

	G	SNAP	TKL	SOLO	AST	SK	INT	FF	FPTS
2023	17	1127	183	96	87	3.5	0	0	254
PROJ	17	1011	159	96	62	2	1	0	230

13 AZEEZ AL-SHAAIR HOU · AGE 27 · BYE 14

Success as an every-down enforcer for the Titans last season earned Al-Shaair a rewarding reunion with DeMeco Ryans in Houston. Al-Shaair might match 2023's LB1-worthy line.

	G	SNAP	TKL	SOLO	AST	SK	INT	FF	FPTS
2023	17	1048	163	84	79	2	0	0	221
PROJ	17	1025	155	94	61	1.5	1	0	225

14 QUINCY WILLIAMS NYJ · AGE 28 · BYE 12

While his younger brother and teammate, Quinnen, is a dominant force up front, Quincy quietly earned All-Pro honors and finished fifth in solo tackles last season.

	G	SNAP	TKL	SOLO	AST	SK	INT	FF	FPTS
2023	17	1047	139	95	44	2	1	2	246
PROJ	17	981	131	79	51	1	2	2	222

15 QUAY WALKER GB · AGE 24 · BYE 10

The switch to Jeff Hafley's 4-3 defensive scheme could unlock a new tier of tackle volume for this former Georgia Bulldog as he enters his prime poised to lead the Packers' front seven.

	G	SNAP	TKL	SOLO	AST	SK	INT	FF	FPTS
2023	14	809	118	59	59	2.5	1	0	172
PROJ	17	1015	147	89	58	2	1	1	218

16 LOGAN WILSON CIN · AGE 28 · BYE 12

With four more interceptions than any other linebacker since he joined the league in 2020, Wilson's deft pass defense combines nicely with a healthy tackle clip to support high-end LB2 value heading into his fifth season.

	G	SNAP	TKL	SOLO	AST	SK	INT	FF	FPTS
2023	17	1028	135	78	57	1	4	3	219
PROJ	17	1021	135	82	53	1	2	2	217

17 FRANKIE LUVU WAS · AGE 27 · BYE 14

Gifted with the name of an old-school crooner, Luvu is a new-school linebacker who blends awesome pass-rush success with atypically high tackle-for-loss production. A move to Washington should prove fantasy-friendly.

	G	SNAP	TKL	SOLO	AST	SK	INT	FF	FPTS
2023	17	954	125	66	59	5.5	0	2	203
PROJ	17	1011	133	81	52	3.5	1	2	221

18 C.J. MOSLEY NYJ · AGE 32 · BYE 12

Mosley has rebounded from an injury-riddled start to his Jets career to rank fourth among linebackers in both snaps and tackles over the past three seasons.

	G	SNAP	TKL	SOLO	AST	SK	INT	FF	FPTS
2023	17	1078	152	81	71	0.5	1	2	214
PROJ	17	1013	141	86	56	1	1	2	214

19 MATT MILANO BUF · AGE 30 · BYE 12

There is no question Milano is among the best defensive playmakers at the position. The concern is whether he returns to top form after a serious knee injury. There is immense upside if he's back at his best.

	G	SNAP	TKL	SOLO	AST	SK	INT	FF	FPTS
2023	5	199	30	18	12	0	2	1	55
PROJ	17	1021	124	75	49	2.5	2	1	214

20 ALEX SINGLETON DEN · AGE 30 · BYE 14

Singleton is tied with Roquan Smith for third in total tackles since the start of 2022 and is third among the top 10 tacklers in pass-rush wins as well. Consistency is now part of his profile.

	G	SNAP	TKL	SOLO	AST	SK	INT	FF	FPTS
2023	17	1042	175	105	70	2	0	0	244
PROJ	17	922	149	90	59	2	1	0	212

21 KYZIR WHITE ARI · AGE 28 · BYE 11

A career-best 95% snap rate as the key every-down 'backer in Jonathan Gannon's defense last season helped fuel an awesome tackle clip that extrapolates to 139 takedowns had White played a full season.

	G	SNAP	TKL	SOLO	AST	SK	INT	FF	FPTS
2023	11	674	90	53	37	2	1	0	143
PROJ	17	1032	141	85	55	1.5	1	1	214

22 JEREMIAH OWUSU-KORAMOAH CLE · AGE 24 · BYE 10

He's one of just four players with at least 100 tackles, 3.5 sacks and two picks in 2023, so it's quite OK to take "JOK" as your second linebacker in fantasy drafts this summer.

	G	SNAP	TKL	SOLO	AST	SK	INT	FF	FPTS
2023	16	721	101	72	29	3.5	2	1	204
PROJ	17	852	117	71	46	2	1	1	213

23 TREMAINE EDMUNDS CHI · AGE 26 · BYE 7

Edmunds flashes as the Bears' ball-hawking playmaker in coverage. With triple-digit tackles in every pro season thus far, he's a safe and steady fantasy selection.

	G	SNAP	TKL	SOLO	AST	SK	INT	FF	FPTS
2023	15	847	113	69	44	0	4	1	191
PROJ	17	988	132	80	52	1.5	1	1	204

24 ROBERT SPILLANE LV · AGE 28 · BYE 10

From undrafted free agent in 2018 to becoming a captain and leading tackler for Vegas last season, Spillane is deployed all over the field by defensive coordinator Patrick Graham.

	G	SNAP	TKL	SOLO	AST	SK	INT	FF	FPTS
2023	17	1056	148	82	66	3.5	3	1	230
PROJ	17	1022	142	86	56	2	1	1	210

DEFENSIVE BACKS

1 ANTOINE WINFIELD JR. TB · AGE 26 · BYE 11

No other player in NFL history has amassed the collection of tackles, forced fumbles, sacks and interceptions in a single season that this man did in 2023. Winfield is in a tier of his own.

	G	SNAP	TKL	SOLO	AST	SK	INT	FF	FPTS
2023	17	1061	122	76	46	6	3	6	258
PROJ	17	1029	108	72	35	2	3	4	211

2 CAMRYN BYNUM MIN · AGE 26 · BYE 6

Third among all defensive backs in snaps last season, Bynum rarely left the field in Brian Flores' aggressive defensive scheme. Another linebacker-like tackle rate could surface.

	G	SNAP	TKL	SOLO	AST	SK	INT	FF	FPTS
2023	17	1086	137	94	43	0.5	2	3	215
PROJ	17	1027	123	83	40	0	3	2	201

3 JESSIE BATES III ATL · AGE 27 · BYE 12

He's second in the league in interceptions the past two years. It's scary to think Raheem Morris could help unlock a new level of production from Bates in 2024.

	G	SNAP	TKL	SOLO	AST	SK	INT	FF	FPTS
2023	17	1083	132	89	43	0	6	3	236
PROJ	17	1029	120	81	39	0.5	3	2	206

4 BRIAN BRANCH DET · AGE 22 · BYE 5

Having spent most of his rookie snaps in a nickel back gig, Branch is likely to take on more safety snaps in the wake of C.J. Gardner-Johnson landing back in Philly.

	G	SNAP	TKL	SOLO	AST	SK	INT	FF	FPTS
2023	15	702	74	50	24	1	3	1	156
PROJ	17	969	97	74	23	2	2	1	196

5 DERWIN JAMES JR. LAC · AGE 28 · BYE 5

Playing at least 16 games last year for the first time since his rookie season, James turned in a top-10 fantasy finish among defensive backs.

	G	SNAP	TKL	SOLO	AST	SK	INT	FF	FPTS
2023	16	971	125	86	39	2	1	0	200
PROJ	17	970	118	80	39	1.5	2	0	187

6 JAQUAN BRISKER CHI · AGE 25 · BYE 7

An effective and efficient blitzer who finished ninth in pressures among DBs last year, Brisker accrued 66 solos last season. Year 3 could include yet another leap.

	G	SNAP	TKL	SOLO	AST	SK	INT	FF	FPTS
2023	15	866	105	66	39	1	1	2	169
PROJ	17	967	111	75	36	1	3	2	192

7 JOSH METELLUS MIN · AGE 26 · BYE 6

As long as he continues to beat out former first-rounder Lewis Cine as the third starting safety in Brian Flores' blitz-driven scheme, Metellus is destined to approach DB1 production.

	G	SNAP	TKL	SOLO	AST	SK	INT	FF	FPTS
2023	17	1031	112	74	38	2.5	1	4	196
PROJ	17	994	105	71	34	3	2	3	193

8 KYLE HAMILTON BAL · AGE 23 · BYE 14

A first-team All-Pro bid in just his second season positions Hamilton near the top of draft boards. Whether he's manning the slot or collapsing the pocket, it's scary to think his best is still to come.

	G	SNAP	TKL	SOLO	AST	SK	INT	FF	FPTS
2023	15	898	81	63	18	3	4	1	190
PROJ	17	1018	95	64	31	2	3	1	188

9 REED BLANKENSHIP PHI · AGE 25 · BYE 5

A top-10 solo tackle tally among defensive backs despite missing two games last season confirms Blankenship could net drafters real profit if he sustains a starting role in Year 3.

	G	SNAP	TKL	SOLO	AST	SK	INT	FF	FPTS
2023	15	897	108	75	33	0	3	0	177
PROJ	17	1010	114	77	37	0.5	3	0	187

10 DEVON WITHERSPOON SEA · AGE 23 · BYE 10

Always around the ball, Witherspoon tied for fifth in passes defended as a rookie. Coach Mike Macdonald will deploy him all over the field in what could be a leap year for the gifted corner.

	G	SNAP	TKL	SOLO	AST	SK	INT	FF	FPTS
2023	14	848	79	56	23	3	1	1	168
PROJ	17	1020	89	68	21	1	3	1	186

11 NATE HOBBS LV · AGE 25 · BYE 10

Just over 60% of Hobbs' snaps came in slot coverage last season. He is the rare corner to prove special in fantasy terms, as his busy role feeds him tons of targets and thus breakup and tackle opportunities.

	G	SNAP	TKL	SOLO	AST	SK	INT	FF	FPTS
2023	13	746	86	59	27	1	1	1	144
PROJ	17	968	101	77	24	1	2	1	181

12 XAVIER MCKINNEY GB · AGE 26 · BYE 10

One of Nick Saban's favorite playmakers from Bama, McKinney has continued this penchant in the pros. Now with the Packers, he'll make plays from the box, blitzing, deep alignments, and even from the slot.

	G	SNAP	TKL	SOLO	AST	SK	INT	FF	FPTS
2023	17	1091	116	78	38	0.5	3	1	195
PROJ	17	1026	106	72	35	1	3	1	180

13 BRANDON JONES DEN · AGE 26 · BYE 14

Capable in zone and man coverage, Jones should see a sizable increase in playing time in a starting role with Denver after being the third safety with Miami last season.

	G	SNAP	TKL	SOLO	AST	SK	INT	FF	FPTS
2023	16	444	46	35	11	0	2	1	89
PROJ	17	976	109	73	36	1	2	2	187

14 JULIAN LOVE SEA · AGE 26 · BYE 10

Mike Macdonald's belief in interchangeable safety deployment should serve Love's statistical profile well as he looks to build on his stellar debut season in Seattle.

	G	SNAP	TKL	SOLO	AST	SK	INT	FF	FPTS
2023	17	907	110	78	32	0	4	2	190
PROJ	17	913	105	71	34	0	3	1	175

15 TARON JOHNSON BUF · AGE 28 · BYE 12

Tied for 14th among all DBs in tackles over the past two seasons, Johnson is arguably the best source of such production from the cornerback position.

	G	SNAP	TKL	SOLO	AST	SK	INT	FF	FPTS
2023	17	907	98	72	26	1	0	3	166
PROJ	17	935	94	71	22	1	1	3	173

16 KAMREN CURL LAR · AGE 25 · BYE 6

Nearly equal snap distribution between the box and free safety alignment in his final season with the Commanders aided Curl's career-best campaign. He could thrive as a chess piece for the Rams' defense this season.

	G	SNAP	TKL	SOLO	AST	SK	INT	FF	FPTS
2023	16	1042	115	74	41	1	0	1	167
PROJ	17	1030	110	74	36	1	2	1	171

17 JUSTIN REID KC · AGE 27 · BYE 6

Chiefs defensive coordinator Steve Spagnuolo revels in leveraging unique blitz packages, evidenced by Reid tying for seventh among safeties last season in pass-rushing snaps. Another season of rewarding usage is on the way.

	G	SNAP	TKL	SOLO	AST	SK	INT	FF	FPTS
2023	16	940	95	74	21	3	1	1	168
PROJ	17	1018	102	69	33	2	2	1	172

18 MINKAH FITZPATRICK PIT · AGE 27 · BYE 9

Health is the main factor in Fitzpatrick's fantasy profile, as this perennial Pro Bowler missed nearly half of last season to various injuries. He's just 27, and a peak year could still be on the way.

	G	SNAP	TKL	SOLO	AST	SK	INT	FF	FPTS
2023	10	518	64	43	21	0	0	0	87
PROJ	17	964	111	75	36	1	2	0	169

19 KYLE DUGGER NE · AGE 28 · BYE 14

Continuity reigns as new head coach Jerod Mayo orchestrated the defenses that saw Dugger become a star. Third among safeties in pass rush snaps last season, he brings a high floor and ceiling to fantasy rosters.

	G	SNAP	TKL	SOLO	AST	SK	INT	FF	FPTS
2023	17	1069	107	70	37	1.5	2	1	175
PROJ	17	1022	101	68	33	1.5	2	1	171

20 GRANT DELPIT CLE · AGE 25 · BYE 10

Blending active coverage skills from the slot and free safety alignments with aggressive downhill work from the box supports a worthy DB2 profile for the former LSU star.

	G	SNAP	TKL	SOLO	AST	SK	INT	FF	FPTS
2023	13	704	77	61	16	2	1	0	137
PROJ	17	1012	105	71	34	1	1	0	171

21 DONOVAN WILSON DAL · AGE 29 · BYE 7

If his strong sack production in 2022 was a bit of an outlier, so was his lack of such production in 2023. Expect a busy, blitz-happy season from Wilson in Mike Zimmer's daring scheme.

	G	SNAP	TKL	SOLO	AST	SK	INT	FF	FPTS
2023	15	693	88	55	33	0	2	1	138
PROJ	17	966	111	75	36	1	1	1	172

22 JALEN THOMPSON ARI · AGE 26 · BYE 11

Splitting time between manning the box and slot coverage helped spur a career high in interceptions and passes defended. A realistic return to triple-digit tackle production would equate to a DB1 outcome.

	G	SNAP	TKL	SOLO	AST	SK	INT	FF	FPTS
2023	15	897	78	59	19	1	4	1	154
PROJ	17	1032	95	64	31	1	3	1	169

23 JALEN PITRE HOU · AGE 25 · BYE 14

Regression from his astounding rookie statistics was expected last season, but Pitre's unique blend of talent and rewarding workload suggests a likely return to triple-digit tackle output.

	G	SNAP	TKL	SOLO	AST	SK	INT	FF	FPTS
2023	15	860	84	58	26	0	0	1	134
PROJ	17	1025	98	66	32	1.5	2	1	168

24 JEVON HOLLAND MIA · AGE 24 · BYE 6

Holland is graded third overall among safeties behind Antoine Winfield Jr. and Jessie Bates III, per PFF. The only holdup from an elite 2023 outcome was injury issues.

	G	SNAP	TKL	SOLO	AST	SK	INT	FF	FPTS
2023	12	676	73	51	22	0	1	3	132
PROJ	17	984	97	65	32	0	2	2	

TEAM PREVIEWS

Depth charts, projections and everything else you need to know for all 32 teams

Under Buffalo's now full-time offensive coordinator Joe Brady (who took over during the 2023 season), the Bills will emphasize the ground game, led by James Cook (No. 4).

ESPN

FANTASY FOOTBALL 2024

ESPN

VP, Fantasy & Sports Betting Content Scott Clark
Senior Deputy Editor Andrew Feldman
Deputy Editor Pierre Becquey
Senior Editor Keith Lipscomb
Editors James Best, Sachin Dave Chandan, Joe Kaiser, Joseph Klingele, AJ Mass
Senior Writers Stephania Bell, Mike Clay, Tristan H. Cockcroft, Eric Karabell
Fantasy Analysts Matt Bowen, Daniel Dopp, Liz Loza, Eric Moody, Field Yates
Sports Betting Analyst Tyler Fulghum
Sports Analytics Content Specialist Seth Walder
Contributing Writers Steve Alexander, Jim McCormick

NFL Nation Reporters Todd Archer, Ben Baby, Sarah Barshop, DJ Bien-Aime, Rich Cimini, Courtney Cronin, Turron Davenport, Rob Demovsky, Mike DiRocco, Alaina Getzenberg, Paul Gutierrez, Brady Henderson, Jamison Hensley, Stephen Holder, John Keim, Jenna Laine, Jeff Legwold, Marcel Louis-Jacques, Tim McManus, David Newton, Daniel Oyefusi, Brooke Pryor, Jordan Raanan, Marc Raimondi, Mike Reiss, Kris Rhim, Kevin Seifert, Adam Teicher, Katherine Terrell, Nick Wagoner, Josh Weinfuss, Eric Woodyard

This work represents the collective reporting, analysis, insights, and creative and production efforts of the entire ESPN enterprise.

Chairman, ESPN and Sports Content, The Walt Disney Company James Pitaro
President, Content Burke Magnus
Head of Digital Content & Audience Expansion Freddy Rolón Jr.
Senior VP, Digital Content & Audience Expansion Nate Ravitz
VP, Investigative and Enterprise Journalism Chris Buckle
VP, Executive Editor, Digital Content Lauren Reynolds
Executive Editors Scott Burton, Cristina Daglas
Senior Deputy Editor, NFL Heather Burns
Director, Analytics & Innovation Allison Loucks
Principal Sports Data Scientist Brian Burke
Senior Sports Analytics Engineer Hank Gargiulo

DOTDASH MEREDITH PREMIUM PUBLISHING

Vice President,Editor in Chief Kostya Kennedy
Creative Director Gary Stewart
Associate Photo Director C. Tiffany Lee
Editorial Operations Director Jamie Roth Major
Editor Rich Sands
Photo Editor Jim Surber
Manager, Editorial Operations Gina Scauzillo
Associate Manager, Editorial Operations Ariel Davis
Copy Chief Tracy Guth Spangler
Reporter Joseph Wilkinson
Production Designer Sandra Jurevics
Premedia Trafficking Supervisor Sophia Mozena
Director, Premedia Imaging Michael Sturtz
Color Quality Analyst John Santucci
Production Director Patrick McGowan
Production Managers Ashley Schaubroeck, Trevi Jones, April Gross
Senior Quality Director Joe Kohler
Associate Quality Director Jason Lamb

Vice President & General Manager Jeremy Biloon
Vice President, Group Editorial Director Stephen Orr
Executive Publishing Director Megan Pearlman
Senior Director, Brand Marketing Jean Kennedy
Associate Director, Brand Marketing Katherine Barnet
Associate Director, Business Development and Partnerships Nina Reed
Senior Manager, Brand Marketing Geoffrey Wohlgamuth
Brand Manager, Brand Marketing Mia Rinaldi

Special thanks Gabby Amello, Brad Beatson, Nicoleta Papavasilakis

DOTDASH MEREDITH

President, Lifestyle Alysia Borsa

Photo and Illustration Credits

Front/back covers [Josh Allen] Ryan Kang/Getty Images; [Patrick Mahomes] Ryan Kang/Getty Images; [Bijan Robinson] Rich von Biberstein/Icon Sportswire/Getty Images; [Amon-Ra St. Brown] Duane Burleson/AP Photo; [Puka Nacua] Ryan Kang/Getty Images **1** Ryan Kang/Getty Images **2–3** William Purnell/Icon Sportswire/Getty Images **5** Illustration by Rafa Alvarez **6-7** Mark J. Terrill/AP Photo **8** Maddie Meyer/Getty Images **9** Ezra Shaw/Getty Images **10** Jessie Rogers/Tennessee Titans **11** Jeffrey T. Barnes/AP Photo **13** David Eulitt/Getty Images **14–15** Illustration by Gluekit; [CeeDee Lamb] Megan Briggs/Getty Images; [Evan Engram] Mike Carlson/Getty Images; [Tyreek Hill] Mike Stobe/Getty Images; [Christian McCaffrey] Ryan Kang/Getty Images; [Patrick Mahomes] Ryan Kang/Getty Images; [Jalen Hurts] Mitchell Leff/Getty Images; [Bijan Robinson] Mike Christy/Getty Images; [Josh Allen] Ryan Kang/Getty Images; [Brandon Aiyuk] Ryan Kang/Getty Images; [Amon-Ra St. Brown] Kevin Sabitus/Getty Images; [Travis Kelce] Kara Durrette/Getty Images; [Tee Higgins] Andy Lyons/Getty Images **16** Ryan Kang/Getty Images **17** Michael Hickey/Getty Images **18** Michael Owens/Getty Images **19** David Berding/Getty Images **21** Adrian Kraus/AP Photo **22** Rich Barnes/Getty Images **23** Jane Gershovich/Getty Images **25** Stephen Maturen/Getty Images **26** Carmen Mandato/Getty Images **27** Courtney Culbreath/Getty Images **29** Michael Reaves/Getty Images **30** Simon Bruty/The Washington Post/Getty Images **31** Rob Schumacher/The Republic/USA TODAY Network **32** Steven Senne/AP Photo **33** Zach Bolinger/Icon Sportswire/Getty Images **34** Robert Kupbens-USA TODAY Sports **35** Tori Richman/Tampa Bay Buccaneers **37** Ryan Kang/Getty Images **38** Leigh Bacho/Getty Images **39** Mike Carlson/Getty Images **41** Dylan Buell/Getty Images **43** Harry How/Getty Images **45** Matt Durisko/AP Photo **46–47** Cooper Neill/Getty Images **49** Ethan Miller/Getty Images **51** Cooper Neill/Getty Images **52** Christian Petersen/Getty Images **57** David Eulitt/Getty Images **58** Cooper Neill/Getty Images **62** Kevin C. Cox/Getty Images **65** Ezra Shaw/Getty Images **67** Timothy T. Ludwig/Getty Images **71** Ryan Kang/Getty Images **75** Brandon Sloter/Image of Sport/Getty Images **77** Ryan Kang/Getty Images **78** Gregory Shamus/Getty Images **82** Michael Owens/Getty Images **87** Megan Briggs/Getty Images **91** Gregory Shamus/Getty Images **92** Dustin Bradford/Icon Sportswire/Getty Images **97** Chris Unger/Getty Images **98** Christian Petersen/Getty Images **100** Nick Cammett/Getty Images **103** Aaron M. Sprecher/AP Photo **108–109** Michael Owens/Getty Images **110** [from top] Mark J. Rebilas/USA TODAY Sports; David J. Griffin/Icon Sportswire/Getty Images **111** [from top] Kevin Richardson/The Baltimore Sun/Tribune News Service/Getty Images; Jamie Squire/Getty Images **112** [from top] Courtesy Carolina Panthers; David Banks/USA TODAY Sports **113** [from top] Jeff Dean/Getty Images; Gregory Shamus/Getty Images **114** [from top] Cooper Neill/Getty Images; Michael Owens/Getty Images **115** [from top] Cooper Neill/Getty Images; Patrick McDermott/Getty Images **116** [from top] Zach Tarrant/Houston Texans; Carmen Mandato/Getty Images **117** [from top] Logan Bowles/AP Photo; Colin E. Braley/AP Photo **118** [from top] John Locher/AP Photo; Mark J. Terrill/AP Photo **119** [from top] Ryan Kang/Getty Images; Megan Briggs/Getty Images **120** [from top] Abbie Parr/AP Photo; Elsa/Getty Images **121** [from top] Cooper Neill/Getty Images; Sarah Stier/Getty Images **122** [from top] Cooper Neill/Getty Images; Chris Szagola/AP Photo **123** [from top] Gene J. Puskar/AP Photo; Ezra Shaw/Getty Images **124** [from top] Michael Hickey/Getty Images; Cliff Welch/Icon Sportswire/Getty Images **125** [from top] Andy Lyons/Getty Images; Emilee Fails/Washington Commanders

2024 NFL SCHEDULE

All 18 weeks

ESPN Fantasy Trade Deadline: Nov. 27, noon ET

WEEK 1 (SEPT. 5–9)

RAVENS @ CHIEFS [Thurs.]
PACKERS VS. EAGLES [Fri.] [São Paulo]
STEELERS @ FALCONS
CARDINALS @ BILLS
TITANS @ BEARS
PATRIOTS @ BENGALS
TEXANS @ COLTS
JAGUARS @ DOLPHINS
PANTHERS @ SAINTS
VIKINGS @ GIANTS
RAIDERS @ CHARGERS
BRONCOS @ SEAHAWKS
COWBOYS @ BROWNS
COMMANDERS @ BUCCANEERS
RAMS @ LIONS
JETS @ 49ERS [Mon.]

WEEK 2 (SEPT. 12–16)

BILLS @ DOLPHINS [Thurs.]
RAIDERS @ RAVENS
CHARGERS @ PANTHERS
SAINTS @ COWBOYS
BUCCANEERS @ LIONS
COLTS @ PACKERS
BROWNS @ JAGUARS
49ERS @ VIKINGS
SEAHAWKS @ PATRIOTS
JETS @ TITANS
GIANTS @ COMMANDERS
RAMS @ CARDINALS
STEELERS @ BRONCOS
BENGALS @ CHIEFS
BEARS @ TEXANS
FALCONS @ EAGLES [Mon.]

WEEK 3 (SEPT. 19–23)

PATRIOTS @ JETS [Thurs.]
GIANTS @ BROWNS
BEARS @ COLTS
TEXANS @ VIKINGS
EAGLES @ SAINTS
CHARGERS @ STEELERS
BRONCOS @ BUCCANEERS
PACKERS @ TITANS
PANTHERS @ RAIDERS
DOLPHINS @ SEAHAWKS
LIONS @ CARDINALS
RAVENS @ COWBOYS
49ERS @ RAMS
CHIEFS @ FALCONS
JAGUARS @ BILLS [Mon.]
COMMANDERS @ BENGALS [Mon.]

WEEK 4 (SEPT. 26–30)

COWBOYS @ GIANTS [Thurs.]
SAINTS @ FALCONS
BENGALS @ PANTHERS
RAMS @ BEARS
VIKINGS @ PACKERS
JAGUARS @ TEXANS
STEELERS @ COLTS
BRONCOS @ JETS
EAGLES @ BUCCANEERS
COMMANDERS @ CARDINALS
PATRIOTS @ 49ERS
CHIEFS @ CHARGERS
BROWNS @ RAIDERS
BILLS @ RAVENS
TITANS @ DOLPHINS [Mon.]
SEAHAWKS @ LIONS [Mon.]

WEEK 5 (OCT. 3–7)

BUCCANEERS @ FALCONS [Thurs.]
JETS VS. VIKINGS [London]
PANTHERS @ BEARS
RAVENS @ BENGALS
COLTS @ JAGUARS
BILLS @ TEXANS
DOLPHINS @ PATRIOTS
BROWNS @ COMMANDERS
RAIDERS @ BRONCOS
CARDINALS @ 49ERS
PACKERS @ RAMS
GIANTS @ SEAHAWKS
COWBOYS @ STEELERS
SAINTS @ CHIEFS [Mon.]
BYE WEEK: LIONS, CHARGERS, EAGLES, TITANS

WEEK 6 (OCT. 10–14)

49ERS @ SEAHAWKS [Thurs.]
JAGUARS VS. BEARS [London]
COMMANDERS @ RAVENS
CARDINALS @ PACKERS
TEXANS @ PATRIOTS
BUCCANEERS @ SAINTS
BROWNS @ EAGLES
COLTS @ TITANS
CHARGERS @ BRONCOS
STEELERS @ RAIDERS
FALCONS @ PANTHERS
LIONS @ COWBOYS
BENGALS @ GIANTS
BILLS @ JETS [Mon.]
BYE WEEK: CHIEFS, RAMS, DOLPHINS, VIKINGS

WEEK 7 (OCT. 17–21)

BRONCOS @ SAINTS [Thurs.]
PATRIOTS VS. JAGUARS [London]
SEAHAWKS @ FALCONS
TITANS @ BILLS
BENGALS @ BROWNS
TEXANS @ PACKERS
DOLPHINS @ COLTS
LIONS @ VIKINGS
EAGLES @ GIANTS
RAIDERS @ RAMS
PANTHERS @ COMMANDERS
CHIEFS @ 49ERS
JETS @ STEELERS
RAVENS @ BUCCANEERS [Mon.]
CHARGERS @ CARDINALS [Mon.]
BYE WEEK: BEARS, COWBOYS

WEEK 8 (OCT. 24–28)

VIKINGS @ RAMS [Thurs.]
RAVENS @ BROWNS
TITANS @ LIONS
COLTS @ TEXANS
PACKERS @ JAGUARS
CARDINALS @ DOLPHINS
JETS @ PATRIOTS
FALCONS @ BUCCANEERS
BEARS @ COMMANDERS
SAINTS @ CHARGERS
BILLS @ SEAHAWKS
EAGLES @ BENGALS
PANTHERS @ BRONCOS
CHIEFS @ RAIDERS
COWBOYS @ 49ERS
GIANTS @ STEELERS [Mon.]

WEEK 9 (OCT. 31–NOV. 4)

TEXANS @ JETS [Thurs.]
COWBOYS @ FALCONS
BRONCOS @ RAVENS
DOLPHINS @ BILLS
SAINTS @ PANTHERS
RAIDERS @ BENGALS
CHARGERS @ BROWNS
COLTS @ VIKINGS
COMMANDERS @ GIANTS
PATRIOTS @ TITANS
BEARS @ CARDINALS
LIONS @ PACKERS
RAMS @ SEAHAWKS
JAGUARS @ EAGLES
BUCCANEERS @ CHIEFS [Mon.]
BYE WEEK: STEELERS, 49ERS

WEEK 10 (NOV. 7–11)

BENGALS @ RAVENS [Thurs.]
GIANTS VS. PANTHERS [Munich]
PATRIOTS @ BEARS
BILLS @ COLTS
VIKINGS @ JAGUARS
BRONCOS @ CHIEFS
FALCONS @ SAINTS
49ERS @ BUCCANEERS
STEELERS @ COMMANDERS
TITANS @ CHARGERS
JETS @ CARDINALS
EAGLES @ COWBOYS
LIONS @ TEXANS
DOLPHINS @ RAMS [Mon.]
BYE WEEK: BROWNS, PACKERS, RAIDERS, SEAHAWKS

WEEK 11 (NOV. 14–18)

COMMANDERS @ EAGLES [Thurs.]
PACKERS @ BEARS
JAGUARS @ LIONS
RAIDERS @ DOLPHINS
RAMS @ PATRIOTS
BROWNS @ SAINTS
RAVENS @ STEELERS
VIKINGS @ TITANS
FALCONS @ BRONCOS
SEAHAWKS @ 49ERS
CHIEFS @ BILLS
BENGALS @ CHARGERS
COLTS @ JETS
TEXANS @ COWBOYS [Mon.]
BYE WEEK: CARDINALS, PANTHERS, GIANTS, BUCCANEERS

WEEK 12 (NOV. 21–25)

STEELERS @ BROWNS [Thurs.]
CHIEFS @ PANTHERS
VIKINGS @ BEARS
TITANS @ TEXANS
LIONS @ COLTS
PATRIOTS @ DOLPHINS
BUCCANEERS @ GIANTS
COWBOYS @ COMMANDERS
BRONCOS @ RAIDERS
49ERS @ PACKERS
CARDINALS @ SEAHAWKS
EAGLES @ RAMS
RAVENS @ CHARGERS [Mon.]
BYE WEEK: FALCONS, BILLS, BENGALS, JAGUARS, SAINTS, JETS

WEEK 13 (NOV. 28–DEC. 2)

BEARS @ LIONS [Thurs.]
GIANTS @ COWBOYS [Thurs.]
DOLPHINS @ PACKERS [Thurs.]
RAIDERS @ CHIEFS [Fri.]
CHARGERS @ FALCONS
STEELERS @ BENGALS
TEXANS @ JAGUARS
CARDINALS @ VIKINGS
COLTS @ PATRIOTS
SEAHAWKS @ JETS
TITANS @ COMMANDERS
BUCCANEERS @ PANTHERS
RAMS @ SAINTS
EAGLES @ RAVENS
49ERS @ BILLS
BROWNS @ BRONCOS [Mon.]

WEEK 14 (DEC. 5–9)

PACKERS @ LIONS [Thurs.]
JETS @ DOLPHINS
FALCONS @ VIKINGS
SAINTS @ GIANTS
PANTHERS @ EAGLES
BROWNS @ STEELERS
RAIDERS @ BUCCANEERS
JAGUARS @ TITANS
SEAHAWKS @ CARDINALS
BILLS @ RAMS
BEARS @ 49ERS
CHARGERS @ CHIEFS
BENGALS @ COWBOYS [Mon.]
BYE WEEK: RAVENS, BRONCOS, TEXANS, COLTS, PATRIOTS, COMMANDERS

WEEK 15 (DEC. 12–16)

RAMS @ 49ERS [Thurs.]
COWBOYS @ PANTHERS
CHIEFS @ BROWNS
DOLPHINS @ TEXANS
JETS @ JAGUARS
COMMANDERS @ SAINTS
RAVENS @ GIANTS
BENGALS @ TITANS
PATRIOTS @ CARDINALS
COLTS @ BRONCOS
BILLS @ LIONS
BUCCANEERS @ CHARGERS
STEELERS @ EAGLES
PACKERS @ SEAHAWKS
BEARS @ VIKINGS [Mon.]
FALCONS @ RAIDERS [Mon.]

WEEK 16 (DEC. 19–23)

BROWNS @ BENGALS [Thurs.]
TEXANS @ CHIEFS [Sat.]
STEELERS @ RAVENS [Sat.]
GIANTS @ FALCONS
PATRIOTS @ BILLS
CARDINALS @ PANTHERS
LIONS @ BEARS
TITANS @ COLTS
RAMS @ JETS
EAGLES @ COMMANDERS
BRONCOS @ CHARGERS
VIKINGS @ SEAHAWKS
JAGUARS @ RAIDERS
49ERS @ DOLPHINS
BUCCANEERS @ COWBOYS
SAINTS @ PACKERS

WEEK 17 (DEC. 25–30)

CHIEFS @ STEELERS [Wed.]
RAVENS @ TEXANS [Wed.]
SEAHAWKS @ BEARS [Thurs.]
JETS @ BILLS
TITANS @ JAGUARS
PACKERS @ VIKINGS
RAIDERS @ SAINTS
PANTHERS @ BUCCANEERS
COWBOYS @ EAGLES
BRONCOS @ BENGALS
CARDINALS @ RAMS
CHARGERS @ PATRIOTS
COLTS @ GIANTS
FALCONS @ COMMANDERS
DOLPHINS @ BROWNS
LIONS @ 49ERS [Mon.]

WEEK 18 (JAN. 5)

49ERS @ CARDINALS
PANTHERS @ FALCONS
BROWNS @ RAVENS
COMMANDERS @ COWBOYS
CHIEFS @ BRONCOS
VIKINGS @ LIONS
BEARS @ PACKERS
JAGUARS @ COLTS
SEAHAWKS @ RAMS
CHARGERS @ RAIDERS
BILLS @ PATRIOTS
DOLPHINS @ JETS
GIANTS @ EAGLES
BENGALS @ STEELERS
SAINTS @ BUCCANEERS
TEXANS @ TITANS

ESPN.com Fantasy Playoff Round 1
ESPN.com Fantasy Playoff Round 2

Did you know that ESPN league managers can now prevent teams that did not make the playoffs from making transactions, and even automatically reseed the playoff bracket?